"In *Love's Trinity* Fred Roden has given us somethii[...] in print for years—a reflection on Julian that follow[...] chapter, instead of forcing her *Revelations of Divine Love* into an abstract system of theology. Only in reading the *Revelations* in this way, following Julian's own narrative, can we fully appreciate her struggle to understand what she experienced of God and savor the spiritual meaning flowing abundantly from her experience into our own. Skillfully applying his training as a professor of literature, Roden interweaves Julian's voice with his voice, proving himself a most helpful guide for anyone seeking a deeper understanding of Julian's experience and the meaning of her *Revelations* for our world."

—The Rev. Gregory Fruehwirth, OJN
Guardian
The Order of Julian of Norwich

"*Love's Trinity* offers to twenty-first century men and women a renewed sense of hope at a time when the human race seems faced with the stark choice between spiritual evolution or annihilation. In one volume we have exquisite translation of Julian's original text by Fr. John-Julian, the founder of the order of Julian of Norwich, and a remarkable commentary by Frederick Roden. Dr. Roden is a fine scholar but he is also clearly a devoted Julian lover. His reflections demonstrate both his scholarship and his love and the result is a commentary that not only does justice to Julian's often complex and challenging theology but also has the power to inspire and to bring the reader closer to God."

—Lay Canon Professor Brian Thorne
Chairman of the Trustees of the Friends of Julian of Norwich

"*Love's Trinity*, a unique commentary on Julian's *Showings*, opens up her long text historically, theologically, prayerfully, chapter by chapter. I unreservedly recommend this book, obviously written by one who has pondered on Julian and her teaching over many years and wants to make her insights available to the people of today. A book to treasure and return to again and again."

—Sr. Elizabeth Ruth Obbard, OCarm
Aylesford Priory, England

"Few books are treasures for the mind and the soul; this is one of them. The text combines the long-awaited translation of Julian's *Showings* by Fr. John-Julian, OJN, a dazzling accomplishment based on a lifetime's study of and meditation upon this remarkable late-medieval treatise. The final result is a translation that voices her visions in radiant English, a version that is both true to Julian's thought and voice and strong enough to render her 'book' in a vivid style. An unexpected delight is the translator's decision to offer the text in poetic form, an ingenious approach that allows the reader to discover the vitality and spaciousness of her visionary language not only as speech but also as song. The commentary by Professor Roden accomplishes exactly what it sets out to do: it probes the spiritual and theological depths of Julian's book in a manner that instructs, challenges, and inspires. The text, with commentary, will be invaluable to those meeting Julian for the first time as well as for those long attentive to the deep mysteries of her wisdom. Take, and read!"

—Dr. Mark S. Burrows
Professor of the History of Christianity
Andover Newton Theological School
Newton Centre, Massachusetts

"Since the 600th anniversary in 1973 of the day when the 14th-century English mystic, Julian, received sixteen 'showings' centered on the crucified Christ, there have been numerous translations of the book in which she recorded their meaning. Now Fr. John Julian—founder of the Order of Julian of Norwich—gives us a new translation, born from decades of meditation on her theology, which by the quality of its scholarship and the clarity of its layout make her message wonderfully accessible. This accessibility is reinforced here with commentaries by Frederick Roden—an associate of the Order—following each chapter of the mystic's writing. These have a depth of insight that is often moving, totally relevant to our lives, and frequently gently challenging. In their intrinsic call to both devotion and action they may well be as significant as the text that inspires them."

—Michael McLean
Retired Canon of Norwich Cathedral
Former Rector of St. Julian's Church, Norwich

Love's Trinity

A Companion to Julian of Norwich

Long Text with a Commentary

Commentary by Frederick S. Roden, PhD, AOJN

Showings of Julian of Norwich
translated by John-Julian, OJN

Foreword by John-Julian, OJN

A Michael Glazier Book

LITURGICAL PRESS
Collegeville, Minnesota

www.litpress.org

A Michael Glazier Book published by Liturgical Press

Cover: St. Julian's Church, Norwich. Photo by Joseph Portanova.

1   2   3   4   5   6   7   8   9

Library of Congress Cataloging-in-Publication Data

Julian, of Norwich, b. 1343.
  [Revelations of divine love. English]
  Love's trinity : a companion to Julian of Norwich / long text with a commentary showings of Julian of Norwich ; translated by John-Julian ; foreword by John-Julian ; commentary by Frederick S. Roden.
    p. cm.
  "Michael Glazier Book."
  ISBN 978-0-8146-5308-1 (pbk.)
  1. Devotional literature, English (Middle)—Modernized versions.
I. Roden, Frederick S., 1970– II. Title.

  BV4832.3.J85513 2009
  242—dc22   2008018877

For the Order of Julian of Norwich,
who teach and live Julian's "lesson of love."

Contents

Foreword

The written works of any true Christian mystic are predictably complicated—John of the Cross was driven to poetry, Teresa of Avila to extended metaphor, Meister Eckhart to an esoteric metaphysics. But even given the general opacity of all mystical writing, Dame Julian of Norwich writes with a density and complexity almost unparalleled and with a compacted literary style that can easily strangle or mislead the casual reader. To unravel this knotted cluster of inspired insight couched in Middle English is a serious literary challenge—one not always adequately met by her translators. As the one who translated Julian's text provided in this book, I can bear witness to this complexity on a textual and literary level, where Julian sometimes invents words when she finds none adequate to her vision, and carries on sentences to such an extent that even a careful reader can easily lose track of the antecedents of her pronouns!

But within this dense literary topography Julian demonstrates a theological acumen that is curiously almost as childlike as it is radical, almost as naive as it is complicated, and this odd paradox is produced not by any intentional ambiguity on her part, but by what can only be called a sanctified simplicity—seemingly unsurprised by its own surprising, complicated, and unique insights.

To track and illuminate the spiritual and theological depths of Julian's work is a tremendous challenge and can be undertaken fruitfully only by someone immersed in the unique spirituality that underlies her writing. In the last thirty years commentaries on Julian's work have sprung up and multiplied by the score, but the major share of them are either scholarly works written by academics for academics, or they have concentrated on some selected aspects of Julian's work—and some, sad to say, have been merely sentimental reflections that never move much below the surface.

The unique aspect of this present book is that it is written by a person who, while an academic himself, has been deeply and significantly engrossed in Julian's teaching on a spiritual and devotional level for many years and is able more than any other writer I have read to bring all of Julian's fourteenth-century insights alive, demonstrating their continuing relevance to our twenty-first-century hunger for a valid Christian spirituality. There is little picking and choosing here: unlike most commentators, the author has drawn out meaning worthy of comment from virtually the entire oeuvre of this outstanding English mystic and theologian. Every chapter of Julian's work and every significant aspect of her spiritual insight is noted, expanded upon, and illuminated here.

As one who has lived with, prayed with, and studied Julian daily for nearly thirty years, and who has founded a religious order under her patronage, I commend these serious meditations on Julian's *Revelations of Divine Love,* a book Archbishop Rowan Williams of Canterbury described as "what may well be the most important work of Christian reflection in the English language."

Fr. John-Julian, OJN
Founder of the Order of Julian of Norwich
May 8, 2008
Feast of St. Julian

Preface and Acknowledgments

The commentary that became this book began as a series of weekly reflections on individual chapters of the Long Text of the *Showings* of fourteenth-century English theologian Julian of Norwich. These were written for the lay affiliate community of the Episcopal Order of Julian of Norwich, of which I am an associate, at the request of its superior, Fr. Gregory Fruehwirth, OJN. I am extremely grateful to have been invited on that narrative pilgrimage, during which time I enjoyed lively dialogue, support, and tremendous encouragement. My thanks go to the entire affiliate community and members regular for being *communitas* in so many ways during my decade of affiliation, but especially to the founder of the Order, Fr. John-Julian Swanson, OJN, whose excellent translation and incisive mind keep us all engaged in the dynamic flow of (in Julian's words) mercy and grace: the union of reason and love working itself out in the world. John-Julian's correspondence was invaluable in making me realize that this book not only fills an important void in "Juliana" but also that I ought to write it. On that note, I am especially appreciative of Hans Christoffersen and Liturgical Press for agreeing with us and taking on the project.

I first met Julian in a secular doctoral program in literature. This book is not the typical publication of a mid-career (or post-tenure, at least) scholar of gender and religion. Its voice is decidedly devotional. But if ever a theologian embodied "faith seeking understanding" (or perhaps "understanding seeking faith"), it is Julian. My commentary details Julian's struggle, and I hope explains why I am drawn to her story.

This is not an "academic" book as much as one that is informed by my academic training and practice. I deliberately avoid extensive footnotes and bibliography, and made a decision while writing my commentaries to commit to as little research on Julian as possible because I would be tempted to create a different kind of scholarly prose. To be sure, I have the highest respect for some of the truly extraordinary studies of Julian and admire many of the fine devotional books available. Both genres have influenced what you read here. My tone in this companion is homiletic insofar as it attempts something that these other works do not: a chapter-by-chapter journey through the text for the reader seeking a particular kind of "understanding." This word is Julian's and it captures that unity of head and heart found in her voice. Whether sermon or close reading, exegesis or *midrash*, I offer this commentary with the hope that it may provide the reader of Julian—secular or religious, scholarly or general—with a perspective she or he may not find elsewhere. I have built my career in writing *about* religion from the humanities academy. Here I write that religion—with, I hope, the reason and love that Julian celebrates as the most fundamental aspects of her God.

Three points require explanation. The first concerns the choice of text and translation. My thanks go to Fr. John-Julian for permission to use his edition of the Long Text of the *Showings* in this book. There are two versions of Julian's work. While a number of provocative formulations are found only in the Short Text, the Long Text offers a much more extensive elaboration of Julian's overall theology. Second is the issue of format. This is not a reference book; commentaries are intended to be read along with Julian's words. Therefore each chapter is followed by its companion reflection rather than locating the commentary elsewhere in the book. Readers may choose to journey from cover to cover or select particular chapters to delve into. A third issue troubles me, which is an entirely good thing for someone who teaches in a Women's Studies Program. In my commentaries I have chosen to avoid gender-inclusive language, instead using the masculine pronoun to refer to the Divine, Whom I call "God." I made the decision to do so, quite simply, because that is how Julian writes in her text. For a theologian whose central metaphor for creation, incarnation, and indeed salvation is the mother-hood of God, this might seem strange. Of course it must be understood with respect to the historical moment, culture, and religion that produced the work. The fact that Julian's Mother God is a He underscores the complicated, indeed limited, nature of gender identification in spiritual experience and the problem with essentializing categories of identity. I invite you to consider Julian's God Who is all there is; Who is Divine Reason longing to fill our understanding but Who in our human reason we can never fully grasp; for Whom "Love was His meaning." In the words of Chapter 84, "at the end, all shall be Love."

12 January 2008
Feast of Aelred of Rievaulx

REVELATIONS

shown to one who could not read a letter.
Anno Domini, 1373

∞ 1 ∞

This is a revelation of love that Jesus Christ, our endless joy, made in sixteen showings or revelations, in detail, of which

The first is concerning His precious crowning with thorns;
    and therewith was included and described in detail
        the Trinity with
        the Incarnation and
        the unity between God and man's soul,
    with many beautiful showings of endless wisdom and
    teachings of love in which all the showings that follow are based
        and united.

The second showing is the discoloring of His fair face in symbolizing His dearworthy passion.

The third showing is that our Lord God—
        all Power,
        all Wisdom,
        all Love
    —just as truly as He has made everything that is, also truly He
    does and causes every thing that is done.

The fourth showing is the scourging of His frail body with abundant shedding of His blood.

The fifth showing is that the fiend is overcome by the precious Passion of Christ.

The sixth showing is the honor-filled favor of our Lord God with which He rewards all His blessed servants in heaven.

The seventh showing is a frequent experience of well and woe—
        the experience of "well" is grace-filled touching and
        enlightening, with true certainty of endless joy;

the experience of "woe" is temptation by sadness and
    annoyance of our fleshly life—
with spiritual understanding that even so we are protected safely
    in love—in woe as in well—by the goodness of God.

The eighth showing is the last pains of Christ and His cruel dying.

The ninth showing is about the delight which is in the blessed
    Trinity because of the cruel Passion of Christ and His regretful
    dying; in this joy and delight He wills we be comforted and made happy
    with Him until when we come to the fullness in heaven.

The tenth showing is that our Lord Jesus shows his blessed heart equally
    cloven in two in love.

The eleventh showing is a noble, spiritual showing of His
    dearworthy Mother.

The twelfth showing is that our Lord is all supreme Being.

The thirteenth showing is that our Lord God wills that we have
    great regard for
        all the deeds that He has done in the great splendor of creating
            all things, and
        of the excellency of creating man (who is above all His other works), and
        of the precious amends that He has made for man's sin,
            turning all our blame into endless honor,
        and here also our Lord says:
            "Behold and see;
                for by the same Power, Wisdom, and Goodness that I have
                    done all this,
                by that same Power, Wisdom, and Goodness I shall make
                    well all that is not well, and
                thou thyself shalt see it."
    And in this showing He wills that we keep us in the Faith and
        truth of Holy Church, not wishing to be aware of His secrets
        now, except as is proper for us in this life.

The fourteenth showing is that our Lord is the foundation of our
    prayer. Herein were seen two elements which He wills both
        be equally great:
            the one is righteous prayer,
            the other is sure trust;

and in these ways our prayer delights Him and He of His
      goodness fulfills it.

The fifteenth showing is that
      we shall without delay be taken from all our pain and from all
         our woe and, of His goodness,
      we shall come up above where we shall
            have our Lord Jesus for our recompense,
            and be filled with joy and bliss in heaven.

The sixteenth showing is that the blessed Trinity our Creator, in Christ Jesus
   our Savior,
      endlessly dwells in our soul,
            honorably governing and controlling all things,
            powerfully and wisely saving and protecting us for the sake of love;
      and that we shall not be overcome by our Enemy.

ಔ   ಔ   ಔ

Chapter 1 of Julian's *Showings* is a table of contents as much as it is a creed. It is a statement of belief that sums up years of reflection on the shocking things Julian came to realize God had worked in her experience. She reached the conclusion that her story was worth telling. The time she spent contemplating her showings leaves no doubt about the seriousness with which she took her endeavor. We revere her commitment, so great that she dedicated her life to making this teaching available. We admire her tenacity and determination as we appreciate those qualities in her argument. Julian's book is literally a labor of love, for love is the heart of her theology.

"Translation" was an important literary form in late medieval England, although it did not mean what it does today. The "translator" made the story his, or her, own. The act of translation created versions far removed from their "originals." The medieval idea of "originality" differed from that of our age. There were no Internet engines to magically translate languages. In Julian we have a particular translation of an Origin. Julian saw herself as a translator of the Incarnate Word. She was not a biblical exegete; she did not claim to interpret Sacred Scripture. In writing her book she translated God's "showing" in her "understanding" into a narrative conveying God's message. Readers could not directly experience what she had known, but hers is not an original message. Her meaning is the love of God. This is outside of time, yet it is literally self-evident in the showings she sees. What is new is how it is explained: first by God in her perception, then in the evolution of this book through which Julian finds and speaks that meaning. The *Showings* concerns origins. In the beginning was Love, and Love was with God, and Love was God. We participate in this translation; we share in Julian's "carrying over" of the Word. We are transformed as we translate God's love into our world—when we translate the significance of her story for our own spiritual growth and development.

❧ 2 ❧

These revelations were shown to a simple creature that had learned
no letter, in the year of our Lord, 1373, the 8th day of May.
This creature had previously desired three gifts from God:
the first was memory of His passion;
the second was bodily sickness in youth at thirty years of age;
the third was to have from God's gift three wounds.

As for the first,
I thought I had some sense of the passion of Christ, but still
I desired more by the grace of God.

I thought that I wished to have been at that time with Mary Magdalen
and with the others who were Christ's lovers,
and therefore I desired a bodily sight wherein I could have more knowledge
of the bodily pains of our Savior, and
of the compassion of Our Lady and
of all His true lovers who at that time saw His pains,
for I wished to be one of them and to suffer with them.

I never desired any other sight or showing
of God until the soul was departed from the body
(for I believed to be saved by the mercy of God).

The purpose for this petition was so that after the showing
I would have a more true consciousness of the Passion of Christ.

The second gift came to my mind with contrition, freely without any effort:
a willing desire to have from God's gift a bodily sickness.
I wished that the sickness would be so severe as to seem mortal
so that I could, in that sickness,
receive all my rites of Holy Church,
myself expecting that I should die,

5

and that all creatures who saw me could suppose the same
(for I wished to have no kind of comfort from earthly life).

In this sickness, I desired to have all the kinds of pains, bodily
and spiritual, that I would have if I were to die, with all the fears
and temptations of the fiends—except the outpassing of the soul.

And this I intended so that
* I would be purged by the mercy of God and*
* afterwards live more to the honor of God because of that sickness,*
* for I hoped that it could be to my benefit when I would have died*
(for I desired to be soon with my God and Maker).

These two desires for the Passion and the sickness I desired of Him with
* a condition (for it seemed to me this was not the common custom of prayer)*
* saying thus:*
* "Lord, Thou knowest what I wish—if it be Thy will that I have it;*
* and if it be not Thy will, good Lord, be not displeased,*
* for I want nothing except what Thou wilt."*

For the third gift, by the grace of God and teaching of Holy Church,
* I conceived a mighty desire to receive three wounds while I was alive:*
* that is to say,*
* the wound of true contrition,*
* the wound of natural compassion, and*
* the wound of earnest yearning for God.*
And, just as I asked the other two with a condition,
* so all this last petition I asked mightily without any condition.*

The first two desires passed from my memory,
* but the third dwelled with me constantly.*

 Chapter 2 is an opening, a wound that might be healed, a womb that might be filled. Can we imagine what Julian's life may have been, that led her to the place where she asks God to enter in? She starts by telling us when it happened. The narrative speaks the voice of experience; Julian begins her story.

 Julian asked for memory of Christ's passion. She may have known some intense pain, loss, suffering, or grief and concluded that a deeper awareness of Jesus' dying would help to heal her own wounds. Julian tells us that her longing was for more love. Her time, and her particular practice of devotion, made the events of the life of Jesus very real and tangible. Julian will not be satisfied with a simple intellectual experience of the Passion. She wants to see it. She wants to know Jesus' pains and the compassion felt by those who loved Him. This is not morbid curiosity. Something had struck a chord in Julian that told her that "if only" she could experience it, everything would be different. Perhaps that would mean a conversion into a deeper faith, a more meaningful life (if life had lost its appeal), or a reprieve from grief. Whatever the situation, the awareness of God in his Passion, greater consciousness of his suffering and death, was what she wanted. In an age that knew crusades, wars, and plagues, a God who suffers like us was easy to recognize. Yet to say "show it to me" is another matter.

Julian's second request is still harder for us to understand. Why would anyone ask for illness? Julian's words suggest dissatisfaction with her life. There was not much left for her here, whatever she had lost or turned away from. It was time to start over. Julian prays for a full awareness of God's human suffering: a full experience of suffering in her own body. Few people invite such drastic measures, yet we are always bidding God to break through, to join us more fully on our journey. Sometimes we don't really want God here with us; at most times it is terrifying to imagine turning everything over to God. But Julian wanted that wound— the hurt place, the open space—that would keep her always desiring her God.

❧ **3** ❧

When I was thirty years old and a half, God sent me a bodily sickness
     in which I lay three days and three nights;
     and on the fourth night, I received all my rites of Holy Church
     and expected not to have lived till day.

After this I lay two days and two nights.
     And on the third night I expected often to have passed away
     (and so expected they that were with me).

And being still in youth, I thought it a great sadness to die—
          not for anything that was on earth that pleased me to live for,
          nor for any pain that I was afraid of
               (for I trusted in God of His mercy)
          but because I would have liked to have lived so that I could have
               loved God better and for a longer time,
               so that I could have more knowledge and
                    love from God in the bliss of heaven.

For it seemed to me that all the time I had lived here—
     so little and so short in comparison to that endless bliss—
     I thought of as nothing.
     Wherefore I thought:
          "Good Lord, let my living no longer be to Thine honor!"

And I understood by my reason and by the experience of my pains
     that I would die.
And I assented fully with all the will of my heart, to be at God's will.

Thus I endured till day,
     and by then my body was dead from the midst downwards as
          regards my feeling.
     Then was I aided to be set upright, supported with help, in order
          to have more freedom for my heart to be at God's will, and
          thinking of God while my life should last.

My curate was sent for to be at my ending, and by the time he came
    I had cast my eyes upwards and could not speak.
He placed the cross before my face and said:
    "I have brought thee the image of thy Maker and Savior.
        Look thereupon and comfort thyself with it."

It seemed to me that I was all right,
    for my eyes were set upwards to heaven
        (where I trusted to come by the mercy of God)
    but nevertheless I consented to fix my eyes on the face of the crucifix
      if I could, and so I did
        (for it seemed to me that I might longer endure to look straight forward
          than straight up).

After this my sight began to fail
    and it grew all dark about me in the chamber as if it had been night,
    except on the image of the cross on which I beheld an ordinary light,
    and I know not how.

Everything except the cross became ugly to me as if it had been much possessed
    by the fiends.

And after this the upper part of my body began to die so noticeably that scarcely
    had I any feeling—
    my worst pain was shortness of breath and waning of life.

And then I expected truly to have passed away.

But, in the midst of this,
    suddenly all my pain was taken from me
    and I was as whole (especially in the upper part of my body)
    as ever I had been before.

I marveled at this sudden change
    (for it seemed to me that it was a secret act of God and not of nature)
but even with the feeling of this comfort, I trusted never the more to live;

    and the feeling of this comfort was no full ease to me,
        for it seemed to me I would rather have been delivered from this world,
        for my heart was wishfully set on that.

Then came suddenly to my memory
    that I should desire the second wound of our Lord's gracious gift:

that my body could be filled with the memory and feeling of
His blessed Passion, as I had prayed before
(for I had wished that His pains were my pains with
compassion, and, afterward, yearning for God).

Thus I thought I could with His grace
have the wounds that I had desired before.

However, in this I never desired any bodily sight
nor any kind of showing from God
(except compassion, such as a natural soul could have with our
Lord Jesus, who for the sake of love willed to be a mortal man).

And therefore I desired to suffer with Him, while living in my mortal body,
as God would give me grace.

     

Julian remembers; she weaves into this story a connection between present and past. Perhaps in narrative reflection she reconstructed her earlier prayer. The beginning of Chapter 3 resonates with Christic references. Julian is about thirty, and she lies for three days in the first part of her illness. In the context of her interpretations of the showings she receives, the miraculous occurrence is not that she has to wait for heaven to receive knowledge and love. Rather, her meditations on the unique experience of this portion of her life become a window into the soul, a greater knowledge and understanding of God. Julian credits God for giving her this "understanding," but it is clear that her long process of exegesis of the "text" of God's showing to her produced an extraordinary theology. Julian is particular not simply because God "showed" her something. She is special because as a woman (rather than a scholastically educated priest) she took what God had put before her and developed a rich and detailed, one might even say "systematic," theology.

When Julian writes that she thought of her life prior to her illness as "nothing," there are a few different ways we can read her. On the one hand, she has the breadth of the theological explanation of heaven before her—the orthodox belief for a medieval person that this world is but a shadow of all that the next one promises. But what was that "nothing"? Medical science has proven that illness often comes at a time when we are psychologically "dispirited," when we have been through trauma and grief. For Julian to have prayed for illness sounds like giving up.

Are these the cries of a desperate person who seeks through faith something more than the world can offer? Should we understand this whole story as a reading and reflection by Julian after the fact, to attempt to construct a narrative frame for the dramatic events that unfold in her life? She remembers she had asked for illness—does that translate into those times when we wish we could escape from our lives? What is the connection between that and the dawn of awareness, when those moments when we are faced with our mortality really arrive?

Julian makes a particular rhetorical gesture of acceptance of forthcoming death. When literally faced with the crucifix, she realizes that she has been inserted into this narrative of the Passion. *Contemplatio* brought the medieval Christian to a quest for so thorough a union with the humanity of the Incarnate God that recollection of his suffering is not through the screen of identification but rather the full union of authentic experience. Julian was not craving some special grace that would set her apart. She asks for what every Christian of her time ought to desire. She asks to be receptive; whatever follows, she argues, is not of her doing; rather, it is God's will. This position is important for anyone who boldly claims to experience God as directly as Julian does in her story. It cannot be forced and must not seem "self-authored." Instead, the experience must be driven by God—who, as Julian maintains, loved us first. Thus she closes this chapter with a prayer for openness, to be receptive to the actions of God in our lives, and goes on to detail what happens when she does so. Can we be so open to the possibilities God offers? If such revelations were to come, would we be willing to commit to discern their meanings as Julian was in the interpretive text she produces?

4

In this showing suddenly I saw the red blood trickling down from under the
garland,
> hot and freshly and most plenteously,
> just as it was at the time of His Passion
>> when the garland of thorns was pressed onto His blessed head.

Just so, I conceived truly and powerfully that it was He Himself
> (both God and man, the Same who suffered thus for me)
> who showed it to me without any go-between.

And in the same showing suddenly the Trinity almost filled my heart with joy.
> (And I understood it shall be like that in heaven without end for
>> all that shall come there.)

>> For the Trinity is God, God is the Trinity;
>>> the Trinity is our Maker,
>>> the Trinity is our Keeper,
>>> the Trinity is our everlasting Lover,
>>> the Trinity is our endless Joy and Bliss,
>>>> by our Lord Jesus Christ.

(And this was shown in the first revelation and in all of them, for whenever
Jesus appears, the blessed Trinity is understood, as I see it.)

And I said: "Benedicite domine!"
> (This I said, for reverence in my meaning, with a powerful voice,
> and full greatly astonished because of the wonder and amazement
>> that I had that He who is so respected and awesome wished
>> to be so familiar with a sinful creature living in this miserable flesh.)

Thus I understood that at that time our Lord Jesus out of His gracious love
> wished to show me comfort before the time of my temptation
>> (for it seemed to me that it could well be that I would—
>> by the permission of God and with His protection—
>> be tempted by fiends before I died).

With this sight of His blessed Passion
   along with the Godhead that I saw in my understanding,
   I knew well that it was strength enough for me
      (yea, and for all creatures living that would be saved)
   against all the fiends of hell and spiritual temptation.

In this showing He brought Our Blessed Lady Saint Mary to my mind.
   I saw her spiritually in bodily likeness,
      a simple maid and humble,
      young of age and little grown beyond childhood,
      in the stature that she was when she conceived with child.

Also God showed in part the wisdom and the truth of her soul
   wherein I understood the reverent contemplation with which she
      beheld her God and Maker,
   marveling with great reverence that He wished to be born of her
   who was a simple creature of His own creation.

And this wisdom and truth
      (knowing the greatness of her Creator
      and the littleness of herself who is created)
   caused her to say full humbly to Gabriel:
      "Behold me here, God's handmaiden."

In this sight I understood truly
   that she is higher in worthiness and grace than all that God made
      beneath her,
   for nothing that is created is greater than she, except the blessed
      Manhood of Christ, as I see it.

Here is the crucifixion. The first image is of blood; notice its sensory qualities. It is red; it trickles; it is hot and fresh and abundant. One can almost feel the pressure of the crown of thorns on human flesh. That puncture wound is an opening into the showings; the blood that flows— here is the narrative of Julian's experience. In one of the text's most straightforward depictions of her experience, Julian simply states: I saw the blood, and I knew this vision came from God, and I knew this God-and-man had suffered for me. Her narrative is direct; her experience is direct. The absolute certainty of these words is stunning. She proceeds to deal immediately with perhaps the most intellectually challenging

aspect of Christian theology: the Trinity. Awareness of the Trinity "fill[s
her] heart with joy." That's it—no philosophical explanation, just a direct
leap from blood to Savior to Trinity. The Trinity is not a logical problem;
rather, it is endless bliss, the experience those in heaven will know. This
Trinitarian theology is crucial at the beginning of the showings, the start
of the story. For Julian, the Trinity is God and is indivisible. She literally
"sees" the Trinity in every one of her showings. That sight may be physical or in her "understanding," but its presence is a *sine qua non*. For the
showings to occur, Julian must own an awareness of God through the
sensory perceptions that allow her to imagine Christ, while the work of
the Spirit in the world may be credited for her visionary experience.

Julian speaks a formulaic "blessed be God!" She is willfully giving
thanks for her showing, but this gesture is also a reflex action—divine/
human threshold crossed in the Incarnation, the heart of mystical experience. The words Julian articulates in repose—her text that we read here—
they too are *"Benedicite domine."* Julian notes that God brought Mary to
her mind. The entire showings (and *Showings*) is a series of multiple
incarnations. She who said "let it be done to me according to thy word"
is born into the mind of Julian by the God who fathered the *Logos*, the
Word, into Mary's own body. The showings allow Julian to be Mary.
Mary bore the Word; Julian bears the Word in her text. Although she had
prayed for this very experience, she is nevertheless awed by it. Her
knowledge of God is Mary's, as it is every one of ours. We are God's
"familiars," God's intimately beloved souls and bodies.

The Passion is a comfort against temptation. Julian's Christianity offers the paradox that God's suffering might both console and give power.
Mary's soul has "wisdom and truth": so, Julian aspires, does her own.
Mary's "wisdom and truth," beholding her Creator and considering her
own self, allowed her to say yes. Julian needs this courage; she too must
say yes. For her it is no struggle; it comes as a reflex. Julian's *"Benedicite
domine!"* is Mary's "Behold me here, God's handmaiden." It is an acceptance without question or doubt. If Mary could say yes, so could
Julian. God offers her this example as a first lesson in love. She in turn
offers it, and herself as text, to the reader who begins her narrative of
the showings. Will we unequivocally say yes to God—no matter what
is shown, whatever we have asked for (or not?) that is set before us? Are
we ready to receive God's gift, God's love? Our souls have this potential
reflex action to receive love. Julian begins to teach God's incredible love;
we are invited just to accept. *Benedicite domine!*

ℭ𝓈 **5** 𝓈ℴ

*At this same time that I saw this sight of the head bleeding, our good Lord
  showed to me a spiritual vision of His simple loving.*

I saw that He is to us everything that is good and comfortable for us.

> *He is our clothing which for love enwraps us,*
> > *holds us,*
> > > *and all encloses us because of His tender love,*
> > > > *so that He may never leave us.*

*And so in this showing I saw that He is to us everything that is good,
  as I understood it.*

*Also in this revelation He showed a little thing,
  the size of an hazel nut
  in the palm of my hand,
  and it was as round as a ball.*

*I looked at it with the eye of my understanding and thought:
  "What can this be?"*

And it was generally answered thus: "It is all that is made."

*I marveled how it could continue,
  because it seemed to me it could suddenly have sunk into nothingness
    because of its littleness.
And I was answered in my understanding:
  "It continueth and always shall, because God loveth it;
  and in this way everything hath its being by the love of God."
In this little thing I saw three characteristics:
  the first is that God made it,
  the second is that God loves it,
  the third, that God keeps it.*

But what did I observe in that?
　　Truly the Maker, the Lover, and the Keeper for,
　　　　　until I am in essence one-ed to Him,
　　　　　I can never have full rest nor true joy
　　　　(that is to say,
　　　　　until I am made so fast to Him
　　　　　that there is absolutely nothing that is created
　　　　　separating my God and myself).

It is necessary for us to have awareness
　　of the littleness of created things
　　　　and to set at naught everything that is created,
　　　　in order to love and have God who is uncreated.

For this is the reason why we are not fully at ease in heart and soul:
　　because here we seek rest in these things that are so little,
　　　　in which there is no rest,
　　and we recognize not our God who is all powerful, all wise, all good,
　　　　for He is the true rest.

God wishes to be known,
　　and He delights that we remain in Him,
　　because all that is less than He is not enough for us.

And this is the reason why no soul is at rest
　　until it is emptied of everything that is created.

When the soul is willingly emptied for love
　　in order to have Him who is all,
　　then is it able to receive spiritual rest.

Also our Lord God showed
　　that it is full great pleasure to Him
　　that a pitiable soul come to Him nakedly and plainly and simply.
　　　　For this is the natural yearning of the soul,
　　　　thanks to the touching of the Holy Spirit,
　　　　according to the understanding that I have in this showing—
　　　　　"God, of Thy goodness, give me Thyself;
　　　　　　for Thou art enough to me,
　　　　　　and I can ask nothing that is less
　　　　　　that can be full honor to Thee.
　　　　　And if I ask anything that is less,

ever shall I be in want,
   for only in Thee have I all."

These words are full lovely to the soul
   and most nearly touch upon the will of God and His goodness,
      for His goodness fills all His creatures and all His blessed works,
      and surpasses them without end,
         for He is the endlessness.

And He has made us only for Himself
   and restored us by His blessed passion
   and ever keeps us in His blessed love.

And all this is from His goodness.

     ℬ ℬ ℬ

"Is it enough"? Is it enough that God so loves us? Can we truly let go? Are we willing to trust? These are not easy questions to answer, particularly when we reflect on the fact that what we hold dearest sometimes stands in our way of fuller communion with our God. Yet he wants us to know that we are enough for him if we will answer his call. This chapter begins with an image of the physical reality of the Passion of Jesus (the bleeding head) joined to the depths of theological understanding (the simple loving). Julian's clothing metaphor—that God's love enfolds us and will never leave us—functions as a kind of safety net. The Christian is given this kind of reassurance and protection in exchange for the trust God asks for. The famous hazelnut metaphor is a lesson in the fragility and minuteness of all creation. It is sustained by God's love. Julian presents an image of a parent-God who cuddles us up in a blanket of love; he literally holds us in his hand. The other side of this comfort is that we must be willing to renounce our ego. Are we willing to turn everything over to him? On the one hand, the "one-ing" described here is a process that will only be fully achieved in heaven. In a very Augustinian sense, as long as we have human bodies we are always going to be looking for rest and joy elsewhere. Yet contained in Julian's message is the call to let go of our "things," to renounce separation and allow ourselves to be drawn only to God. For Julian the writer we must contextualize these words with respect to her visionary experience. She had to let go and trust enough to believe that wherever it was taking her, she would be safe. The barriers raised by her subjectivity and ego would only get in the way of what God was doing. For some of us it may take mortal illness and a vision to convince us to drop what we are doing and listen. But the message here is that God offers love and rest wherever we are, whatever we are doing, if only we will let go.

Julian makes a distinction between the littleness of the created and the greatness of the uncreated. To such a degree God's uniqueness stands in relation to our "doing." What we "do" or "make" is nothing compared to That Which Is, what was never created. Here is the call to stop what we are "doing" and just "be." Julian does not say that we necessarily must throw down our lives as we know them, the failed rests in which we are already enfolded. But she certainly does challenge our attachment to what is familiar, what we are most invested in. There may be many ways in which our God is working through every aspect of our lives. Yet if we see the things themselves and not the hand of God in them, we surely miss the mark. Neither Julian nor God commands us to toss aside our relationships in this world or the work that we do. However, God invites us to be willing to do so; that is the challenge. This philosophy is not about self-abnegation. Rather, we are called to reimagine all of our attachments.

Julian did not die after her showings. Instead, she stayed around for many more decades to refine the theology she had experienced directly, so that six hundred years later we read it and interpret its meaning for our own lives. Julian became a much-trusted spiritual adviser. This is transformation of life, not utter and complete dismissal of the world. There is no quick "escape" into the arms of bliss. The lesson we learn from Julian is that we are all called to allow the hand of God to work in us and through us. We are called to find the courage within ourselves to say yes. Spiritual rest in this world is not inactivity. It is work and relationships here and now, within which we can know a dynamic kind of peace, a positive spiritual inertia in which we feel propelled forward not by our own will but in an awareness of God operating through us.

Julian writes a remarkable love letter to a God who desires his creatures to demand all of him. God is our sole desire, and God wants to give us all of himself. God is enough. God asks for all of us— knowing, as Augustine says, that it is an impossible request while we still have human bodies. So God gives us grace, the Holy Spirit awakening us to allow God to work in and through our lives. It is a fine line to walk, between the awareness that it is God whom we seek and the necessary mindfulness that we seek him in so many of the places and spaces that already infuse our worlds. When we realize that it is indeed he whom we love, desire, and care for, our reverence increases. I do not love my parent, spouse, or child less because I know it is God I seek and love in them; rather, this consciousness allows me to love better, putting our limited humanity into a broader divine context. I do not love my work less because it is some kind of substitute for God; rather, I can function with greater passion and integrity in the knowledge that if I am open to God, God will always work through me. The magic is that I get to let go. It does not all have to depend on me. The secret is that, whether I know it or not, thanks to the grace of the Holy Spirit's touch God is already working through me in my relationships and activities. Julian held on so tightly that the only way God could invite her to let go was through these visions of Christ's passion. We can identify with her struggle. We can also identify with her epiphany, that it was God alone whom she desired. May this knowledge seep into our lives and transform us, allowing grace to operate more fully, calling us to let go and let God.

ଔ **6** ଐ

This showing was made to teach our soul wisely to cleave to the goodness
of God.
At that time the custom of our praying was brought to mind:
how for lack of understanding and recognition of love,
we are used to creating many intermediaries.

Then saw I truly that it is more honor to God and more true delight
that we faithfully pray to Himself out of His goodness,
and cleave to that goodness by His grace with true understanding
and steadfast belief,
than if we created all the intermediaries that heart can think of.

For if we create all these intermediaries,
it is too little,
and not complete honor to God,
whereas all the whole of it is in His goodness,
and there absolutely nothing fails.

For this, as I shall say, came to my mind at the same time:
we pray to God
by His Holy Flesh
and by His Precious Blood,
His Holy Passion,
His dearworthy Death and Wounds,
by all His blessed Human Nature,
but the endless life that we have from all this is from His goodness.

And we pray to Him by His sweet Mother's love who bore Him,
but all the help we have from her is of His goodness.

And we pray by His Holy Cross that He died on,
but all the strength and the help that we have from the cross is from
His goodness.

And in the same way, all the help that we have from special saints
    and all the blessed company of heaven—
the dearworthy love and endless friendship that we have from
    them—it is from His goodness.

For God of His goodness has ordained intermediaries to help us, all fair
    and many,
        of which the chief and principal intermediary is the blessed Human
            Nature that He took from the Maid,
        with all the intermediaries that go before and come after which
            are part of our redemption and our endless salvation.

Wherefore it pleases Him
        that we seek Him and worship Him by intermediaries,
            understanding and recognizing that He is the goodness of all.

For the goodness of God is the highest prayer and it comes down to
    the lowest part of our need.
        It vitalizes our soul
        and brings it to life
        and makes it grow in grace and virtue

        It is nearest us in nature
        and readiest in grace
            (for it is the same grace that the soul seeks and ever shall,
                till we know our God truly who has us all in Himself enclosed).

A man goes upright
        and the food of his body is sealed as in a purse full fair;
        and when it is time of his necessity, it is opened
        and sealed again full honestly.
And that it is He who does this is shown there where He says that He
    comes down to us to the lowest part of our need.

For He does not despise what He has created,
        and He does not disdain to serve us even at the simplest duty that
            is proper to our body in nature, because of the love of our soul
                which He has made in His own likeness

        For as the body is clad in the clothes,
        and the flesh in the skin,
        and the bones in the flesh,
        and the heart in the breast,

so are we, soul and body, clad in the goodness of God and enclosed
   —yea, and even more intimately,
      because all these others may waste and wear away,
      but the goodness of God is ever whole,
      and nearer to us without any comparison.

For truly our Lover desires that our soul cleave to Him with all its might
  and that we evermore cleave to His goodness,
    for of all things that heart can think,
    this pleases God most and soonest succeeds.

For our soul is so especially beloved by Him that is Highest that it
  surpasses the knowledge of all creatures
    (that is to say, there is no creature that is made that can know
      how much and how sweetly and how tenderly our Creator loves us).

Therefore we can, with His grace and His help, remain in spiritual
  contemplation, with everlasting wonder at this high, surpassing,
  inestimable love which Almighty God has for us of His goodness.

And therefore we can ask of our Lover with reverence all that we wish,
    for our natural wish is to have God
    and the good wish of God is to have us.

And we can never leave off wishing nor longing until we have Him in
  fullness of joy, and then can we wish for nothing more,
    for He wills that we be occupied
    in knowing and loving
    until the time that we shall be fulfilled in heaven.

      And for this purpose was this lesson of love shown (along
         with all that follows, as you shall see)—for the strength
         and the basis of all was shown in the first vision.

For of all things,
  the beholding and the loving of the Creator
    makes the soul seem less in its own sight,
    and most fills it with reverent fear and true humility,
    with an abundance of love for its fellow Christians.

      ജ   ജ   ജ

What does it mean to "cleave to the goodness of God"? This chapter describes that experience in a range of different forms. Julian's Christianity shows its metaphor and mysticism. How else can she dismiss intermediaries and then demonstrate, in the Incarnation, how interconnected are all creatures, including the human person made in the image of God? When the soul cleaves to the goodness of God it is cleaving to the source of its creation. The body of God is the doorway into our share in that creation. Julian repeats the word "goodness" often in this chapter. In prayer, this is what we adhere to. It is natural for us to cleave to divine goodness, because it made us. In the monotheistic God of this incarnational Christianity, God is good. This is no cliché; God is goodness itself, manifest through all things. When Julian prays in Chapter 5 that God might give her himself, she says it is of that very goodness. Here is the foundation of the incarnational process: the manifestation of goodness. Incarnation is the extension of goodness. The body of Jesus itself is an intermediary, an answer to a prayer. The need is a prayer unspoken, embodied in goodness, the answer. There is dynamism here in the process of creation that is not about an active/passive deed but rather a continual interaction between this force that is goodness itself addressing every reaction. It is not asking and answering: it is exchange and application. The substance is like our substance; it is prepared to act through the order of the incarnate Spirit. It is, as Julian explains earlier, that which we are driven to desire. Julian's human being longs for the familiar grace that is goodness made manifest. It is of this very stuff that we are made. We are already enclosed in God's goodness, so we need not seek it out. This is grace; this is the goodness of God. This is the same God that always already has enclosed us, that always already has solved every need through the action of grace. The goodness of God quite literally cleaves to us in these metaphors of the Incarnation. Our every need is met through prayers that never need to be spoken yet are acted upon through grace. The human mind may wake up to this reality and willingly cleave to this very goodness that is constantly operating on it and in it, without memory of beginning or awareness of end. Julian, in her illness, awakened to the knowledge of a creation tended to and infused by such goodness—and she cannot refrain from sharing it with her fellow human beings.

The act of will is real. Grace, active goodness in the world, answers prayers without need of their utterance. Prayer is radically redefined as the dynamic exchange between a need and an action of grace made manifest. Yet in this great creation that is so loved—so "gooded"—the

Creator still wants us to love and cleave to him as much as he loves and enfolds us. Goodness attracts more goodness. The manifestation of goodness in our share in the Incarnation leaves us desiring that from which we were made and in which we are enclosed. The trajectory of grace travels in both directions, leading the human mind and soul to the desire of God. We are not off track; we are not lost. We are simply loved and ready to love. We are always going to keep longing. Julian writes that it is God's will that it is so, knowing and loving and desiring. We see how small we are, not so that we might despise ourselves but so that we may realize the literal goodness of God working in us and through us, connecting us to the shared goodness that is the wonderful web of incarnation on earth and glorious communion of saints in heaven.

7

And to teach us this, as I understand it, our Lord God showed
Our Lady Saint Mary at the same time
(which is to signify the exalted wisdom and truth she had in contemplating
her Creator
so great,
so high,
so mighty,
and so good).

This greatness and this nobility of her vision of God filled her with reverent fear
and with this she saw herself
so little and so lowly,
so simple and so poor, in relation to her Lord God,
that this reverent dread filled her with humility.

And thus, for this reason, she was filled full of grace
and of all kinds of virtues
and surpasses all creatures.
During all the time that He showed this which I have just described in spiritual
vision, I was watching the bodily sight of the abundant bleeding of the Head
continuing.
The great drops of blood fell down from under the garland like pellets,
seeming as if they had come out of the veins;
and as they emerged they were brown-red
(for the blood was very thick)
and in the spreading out they were bright red;
and when the blood came to the brows,
there the drops vanished;
and nevertheless the bleeding continued until many things were seen
and understood.

The beauty and the lifelikeness was comparable to nothing except itself.

The abundance was like the drops of water that fall off the eaves
of a house after a great shower of rain which fall so thick that
no man can number them with earthly wit.
And because of their roundness, the drops were like the scales of
herring as they spread over the forehead.

> *These three things came to my mind at the time:*
> *pellets, because of roundness, in the emerging of the blood;*
> *the scales of herring, in the spreading over the forehead,*
> *because of the roundness;*
> *the drops off the eaves of a house,*
> *because of the immeasurable abundance.*

This showing was alive and active,
and hideous and dreadful,
and sweet and lovely.

And of all the sights it was most comfort to me that our God and Lord,
who is so worthy of respect
and so fearsome,
is also so plain and gracious;
and this filled me almost full with delight and security of soul.

> *For the interpretation of this He showed me this clear example: it is the most*
> *honor that a solemn king or great lord can do for a poor servant if he is*
> *willing to be friendly with him, and, specifically, if he demonstrates it him-*
> *self, from a full, true intention, and with a glad countenance, both privately*
> *and publicly. Then thinks this poor creature thus: "Ah! How could this*
> *noble lord give more honor and joy to me than to show me, who am so little,*
> *this marvelous friendliness? Truly, it is more joy and pleasure to me than*
> *if he gave me great gifts and were himself distant in manner."*

This bodily example was shown so mightily that man's heart could be
carried away and almost forget itself for joy over this great friendliness.

Thus it fares between our Lord Jesus and ourselves;
for truly it is the most joy that can be, as I see it,
that He who is highest and mightiest,
noblest and worthiest,
is also lowliest and meekest,
most friendly and most gracious.

And surely and truly this marvelous joy shall be shown us all when we see Him.
   And this wishes Our Lord:
      that we believe and trust,
         enjoy and delight,
         comfort and solace ourselves, as best we can,
         with His grace and with His help,
         until the time that we see that joy truly.

For the greatest fullness of joy that we shall have, as I see it, is the marvelous
   graciousness and friendliness
      of the Father who is our Creator,
      in the Lord Jesus Christ who is our Brother and our Savior.

But no man can be aware of this marvelous friendliness in this life,
   unless he receives it by special showing from Our Lord,
   or from a great abundance of grace inwardly given from the Holy Spirit.

But faith and belief with love are worthy to have the reward,
   and so it is received by grace—
   for in faith with hope and love, our life is grounded.

The showing (made to whom God wishes) plainly teaches the same, uncovered
   and explained with many secret points which are parts of our Faith and
   Belief which it is honorable to know. And when the showing, which is
   given at one time, is past and hidden, then the Faith keeps it by the grace
   of the Holy Spirit until our life's end.

And this is the showing—it is none other than the Faith, neither less nor more
   (as can be seen by our Lord's meaning in the earlier matter)
   until it comes to the final end.

ℬ ℬ ℬ

Chapter 7 begins with one of those "intermediaries" discussed in Chapter 6. Julian again puts forward Mary with a clear sense of identification. The theology of the Incarnation, the "good-ing" "intermediariness" of God/goodness unites Mary and Julian in the web of connection. Julian has become aware of God as goodness-by-definition that keeps desiring us. Mary allowed herself to be desired by God for his purpose. Mary literally "beheld" the Creator in her womb in the process of giving flesh to God. These details follow Julian's long discussion of God's enclosure of the soul through goodness. Here we have the female form that gave God a body. In turn, we have Julian who gives the Word words. His goodness cleaves to Mary in her womb; she, in her mind's eye, cleaves to him by her acceptance. Julian, in the showings, experiences the Divine Word conceived within her soul, known in body, intellect, and spiritual vision. She then mothers forth the text.

We are all these intermediaries of Chapter 6. The text is born to us in Julian's composition, and that Word is born anew to us each time we contemplate it. Intellectually, spiritually, bodily, its goodness cleaves to us and we cleave to it like drops of blood. At the same time that this process is unfolding, the ongoing Passion of God is occurring. The suffering must keep happening; the act of salvation is a process forever being made and remade in Julian's composition of the text and our consumption of its body. She celebrates the mass of her showings in making this Word Incarnate. The blood of Chapter 7 is the stuff of enclosure, holding in the goodness of God and wrapping up our souls. The goodness of God is that sacramental, sacrificial, corporeal liquid that is the ink of Julian's text. The action of the Creator allows goodness to be spilled forth through the first making of flesh; the living of that *Logos*-flesh—the life of the Son—is pained in its passion; yet by the movement of grace, the goodness of God in the action of the Spirit bleeds through.

Julian's metaphor of the blood's flow is a contemplative meditation on a stream, moving more deeply into prayer. In the mind, in the body, the unfolding of understanding begins to take shape like those drops of blood changing in color and form. The images—ideas—are the germs and gems of understanding beginning to coagulate for Julian. It is as impossible to count these drops as it is to convey what they are really like. Our God is known yet unknown: Julian strives to describe what the blood resembles, but everything falls short of the ineffable Word. Yet they are all we, as we are all he. This God is "plain and gracious" because he bleeds like us. That material form of the blood that encloses Goodness is the same blood any mortal might bleed. Julian surely encountered deaths from illness, probably plague. God willfully came down not in disease but in goodness, a God who does not need us but desires us all the same. Julian's age struggled to accept that "gentle deeds" more than "gentle birth" made the gentleman, that true courtesy was of actions, not blood. Julian's "bodily example" is one of "friendliness," the lord who humbles himself. The radical nature of this theology must be understood in the context of its social history. This element of shared humanity—with God and one's fellow incarnate-intermediaries—is central to Julian's showings. Julian puts forth a theology of humbling Incarnation by goodness/God and the egalitarianism of all creatures before a God who so humbled himself. Does she speak as a woman writer here, claiming her voice and right to this vision despite the female body that may separate her from the male clerical theologians of her world? Or had the Julian whose life we do not know experienced some kind of humbling in material circumstances or rank? Whatever the case may be, the author revels in the "friendliness" of God, a notion that she maintains one can only learn through God's explicit individual revelation. In those drops of blood that continuously fall, the Passion is ever occurring. The "friendliness" of our God ever bends down to us in our need, making us one with him. The goodness of God fills each of us "intermediaries" as we realize our connection with one another. The goodness of God pours out, making friends of us in the repair of the world.

8

*As long as I saw this sight of the plenteous bleeding of the head, I
could never cease these words: "Benedicite domine!"*

In this showing of the bleeding I interpreted six things:
    *the first is the sign of the blessed Passion and the plenteous shedding
        of His Precious Blood;*
    the second is the Maiden who is His dearworthy Mother;
    *the third is the blessed Godhead that ever was, is and ever shall be,
        all Power, all Wisdom, all Love;*
    *the fourth is everything that He has created (for well I know that
        heaven and earth and all that is created is ample and large,
        fair and good,*
        *but the reason why it appeared so little in my vision was because
        I saw it in the Presence of Him who is the Creator of all things,
        and to a soul that sees the Creator of everything, all that is
        created seems very little);*
    *the fifth is that He created everything for love
        and by the same love everything is protected
        and shall be without end;*
    *the sixth is that God is everything that is good, as I see it,
        and the goodness that everything has, it is He.*

*All this our Lord showed me in the first vision
    and gave me time and space to contemplate it,
        and the bodily sight ceased,
        and the spiritual sight remained in my understanding.*

And I waited with reverent fear, rejoicing in what I saw.

*And I desired, as much as I dared, to see more, if it were His will
    (or else the same thing for a longer time).*

In all this, I was much moved in love for my fellow Christians—that they could see and know the same that I saw, for I wish it to be a comfort to them—because all this sight was shown universally.

Then I said to those who were around me:
    "It is Doomsday today for me."
    (This I said because I expected to have died—for on the day that
    a man or woman dies, that person experiences the particular
    judgment as he shall be without end, as I understand it.)

I said this because I wished they would love God the better,
    in order to remind them that this life is short,
    as they might see in my example
        (for in all this time I expected to have died, and that was a wonder
            to me and sad in part, because it seemed to me that this vision was
            shown for those who would live).

All that I say concerning myself, I say in the person of all my fellow Christians, for I am taught in the spiritual showing of our Lord God, that He intends it so.

Therefore I beg you all for God's sake,
    and I advise you for your own benefit,
    that you believe this vision of a sinner to whom it was shown,
    and powerfully, wisely, and humbly look to God
    who of His gracious love and endless goodness wishes to show the vision
        universally in reassurance for us all.

It is God's will that you receive it with great joy and delight since Jesus has shown it to you all.

ЄЭ   ЄЭ   ЄЭ

Julian steps back to parse her text, providing an exegesis of the preceding events, a theological summary. Her analysis begins with the literal. She moves from the bleeding head of Christ to the Passion. We know the difficulties of our lives—the pain, the literal and metaphorical shedding of blood. We seek and hope that there is a purpose to what we experience, as the church taught Julian there was meaning in Christ the saving victim. Julian's second point concerns Mary, who recorded in her body the sufferings of her son, who kept them in her heart. Mary is the prototypical human, the original Julian, inscribed with the Word by the Incarnation. We are who she is, in that we give body to the Holy Spirit's actions in the world. We likewise suffer the world's pains. Julian is look-ing for the bleeding head to make some sense. First she looks to the *mater dolorosa* who had to interpret these things, as Julian is likewise trying to make sense of her own experience. Mary said yes; Julian, in her *"Bene-dicite domine,"* also says yes. But sense must come from God, whom she articulates in terms of time, endlessness, and lacking in beginning. The power of God the creator, the wisdom in the embodiment by the Spirit, all love in the Passion—suddenly, perspective happens for Julian. She moves from grasping at the skirts of the infinite to an awareness of All Created Thing humbled in the Presence. The trajectory begins to climb: from Jesus' sufferings to Mary's memory to God who is responsible for it all. We are back to the hazelnut, the microcosm of the macrocosm. The notion of interconnectedness returns Julian to our utter dependence on God, whose every action is love. The climax comes in a restatement of Julian's "goodness" litany, a characterization of a God whose philosophi-cal definition is goodness and whose will is love. Julian moves from suffering humanity to the mode of incarnation to the singular God; then back again from God the creator to the work of love in the world to ul-timate goodness/Godness embodied in all materiality.

Julian waits, she desires, and she hopes that others might know what she has known. She believes this experience of the goodness and love of God would comfort others. In a sense the project that is her book began during the time of reflection recounted in this chapter. Julian returns from her near-death experience ready to share a lesson of love. There was meaning in her suffering. Her evangelism begins here, but it is hardly a "repent, the end is near" theology. "Fear" as we know it is not part of this narrative; rather, love is. Julian realizes that she may live, and perhaps it is God's will that she show what she has been shown. She is called to teach God's "reassurance." Julian moved back and forth, struggling to describe what she had seen. We join her in this process, looking once at our circumstances, next at their meaning. This is an opening, as the narrative of spiritual sight and understanding continues. Julian discerns, as do we.

❦ 9 ❧

I am not good because of this showing,
   but only if I love God better;
   and in so much as you love God better,
   it is more to you than to me.

I do not say this to those who are wise, for they know it well,
   but I say it to you who are simple,
   for your benefit and comfort,
   for we are all one in love.

Truly it was not shown to me that God loved me better than the least soul that
   is in grace,
   for I am certain that there are many who never had showing nor vision
   (except from the common teaching of Holy Church)
   who love God better than I.

If I look individually at myself, I am just nothing;
   but in general terms, I am, I hope, in unity of love with all my
      fellow Christians.
   On this unity is based the lives of all mankind that shall be saved,
         for God is all that is good, as I see it,
         and God has created all that is created,
         And God loves all that He has created,
      and he who broadly loves all his fellow Christians because of God,
         he loves all that is.

For in mankind that shall be saved is contained all
      (that is to say, all that is created and the Creator of all)
   because in man is God,
         and in God is all,
         and he who loves thus, loves all.

And I hope by the grace of God that he who sees it in this way shall
  be truly taught and mightily comforted if he needs comfort.

I speak of those who shall be saved, because at this time God showed me
  no other.

  But in everything I believe as Holy Church believes, preaches, and teaches
    (for the Faith of Holy Church which I had beforehand believed
      and, as I hope, by the grace of God, willingly observe in use and
      custom, remained constantly in my sight)
  wishing and intending never to accept anything that could be contrary to it.

And with this intent, I watched the showing with all my diligence,
  because in this whole blessed showing,
    I saw it as one with that Faith in God's intention.

All this was shown in three parts: that is to say,
  by bodily sight,
  and by word formed in my understanding,
  and by spiritual sight.
    (However, the spiritual sight I do not know how nor am I able
      to show it as openly nor as fully as I wish,
    but I trust in our Lord God Almighty that He shall of His
      goodness, and because of your love,
    cause you to receive it more spiritually and more sweetly than I
      know how or am able to tell it.)

ଓ   ଓ   ଓ

Julian proceeds with the meta-narrative of her experience, the reflection on the process that is unfolding for her. She seeks to explain what is happening, how she sees it, and what its implications are. If Julian's narrative of her showings helps one soul to love God better, then the whole experience of the showings means more to that soul than to Julian herself who knew it directly. God has acted in the showings; now it is humanity's responsibility to respond. The love of God is for everyone, and Julian's point is to emphasize that her visions do not set her apart except insofar as they enable her to share a message. The showings are thus scripted in terms of service, what Julian must do. They are her wake-up call, her calling to interpret God's meaning. They "one" her to God and to all creation. Through her text, they one her to us. Unity—defying the mystery of Trinity—is the grounding of salvation. Incarnation makes possible the redemption. If we will to love one another, we will to love all. In order to express love, we must love all. This incarnational love does not admit exceptions. God's goodness in the Incarnation spreads love out into All Created Thing. In humankind—the realized potentiality of salvation—is all creation, the very electric charge of the Incarnation in its chemical/physical bonds. Through the act of creation, God/goodness is embodied. Through that enfolding in love of material enclosure, all that is embodied is clothed in God/goodness. There is no separation; there is no break, no distinction in the material world of an "us" versus "them." We need not seek to "get to" God. We are already there by love. In our love for one another, we are in God. God in us is what causes us to love, and to recognize this love in one another. This goodness is a verb: it is the communion of saints on earth that is the Incarnation, the interconnectedness of all things. We are not alone with our God. Our God is in us and with us in the bodies of one another. In and through them and ourselves we are in God.

When Julian speaks of "those who shall be saved," she does not explain where the "unsaved" stand in relation to this unity. Rather, she states that God did not show her anything but the "saved." What distinctions God makes within oneness were never revealed to her. God's will in the showings was not to contradict what she had been taught but, rather, to speak to it in some way. What Julian teaches and what she had been taught must both maintain their integrity, especially for her to proclaim God's message to a culture suspicious of heresy. The church's teaching, the showing, and the intention of God are all one in love, according to her. Julian concludes the chapter with a statement about her experience: an explication of what she cannot explain, partly in response to this question of salvation. Julian was shown God's teaching in three ways: "bodily sight," "word formed in [her] understanding," and "spiritual sight." Julian claims actually to have seen those images of Jesus' passion that she described so vividly, and to have heard, in her "mind's ear," as it were, God's message. But she also knew God's meaning by what she called "spiritual sight." Julian writes that she neither knows how nor is she able to show the "spiritual sight" more clearly. That, for us, is the source of all that cannot easily be explained, the questions whose answers defy easy dichotomies.

10

And after this, I saw with bodily sight
    on the face of the crucifix which hung before me
        (on which I gazed constantly)
    a part of His Passion:
        contempt,
        and spitting
        and defiling
        and smiting
    and many distressing pains—more than I can count,
        and frequent changing of color.

And at the same time I saw how half the face, beginning at the ear, was
    overspread with dried blood until it was covered up to the middle of the face,
    and after that, the other half was covered in the same way,
    and then it vanished in the first part just as it had come.

This I saw physically, sorrowfully and obscurely,
    and I desired more physical light in order to have seen more clearly.
        But I was answered in my reason:
            "If God wishes to show thee more, He shall be thy light.
            Thou needest none but Him."

For I saw Him and still sought Him,
    for we are now so blind and so unwise that we never seek God
        until He of His goodness shows Himself to us;
    and when we see anything of Him by grace, then are we moved by
        the same grace to try with great desire
        to see Him more perfectly.

And thus I saw Him and I sought Him,
    and I possessed Him and I lacked Him.
And this is, and should be, our ordinary behavior in this life,
        as I see it.

At one time my understanding was taken down into the sea-bed,
   and there I saw hills and green dales,
   seeming as if it were overgrown with moss,
     with seaweed and gravel.

Then I understood this:
   that even if a man or woman were there under the broad water,
    if he could have a vision of God there
     (since God is with a man constantly)
   he would be safe in body and soul and receive no harm
   and, even more, he would have more solace and more comfort
    than all this world can tell.

Because He wills that we believe that we experience Him
   constantly (although we imagine that it is but little)
and by this belief He causes us evermore to gain grace, because
    He wishes to be seen and He wishes to be sought,
    He wishes to be awaited and He wishes to be trusted.

This second showing was so lowly and so little and so simple that my spirits were in great travail over the sight—mourning, fearful and yearning—for I was sometimes even in doubt whether it was a showing.

And then at different times our good Lord gave me more insight
   whereby I understood truly that it was a showing.

It was a shape and image of our foul mortal flesh that our fair, bright, blessed Lord bare for our sins.
   It made me think of the holy Veronica's Veil of Rome which He
    has imprinted with His own blessed face
     (when He was in His cruel Passion, willingly going to His death)
   and often changing color.

     From the brownness and blackness, pitifulness and leanness of
      this image, many marvel how it could be so, given that He
      imprinted it with His blessed Face
       which is the fairness of heaven,
        the flower of earth,
        and the fruit of the Maiden's womb.
      Then how could this image be so discolored
       and so far from fair?

I desire to say just as I have understood it by the grace of God.

We know in our Faith and believe by the teaching and preaching
of Holy Church that the entire blessed Trinity created mankind in
His image and to His likeness.

In the same sort of way we know that when man fell so deep and
so wretchedly by sin, there was no other help to restore man
except through Him who created man.

And He that created man for love, by the same love He wished to
restore man to the same bliss, and even more.

And just as we were created like the Trinity
in our first creation,
our Maker wished that we should be like Jesus Christ our Savior,
in heaven without end,
by the strength of our re-creation.

Then between these two He was willing
(for love and honor of man)
to make Himself as much like man in this mortal life
(in our foulness and our wretchedness)
as man could be without sins.

From this comes what the showing signifies.
As I said before, it was the image and likeness of our foul,
black, mortal flesh wherein our fair, bright, blessed Lord
hid His Godhead.
But most surely I dare to say (and we ought to believe) that
no man was as fair as He until the time that His fair
complexion was changed with toil and sorrow,
suffering and dying.

(Of this it is spoken in the eighth revelation where it tells more about
the same likeness—and there it says of the Veronica's Veil of Rome, that it
moves through different changes of color and expression—
sometimes more reassuring and lifelike,
and sometimes more pitifully and deathly—
as can be seen in the eighth revelation.)

This vision was a teaching for my understanding that the constant seeking
of the soul pleases God very much
for the soul can do no more than seek, suffer, and trust, and this is

*brought about in the soul that has it by the Holy Spirit, but the
clarity of finding is by His special grace when it is His will.*

*The seeking with faith, hope, and love pleases our Lord,
and the finding pleases the soul and fills it full of joy.*

*And thus was I taught for my own understanding that seeking is as good as
beholding during the time that He wishes to permit the soul to be in labor.*

*It is God's will that we seek Him until we behold Him,
for by that beholding He shall show us Himself
by His special grace
when He wishes.*

*How a soul shall behave itself in beholding Him,
He Himself shall teach;
and that is most honor to Him
and most benefit to the soul
and mostly received from humility and virtue
with the grace and leading of the Holy Spirit.*

*A soul that simply makes itself fast to God with true trust—either by seeking
or in beholding—that is the most honor that it can do to Him, as I see it.*

*These are two workings which can be seen in this vision:
the one is seeking,
the other is beholding.
The seeking is universal so that every soul can have with His grace
(and ought to have) the moral discernment and teaching of the
Holy Church.*

*It is God's will that we have three objects in our seeking:
The first is that we seek willingly and diligently, without laziness,
as much as possible through His grace, gladly and merrily
without unreasonable sadness and useless sorrow.
The second is that we await Him steadfastly because of His love,
without grumbling or struggling against Him, until our life's end
(for it shall last only a while).
The third is that we trust in Him mightily in fully-certain faith, for
it is His will that we know that He shall appear without
warning and full of blessing to all His lovers—
for His working is secret,
but He wishes to be perceived,*

and His appearing shall be truly without warning,
      but He wishes to be trusted,
because He is most simple and gracious.

Blessed may He be!

૪ઠ   ૪ઠ   ૪ઠ

We glimpse the face of God. It is not a pretty sight. The body of Christ is in pain; the body of Christ as the church, humanity on earth, is suffering. Julian feels this deeply and seeks answers, looks for meaning. She gets only a partial view of the Savior. Still, she sees what Jesus endured: what we do to one another and to our world. In this gory depiction the water of life, the blood of the Christ, is so dried out and devoid of its essence that gradually the face of Jesus is obscured. Sin and suffering in the world are so great that it is impossible for Julian—or for us—to look on the divine. How do we watch a God in pain? It is counterintuitive. Julian hangs on, wanting to see more, yet she is blocked. She is frustrated. Julian must have known great human suffering to be able to depict Jesus' pain so dramatically. She must have had a painful desire for answers. She describes the state of the lover of God: that awkward place where one is not perfectly comfortable with or without divine union. Julian experiences just enough of God to whet her appetite. That comes in our human nature, one-ed with a divine that has inculcated us with desire for more. It renewed as we endure pain and loss and witness human suffering. We are conscious of our need for God. We know God's presence somehow and are aware that we want more than a glimpse.

God wants us to want him. Is the glimpse of God enough of a mustard seed to hold on to? Our lack, particularly of understanding, means difficult days. We are told to hang on. Jesus' suffering has meaning; so does ours. He feels our pain; his one-ing with us allows for pain's transcendence. How could Julian see so little and know so little? Is this really God? How can our image of God be so distorted and wounded at times? Our lives and loves are imperfect. Julian wants to see answers in the face of God. Psalm 27:11 beseeches: "Your face, Lord, will I seek. Hide not your face from me." She shakes her fist at him. She is willing to seek the Face, but she is impatient. First Corinthians 13:12 asserts that "now we see in a mirror, dimly, but then we will see face to face." Julian's "face-to-face" encounter with God is extraordinary, yet the answers she craves cannot all be revealed in this life. Sinful, fallen humanity is one with the sufferings Jesus endured that literally appeared on his visage. Jesus' saving act is all love, yet the Incarnation alone ones us with him. He takes on our sufferings not only in the cross but also fully in the act of taking a body. The Incarnation cannot be separated from the atonement. The human Jesus is not that valiant Savior doing battle on the cross. He is the person who lived, loved, died, and understood our grief.

We might appreciate actually beholding an aspect of God, but for God there is no difference. The beholding comes from him; the route of getting there is the shared burden of necessary work on our part and freely given grace. Labor leads to creation born forth. Our search for God is not in vain. We journey on with remembrance of what has been revealed and commitment to doing the work we need to do in order to be receptive to the gracious gift of beholding our God.

11

And after this, I saw God in a point
(that is to say in my mind)
by which vision I understood that He is in all things.

I gazed with deliberation,
seeing and knowing in that vision that He does all that is done.

I marveled at that sight with a mild fear, and thought: "What is sin?"
(for I saw truly that God does everything no matter how little,
and I saw truly that nothing is done by luck or by chance
but everything by the foreseeing wisdom of God).

(If it is luck or chance in the sight of man, our blindness and our lack of foresight is the cause, for the things that are in the foreseeing wisdom of God from without beginning [which rightfully and honorably and constantly he leads to the best end as they come about] happen to us without warning, ourselves unaware; and thus, by our blindness and our lack of foresight, we say these are luck and change; but to our Lord God, they are not so—
wherefore, it is necessary to concede that everything that is done, it is well done, for our Lord God does all
[for at this time the action of creatures was not shown, but of our Lord God in the creature]).

He is in the midpoint of everything and He does everything, and I was certain He does no sin.

And here I saw truthfully that sin is no deed,
for in all this revelation sin was not shown.

And I wished no longer to wonder at this, but I looked to our Lord for what He wished to show.

And thus insofar as could be shown for the present, the rightfulness
  of God's action was shown to the soul.

   Rightfulness has two fair qualities:
      it is right,
      and it is full;
   and so are all the actions of our Lord God;
   and to them is lacking neither the action of mercy nor of grace,
   for it is all right-full, in which nothing is wanting.
         (and at a different time He made a showing in order for
            me to see sin nakedly, as I shall say later, where He uses the
            action of mercy and grace.)

This vision was shown to my understanding,
      for our Lord wished to have the soul turned truly
   unto the beholding of Him,
   and generally of all His works
      (for they are most good
      and all His judgments are comfortable and gracious,
      and they bring to great comfort the soul
      which has turned from paying attention to the blind judgment of man
      to the fair, gracious judgment of our Lord God).

A man looks upon some deeds as well done
      and some deeds as evil,
   but our Lord does not look upon them so;

   for just as all that has being in nature is of God's creating,
   so everything that is done is in the character of God's doing.

   It is easy to understand that the best deed is well done,
      but just as well as the best and most exalted deed is done,
      so well is the least deed done—
         and all in the character and in the order
         in which our Lord has it ordained from without beginning.

   For there is no doer but He.

   I saw full certainly that He never changes His purpose in anything,
      nor ever shall, without end.

   There was nothing unknown to Him in His rightful ordering from
      without beginning.

and therefore everything was set in order before anything was
  created, just as it would stand without end,
and no manner of thing shall fall short of that mark.

He made everything in fullness of goodness,
  and therefore the Blessed Trinity is always completely pleased with all
    His works.

And all this He showed most blessedly, meaning this:
    "See, I am God.
    See, I am in everything.
    See, I do everything.
    See, I never lift my hands from my works, nor ever shall,
      without end.
    See, I lead everything to the end I ordained for it
      from without beginning
    by the same Power, Wisdom, and Love with which I made it.
  How would anything be amiss?"

Thus powerfully, wisely, and lovingly was the soul tested in this vision.

Then I saw truthfully that it was appropriate that I needs must assent with
  great reverence, rejoicing in God.

ဗ္၀   ဗ္၀   ဗ္၀

To see God in a point is to see him in everything. The goodness of
God is found in all creation. Deeds and doing are not single acts so much
as actions made manifest everywhere. The nature of God is love, and
love is in every created thing. The workings of mercy and grace infuse
nature. This showing challenges randomness and a kind of dualism: a
dichotomy of making certain things good, certain things bad. Julian does
not say that every human act was a good act. Rather, in the created world,
in this materiality of incarnation that is God manifest, rightfulness shines
through. Julian's God, in the midpoint and doing everything, is creator.
Creation is an ongoing process; so too is incarnation. Incarnation is action
made manifest, not in a single act but in the continuous process of creation. We cannot see what God sees. Chance, randomness, or variety (even
"sin") might seem to be the outward manifestation. Gerard Manley
Hopkins's poem "Pied Beauty" celebrates the variation to be found in
the natural world. The same is found here: difference is not "sin," error,

or missing the mark. Unpredictability, randomness—these are not accidents. This Gospel is cosmological and experiential theology for Julian. It explains the seeming incomprehensibility of phenomena of the natural world as well as the inexplicability of the experiences of our own lives.

There is a humble cliché that "God doesn't make junk." The Incarnation glorifies all material things, and there is no such thing as a mistake in God's eyes. In this showing, incarnation is articulated as God made manifest. To say that sin is no deed is to stress its impermanence. It is not action made manifest. In the ongoing process of incarnation/creation it is impossible to conceive of something that misses the mark. Julian challenges the very idea of a dichotomy, good versus evil in the created world. There is no "us" versus "them." Incarnation, God at the center of it all, is the completion of the good, action made manifest. God wills that humans behold him and his works. In a theology of the Incarnation where deeds are realized actions—God dynamically working through matter, form, and movement—the human tendency to judge is the missing of the mark. It is the sin. Nothing is, except through God. This God is not just a First Mover, a *Primum Mobile*. God is alive and dynamic in all the created world, working for good. The material world is not created and then set adrift. The goodness (mercy, grace) of God is ever operating in us and through us in the ongoing process of creation/incarnation. Can we realize how powerful we are as vectors of God's grace and mercy? Can we ever relinquish control in favor of trust?

⌘ **12** ⌘

After this, as I watched, I saw the body plenteously bleeding
  (as could be expected from the scourging)
    in this way:
        the fair skin was split very deeply into the tender flesh by the
            harsh beating all over the dear body;
        so plenteously did the hot blood run out that one could see
            neither skin nor wound, but, as it were, all blood.

And when it came to the place where it should have fallen down,
  there it vanished.

Nevertheless, the bleeding continued a while until it could be seen
  with careful deliberation.

And this blood looked so plenteous that it seemed to me, if it had
  been as plenteous in nature and in matter during that time,
    it would have made the bed all bloody
    and have overflowed around the outside.

And then it came to my mind that God has made plentiful waters on earth for our
assistance and for our bodily comfort because of the tender love He has for us,
    but it still pleases Him better if we accept most beneficially His
      blessed blood to wash us from sin.
There is no liquid that is made
      which it pleases Him so well to give us,
          for just as it is most plentiful,
          so it is most precious
              (and that by the virtue of His blessed Godhead).

And the blood is of our own nature, and all beneficently flows over
  us by the virtue of His precious love.

The dearworthy blood of our Lord Jesus Christ,
    as truly as it is most precious,
    so truly it is most plentiful.

Behold and see.

    The precious abundance of His dearworthy Blood
        descended down into hell,
        and burst their bonds
        and delivered all that were there
            who belonged to the court of heaven.

    The precious abundance of His dearworthy Blood
        flows over all earth
        and is quick to wash all creatures from sin who are of good will,
            have been, and shall be.

    The precious abundance of His dearworthy Blood
        ascended up into heaven
        to the blessed Body of our Lord Jesus Christ,
        and there it is within Him,
            bleeding and praying for us to the Father—
        and it is and shall be so as long as it is needed.

    And evermore it flows in all heavens
        rejoicing in the salvation of all mankind that are there
            and shall be,
        completing the count that falls short.

ॐ   ॐ   ॐ

Chapter 11's "God in a point," "in the midpoint of everything," means that God is in each drop of Jesus' blood. This might seem intuitive: Jesus is the Son of God; genetically, as it were, it is God's blood that is being spilled. That is the doctrine of the Incarnation. But God is in every drop of blood, not just Jesus', because God is in everything. Humanity's blood, creation's blood, is spilled in Jesus' death; God's blood likewise flows from every human wound. The divine exists in every nucleus of every cell, in the amino acids making up the strands of DNA, in the atoms, protons, electrons, neutrons, their energy. There is God, literally at the center of it all. God is at the very center of everything at Jesus' crucifixion. This is a difficult teaching because it is part of Julian's struggle to deal with the place of evil in the world. How can the suffering of Jesus the Christ be justified in God? How can we say that "sin is no deed" when the Son of God bleeds? Perhaps "nothing is done by luck or by chance but everything by the foreseeing wisdom of God"; but where does that leave Jesus in the role he was to play? When we remember the six million Jews killed in the Holocaust, plus all those slain in crusades and pogroms throughout the centuries, how can we read the chilling words of Matthew 27:25: "His blood be upon us and upon our children"?

Julian returns to the ongoing crisis of human suffering, the body of Christ that continues to bleed every day as long as creation endures. Her age did not have our modern understanding of contagion. She lived through plagues and knew arguments about the nature of disease and its capacity to spread. We moderns see in a drop of infected blood the possibility of illness. We live in a world haunted by AIDS, where contagion is understood through blood, the seropositives and seronegatives dichotomized as bad versus good. Some theologians seek God's judgment within a drop of blood. Julian's frustration survives: How can everything done be well done when human suffering continues? How can we read the signs of God's active participation in our broken world? Under Nazism, elaborate rules were constructed based on bloodlines to distinguish who would live from who would die. Elsewhere, racial purity laws have also been employed in the service of oppression and extermination. What eugenic choices do we make in the termination of pregnancy? What are we selecting for, and where in this elaborate human process is the hand of God making all things well?

The material world may give us some relief, but the remedy offered by the Christ is greater. His blood is ours. His suffering is ours. So let his salvation be ours too. In divine physics, "God-in-a-point" releases the energy contained in the "bonds" of all chemical compounds. God's benevolent determinism of love flows. That holiness of the Incarnation, embodied in the blood, is contained within us. It yearns for full union and return to God. It is attracted to him like miniscule physical particles drawn to a point. That point is God. It is in heaven, not on earth, that the blood is most fully within him. As long as we suffer on earth, that saving blood ones us to him. The bonds keep breaking, for this blood is of love, propelled by the heart—midpoint, or point—that is God. It ones us to him through salvation. There are no inadequacies; there is total healing.

❧ **13** ❧

Afterwards,
> *before God showed any words,*
He permitted me to gaze on Him a suitable time—
> *and on all that I had seen*
> *and all the comprehension that was in it*
> *(as much as the simplicity of the soul could receive it).*

Then, without voice or an opening of lips, He formed in my soul these words:
"With this the Fiend is overcome."

> *(Our Lord said these words, referring to His Blessed Passion*
> *as He showed it before.)*

In this our Lord showed that His Passion is the overcoming of the Fiend.

God showed that the Fiend
> *has now the same malice that he had before the Incarnation;*
> *and no matter how vigorously nor how constantly he labors,*
> *he sees that all salvation's souls escape him gloriously*
> > *by virtue of Christ's precious Passion.*

> *That is his sorrow, and most unpleasantly is he brought down,*
> > *because all that God allows him to do*
> > > *brings us to joy*
> > > *and him to shame and woe and pain.*

And he has as much sorrow
> *when God gives him leave to work*
> > *as when he does not work*
> > > *(and that is because he can never do as much evil as he*
> > > *would like, for his power is all locked in God's hand).*

> *(But in God can be no wrath, as I see it,*
> > *for our good Lord endlessly has regard for His own honor*
> > *and for the benefit of all that shall be saved.)*

With power and justice He withstands the Reprobate
   who because of malice and shrewdness
      busies himself to conspire and to act against God's will.

Also I saw our Lord scorn the Fiend's malice
   and totally discount his powerlessness
      (and He wills that we do so, too).

Because of this sight I laughed mightily,
   and that made them laugh that were about me,
   and their laughing was a delight to me.

I thought that I wished that all my fellow Christians had seen as I had seen,
   and then would they all laugh with me.

> (Except I saw not Christ laughing; even though I was well
> aware that it was the sight that He showed which made me
> laugh, because I understood that we can laugh in comforting
> ourselves and rejoicing in God, because the Devil is overcome.
> And when I saw Him scorn the Devil's malice, it was only by a
> leading of my understanding into our Lord, that is to say, an
> inward showing of constancy, without alteration of outward
> expression for, as I see it, constancy is a worthy quality that is
> in God, which is enduring.)

After this I fell into a soberness and said:
   "I see three things: amusement, scorn, and seriousness.
      I see amusement in that the Fiend is overcome.
      I see scorn in that God scorns him and he shall be scorned.
      And I see seriousness in that he is overcome by the blissful
         Passion and Death of our Lord Jesus Christ which was done
         in full earnest and with weary labor."
      (When I said, "He is scorned," I mean that God scorns
      him—that is to say: because He sees him now as He shall
      see him without end.)

In this God showed that the Fiend is damned
   (and this I meant when I said, "He shall be scorned":
      at Doomsday generally by all who shall be saved—
      for whose salvation he has great envy).
   Then he shall see that all the woe and tribulation that he has done
      to them shall be turned into increase of their joy without end,

and all the pain and tribulation to which he would have brought
them, shall endlessly go with him to hell.

ও　　ও　　ও

Evil is overcome by Christ's sacrifice, yet it is not simply a tit-for-tat.
God, in taking human form, in suffering and dying with us, overcomes
evil in the world. It is not especially helpful to imagine salvation as a
form of exchange—"for the sheep the Lamb has bled." Rather, our personal sufferings are transformed and evil is exorcised by the ongoing,
without-beginning-or-end reality of the Incarnation, which cannot be
separated from the Passion. God's presence in the world—was, is, and
to be—overcomes the absence of God. Julian's awakening to the awareness of the Fiend overcome is as much dependent on her realization of
"God-in-everything" as it relies on some sense of Christ's conquest
through the cross. The image of Jesus bleeding that dominates several
of the chapters reminds us of the blood that contains multitudes: by the
workings of grace, God's Spirit in us as much as his human suffering.

Julian's lesson in this chapter is that evil is real. In our modern world
we are less likely to talk about the work of the Devil. It is important for
us to admit to the fact that there are places and spaces where there is
"not-God." We don't like to speak of this; it is hard for us to do so. Yet
it is crucial for our spiritual and psychological development. We can
understand, following Julian's beautifully incarnational theology, that
the indwelling of God in us and for us overcomes those forces of evil—
pain, suffering, grief, and loss. Milton wrote of hell as "darkness visible."
We all know a bit of hell by that definition. Evil incarnate is always trying to do more; it is in Evil's power to keep trying. We can certainly
understand this as metaphor for our own struggles and frustrations.
Julian notes that this suffering is not of God. In fact, God disdains such
evil; it is of nothing, it truly does not have power. God wills that we join
him in seeing how insignificant is evil compared to God. Julian had
prayed for the experience of the Passion and, in effect, for a near-death
experience. What she gets is a teaching that human suffering is of nothing because of divine compassion. God's willingness to suffer with us
and for us—in the transformative action of grace called the Passion—
changes everything. God is with us for always in the Incarnation; God
overcomes all in the Passion.

Teresa of Avila called the resurrection the divine joke played on the
Devil. Theologically, this rhetoric of laughter suggests the importance

of irony as we struggle to understand evil in the world. Psychologically, it also points to the value of a sense of humor as we grapple with our own experiences of suffering—however grave they may be. Julian observes that she does not see Christ laughing. Jesus suffered; when we are in the midst of our pain we cannot have the perspective others may claim. His full humanity and oneness with us is underscored by the Son's inability to utter the laugh of scorn at evil. The Roman poet Virgil wrote of human suffering, "Perhaps at some time it may be pleasant to remember even this." Julian's practice of narrative is grounded in memory. The suffering of Jesus the human, even in the face of his cosmic role, stands as the model for all our pain—and all overcoming of evil.

❧ **14** ❧

After this our good Lord said:
   "I thank thee for thy labor and especially for thy youth."
   *And in this showing my understanding was lifted up into heaven where I
   saw our Lord as a lord in his own house, who has called all his dearworthy
   servants and friends to a solemn feast. Then I saw the lord take no special
   high-ranked seat in his own household, but I saw him royally reign throughout his house, and he filled it full of joy and mirth himself, in order endlessly
   to cheer and comfort his dearworthy friends most plainly and most graciously, with marvelous melody of endless love in his own fair blessed face
   (which glorious face of the Godhead fills up heavens of joy and bliss).*

God showed three degrees of bliss that every soul shall have in
   heaven who has willingly served God in any degree on earth.
      The first is the honor-filled favor of our Lord God which the soul
         shall receive when it is delivered from pain.
            This favor is so exalted and so full of honor that it seems to the
            soul that it fills him completely even if there were nothing more,
            for it seemed to me that all the pain and labor that could be
            suffered by all living men could not deserve the honorable
            gratitude that one man shall have who has willingly served God.
      The second, that all the blessed creatures that are in heaven shall see
         that honorable favor, and He makes that man's service
         known to all that are in heaven.
            And at this time, this example was shown: a king, if he thanks
            his servants, it is a great honor to them, and if he makes it
            known to all the realm, then is the servant's honor much
            increased.
      The third is that as new and as pleasing as it is to receive it at that
         moment, just so shall it last without end.
            And I saw that simply and sweetly was this shown: that the age
            of every man shall be known in heaven, and shall be rewarded

for his willing service and for his time; and especially is the age
of those who willingly and freely offer their youth to God
excellently rewarded and wonderfully thanked.

For I saw that whenever or at whatever time a man or woman is
truly turned to God,
for one day's service and in order to fulfill His endless will,
that one shall enjoy all these three degrees of bliss.

And the more that the loving soul sees this graciousness of God,
the more it prefers to serve Him all the days of its life.

ৎ৹   ৎ৹   ৎ৹

God has come into the world; God has become Incarnate in Jesus the
Christ. By grace, God's work in the world now depends on us. It depends
on our willingness to listen in the stillness to hear what God may be
asking of us. It depends on our willingness to say "Yes, we are able" and
to dedicate our lives. God as lord of all offers the eucharistic banquet of
the body and blood, but that is not simply the sacrament of communion
taken literally. It is the call, through his hospitality, to accept God's love
and to realize his incarnation in this world through our bodies and our
own willingness to serve. In us he is reborn; through him the "Fiend" is
overcome, but we are called upon to continue living this out. First we
must know how very much he loves us and welcomes us; then we can
say "yes." God's presence is not limited by the single Incarnation in the
body of Jesus the Christ. That presence in the "reign of God"—in the
glory that is creation—resides in All Created Thing. In this *kenosis* God's
essence is poured out into every aspect of the material world. We are
made in God's image. We are loved by God; we are God's love. We are
God's incarnation here on earth and so we are called to serve. That call
can take many forms: literal hospitality, nurturing one another, is sacrament. These are "outward visible signs" of "inward spiritual graces."
They can be forms of spiritual practice that are not always easy but are
means by which we express love for one another. God appreciates us;
this sounds trivial and potentially blasphemous. But however and in
whatever way we allow God to work through us in saying "yes" to the
call, God is made manifest in the world. This too is sacrament: by this
affirmation our bodies celebrate his eucharist. The solemn feast of the
body and blood is the literal "thanksgiving." Our bodies' presence and
actions celebrate this communion. When we say yes, human hands and

hearts can participate in *tikkun olam,* the repair of the world. Saying "yes" makes us more fully part of the community of God. We realize what we already are: God's beloved children.

The sooner we awaken to God's call and affirm it in our lives, the more service we can render, the more fully we are part of the incarnate *communitas,* the greater the gratitude of our God. God says "thank you" when we release what is inside ourselves. His eucharist occurs when we let the Godself out. This is not ego talking. As part of God's creation we are one-ed with his incarnation. When we fail to realize God, to recognize who we are and who we need to be, we hinder grace from working through us. As with metaphors of service and hospitality, this does not mean that we must be doormats and submit to self-abnegation. These attitudes have historically been used to justify slavery and the exploitation of women. Rather, saying "yes" allows us to be whatever we need to become. It is not frustration or repression; it is liberation and realization of the gifts and talents God has given each of us for the improvement of our world.

Having reflected on the place of evil—expressed through all sorts of forms, if embodied in the personification of the Fiend in Chapter 13—Julian is ready to say "yes." If the showings invited her into a love relationship through God's passion, the awareness of a broken world serves as a doorway for the grace-filled realization of God's incarnation within herself. Turning to God rarely happens in the way of the cliché conversion narrative. It is a process, an ongoing and ever-present revelation and epiphany. As in twelve-step spirituality, we can only say "just for today." In that present moment of mindfulness we are able to realize and incarnate the grace of God. Even Augustine's 1500-year-old narrative of his turn to God demonstrates how "just for today" is a working-out, an unfolding awareness of God's place in our lives. Julian articulates how our answer to the call can only be here in this moment. That is grace, that is the gratitude of God, thus we have our spiritual practice. Julian, who asked for mortal illness and a fuller experience of God, begins to say yes to all that she was shown and its implications for her future life. May we too, as we awaken to the working of God in our lives, feel compelled to say yes and let the God out—if only for this moment.

∝ **15** ∞

After this He showed a most excellent spiritual pleasure in my soul:
    I was completely filled with everlasting certainty,
        powerfully sustained without any painful fear.
This feeling was so joyful and so spiritual that I was wholly in
peace and in repose and there was nothing on earth that would
have grieved me.

This lasted only a while, and I was changed
    and left to myself in such sadness and weariness of my life, and
    annoyance with myself that scarcely was I able to have patience
    to live. There was no comfort nor any ease for me except faith,
    hope, and love, and these I held in truth (but very little in feeling).

And immediately after this, our Blessed Lord gave me again the
    comfort and the rest in my soul,
        in delight and in security so blissful and so powerful
        that no fear, no sorrow, no bodily pain that could be suffered
        would have distressed me.

And then the pain showed again to my feeling,
and then the joy and the delight,
and now the one,
and now the other,
various times—I suppose about twenty times.

And in the times of joy, I could have said with Saint Paul
    "Nothing shall separate me from the love of Christ."
And in the pain I could have said with Peter:
    "Lord, save me, I perish."

This vision was shown me, for my understanding,
    that it is advantageous for some souls to feel this way—

sometime to be in comfort,
and sometimes to fail and to be left by themselves.

God wants us to know that He protects us equally surely in woe and in well.

But for the benefit of man's soul a man is sometimes left to himself
    (although sin is not always the cause—for during this time I
      committed no sin for which I should be left to myself, for it
      was so sudden).
    (Equally, I deserved not to have this blessed feeling.)

But freely our Lord gives when He wishes,
    and permits us to be in woe sometimes.

And both are one love,
    for it is God's will that we keep us in this comfort with all our might,
      because bliss is lasting without end,
        and pain is passing and shall be brought to nothing for those who
        shall be saved.

And therefore it is not God's will
    that we submit to the feeling of pains, in sorrow and mourning
      because of them,
        but quickly pass over them and keep ourselves in the endless
        delight which is God.

           C3   C3   C3

Julian receives a gift of the Spirit, a kind of divine goodie to nourish and sustain her. It comes from God to provide encouragement, but it is transient. Julian makes a distinction between the affective and the intellectual. It is rather like experiencing depression with some self-awareness: one knows rationally that life may be worth living, but one can hardly *feel* such a *belief* at the time. Shilly-shallying back and forth, Julian has peace of mind and trust in God, and desperate white-knuckled clinging to something, whatever, that might allow her just to hold on. How familiar this journey sounds! At one moment we feel nourished, we feel held in God's loving arms; at other times we are like frightened children longing for our parents. Yet this is the way, the journey to spiritual growth. We must face the fear and just hang on. For here is the teaching, the growth in Julian's self-understanding that becomes part of her lessons through her book. So far, she has been guided on. When we step away from the loving God who keeps us in spiritual kindergarten and are ready to go to graduate school in the devotional life, we had better be prepared for the risks maturity entails. In the decades following her showings, Julian stands alone in the love of God, discerning and deciphering the meaning of these events—for herself and for those who might read them. We must know in the depth of our souls that God is with us even if we cannot feel his presence. This is true in the dark times of our outward lives, but also in the dark nights of our souls, as spiritual growth proceeds because of, rather than despite, challenges.

Sin, separation from God, does not enter into this sense of walking the lonely road; as Julian affirms in her strength, nothing can separate us from the love of Christ. But as she points out, the "*blessed* feeling" was not something she deserved either. Feeling that God is with us, leading us on, versus feeling that we are cast adrift, has nothing to do with our merit. We do not earn such experiences, nor are we punished by them. Rather, they are given to us as our own soul's journey is being worked out. Julian's message here is to wait on no mood. We must not pay too much attention to how we "feel" on our spiritual journey. The love of God is there whether we sense it or not. Keep one's eyes on the prize, and keep on truckin'! The prize is the ever-present if sometimes intangible reality of a God whose unchanging meaning is love.

Here is Julian's spiritual growth; here she continues to learn what God is calling her to do as an interpretive theologian of an extraordinary mystical experience. The spiritual life is a process toward greater maturity and memory: recollection that the feelings of the moment play little role in our permanent place as beloved children of God, whose love and *protection* are there for us through it all. Julian had plenty of time to reflect on these thoughts as she worked to unravel the meaning of her experiences. We live in a time and place that sometimes gives too much credence to the feelings of the moment. We must acknowledge and bless our feelings; we must assert our needs and permit God's love to work in us and through us, allowing God to flow out into the world through our actions. But through it all—thick and thin, sick and sin—Julian reminds that God's love and support are the same no matter how we feel.

☙ **16** ❧

After this Christ showed a portion of His Passion near His death.
   I saw His sweet face
        and it was dry and bloodless with pale dying and deathly ashen;
        and after that more pale, grievous, distressing,
        and then turned more lifeless into blue,
        and after that more brown-blue, as the flesh changed into more
           profound death.

His suffering revealed itself to me most distinctly in His blessed face,
      and especially in His lips where I saw these four colors
         (though before those lips were fresh, ruddy, and pleasant to my sight).

This was a sorrowful change to see this profound dying,
      and also the nose was shrivelled together and dried, as I saw it,
      and the sweet body became brown and black,
      all changed from the fair life-like color of Himself into dry dying;
           because at the time that our Lord and Blessed Savior died
           upon the rood, there was a dry, sharp wind and wondrous
           cold, as I see it.

And by the time all the Precious Blood was bled out of the sweet body
   that could pass from it,
      yet there remained a moisture in the sweet flesh of Christ,
         as it was shown.

   Bloodlessness and painful drying within
   and the blowing of wind and cold coming from without
   met together in the sweet body of Christ.

   And these four,
         two without,
         and two within,
   dried the flesh of Christ over the course of time.

And though this pain was bitter and sharp,
  it was most long-lasting, as I saw it,
  and it painfully dried up all the living elements of Christ's Flesh.
Thus I saw the sweet Flesh die,
  apparently part after part,
  drying with awesome pains.

And as long as any element had life in Christ's flesh,
  so long He suffered pain.

This long torment seemed to me as if He had been seven nights lifeless,
  dying,
  at the point of passing away,
  suffering the last pain.
    (And when I say it seemed to me as if He had been seven nights
    lifeless, it means that the sweet body was as discolored, as dry,
    as shrivelled, as deathlike and as piteous as though He had been
    seven nights lifeless, constantly dying.)

And it seemed to me that the drying of Christ's Flesh
    was the worst pain,
  and the last,
  of His Passion.

ঝ   ঝ   ঝ

Julian literally watches the life drain out of the face of God. This return to the Passion interweaves her story with that of the One who came to redeem humanity. To watch Jesus die, to stare him in the face, after the "God wants us to know that he protects us equally surely in woe and in well" of Chapter 15, is a challenge. Julian may assert there that "pain is passing," and we ought not to submit ourselves to sorrow and mourning. But then death stares her in the face. Surely it is her own death, as Julian lay between this world and the next in her illness. But the pathos and compassion evoked also suggest that Julian's awareness of suffering comes from watching death and dying in her world, probably among those she had loved most. Julian has fully inserted herself into the Passion narrative: she is dying with/as the Christ as a manifestation of his ongoing incarnation. But she also stands as a bystander on the road, enacting the *via dolorosa* of Good Friday. Is there any sorrow like unto her sorrow?

The metaphors Julian employs depend on color and moisture. Earlier the red blood flowing permeated her description of the suffering body of Jesus. Here is the darkening and the drying up, the cold wind blowing. We cannot read Julian's *Showings* without being struck by the intensity of the gore. We live in a culture that has sanitized its death and dying. Not so in Julian's age, lacking the cleansing power of running water or the icy sterility of a hospital room. Having lived through plague and residing in a city, it would have been next to impossible for Julian not to have known the revulsions of the suffering, dying body. She speaks of the bleeding-out of the body of Jesus as if it were an animal slaughtered for food or hide. Julian observes the cold wind blowing as if it were the Holy Spirit witnessing the death of the Christ. The God who had taken human form could never quite give up the infectiousness of the Incarnation: from him all life proceeds, even in the literal "face" of death. As in Hopkins's poem "God's Grandeur," the world is charged with the goodness of God. Despite all destruction at humanity's hand, there remains the deep-down thing within that has the power to redeem all.

The body of Christ is an array of earth/wind/water/fire—All Created Thing in the Real Presence. In this incarnate God all forces meet: the flesh, its inherent moisture and resounding life; the drying elements working away at this. At last, the body of Christ is sealed by this preservation in death. In life and birth God became most fully human. In death the process is completed. Jesus could not be one of us without death. By literally facing death, and the death of God in Jesus the Christ, Julian confronts the ultimate incarnation. Here in her text there is no chiding and no blame: no lamenting about this unjust sacrifice or punishment. Rather, in the dying body of God we have the reality of human suffering. Julian has begun to grapple theologically with the place of evil in the world, and why there seems no rhyme or reason to human suffering and chance. Here that discernment fades away and we are left with the stark reality of death.

But in that death is the greatest of life. If the Christ could suffer as we suffer, his body the source for all creation, so too we can join him in bliss. Again, this is not a matter of exchange. There is no reward for those who suffer. We do not get the good because we are being compensated for the bad. The bad just is; suffering, pain, death cannot be accounted for. But through all of this there is life, and thus there is love from an eternal source. If Jesus the incarnate God will suffer and die, so can we. And, as we will hear many times before the end of the *Showings*, all shall be well. The whole of Julian's message is that ultimately there is only good and only love.

Chapter 16 begins a whole series of reflections on the Passion of Christ that allow Julian to explore the theological basis for suffering. It follows a turn where Julian had been able to find comfort in God's rest and assurance that evil could not triumph—that God's love is the literal "midpoint" of all there is. But such intellectual insights or affective anchors cannot sustain us all the time, as Julian observes in Chapter 15. How do we make sense of a world in which the Incarnate—in the body of Jesus and in every living thing—must suffer and die? Julian does not shy away from the vivid depictions of this aspect of life. As a medieval woman she is convinced that peering into the wounded side will literally show her something. Living Christ's suffering becomes the stuff of contemplation. As a ray of the Incarnation herself, it is through such awareness that she can process her physical and emotional pain.

We live in a culture that hesitates to look at the sacrament of suffering—the transcendence of that pain and loss of a beloved present is the Real Presence that is a gift in the presence of death. None of us would ask for it, but have not loss and death been remarkably transformative in some way to our souls? Few of us today would claim to live in a society in which the suffering of God is central to our devotional life, but we surely live in a world of great pain. The sufferings of vast manifestations of the Incarnation are all too real to us. I do not believe that media representing religious violence are the best sources for our spiritual growth. Mel Gibson's "Passion" aesthetic will not heal the spiritual or physical pain of our world. We do not need more lenses through which to view the suffering of the Body of God. We can find that Christ well enough in our lives and in the pain of a creation we are called to heal. We stand with Julian watching a dying body, our drying Mother Earth. We stand with Julian watching brothers and sisters languish from physical and spiritual starvation. We stand with Julian as our own souls die from lack of nourishment. We are called, incarnate victims, clones of the redeeming Love made manifest in the Christ, to set the world free. For we are one with his Body just as we are also one with Julian. We stand powerless, waiting for the God in us to break through. We must allow ourselves the necessary grief—huddling with Julian, watching the death. But we then need to allow the Resurrection to happen in our lives: to rise up and allow the God-force of our call to work through us in the repair of the world. For the world is charged with the glory of God.

☙ 17 ❧

In this dying was brought to my mind the words of Christ: "I thirst,"
  for I saw in Christ a double thirst:
    one bodily,
    another spiritual
        (which I shall speak of in the thirty-first chapter).

I was reminded of this word
  because of the bodily thirst
    which I understood was caused by the lack of moisture,
    for the blessed flesh and bones were left all alone
    without blood and moisture.

The blessed body dried all alone a long time,
  with the twisting of the nails
  and weight of the body
      (for I understood that because of the tenderness of the sweet
          hands and of the sweet feet, and by the large size, cruelty,
          and hardship of the nails, the wounds grew wider),
  and the body sagged because of the weight by hanging a long time
  and the piercing and wrenching of the head
and the binding of the crown,
  all parched with dry blood,
    with the sweet hair and the dry flesh clinging to the thorns,
    and the thorns to the drying flesh.
And in the beginning
    while the flesh was fresh and bleeding,
  the constant settling of the thorns made the wounds wide.

Furthermore I saw that the sweet skin and the tender flesh,
  with the hair and the blood,
    were all raised and loosened about from the bone with the thorns,
    and gashed in many pieces,

*and were hanging like a cloth that was sagging as if it would
        very soon have fallen off because of the weight and looseness
        while it had natural moisture.
    (And that was great sorrow and fear for me, because it seemed to me
        that I would not for my life have seen it fall.)*

*How it was done, I saw not, but understood it was with the sharp
thorns and the violent and painful setting on of the garland
unsparingly and without pity.*

*This continued a while, and soon it began to change,
    and I beheld and wondered how it could be.
    And then I saw it was because the flesh began to dry
        and lost a part of the weight that was round about the garland.
    With this it was surrounded all about, as it were garland upon garland.
    The garland of the thorns was dyed with the blood, and the other
        fleshly garland and the head were also the same color—
        like clotted blood when it is dry.*

*The skin of the flesh of the face and of the body which showed had small
    wrinkles,
        with a tanned color,
        like a dry board when it is old,
        and the face was more brown than the body.*

*I saw four kinds of dryings:
    the first was bloodless;
    the second was pain following after;
    the third was that He was hanging up in the air the way men hang
        a cloth to dry;
    the fourth, that His bodily nature demanded fluid and there was no
        kind of comfort administered to Him in all His woe and distress.*

*Ah! cruel and grievous was His pain,
    but much more cruel and grievous it was
    when the moisture was lacking and all began to dry,
    shrivelling this way.*

*These were two pains that showed in the blessed head:
    the first caused the drying while it was moist;
        and the other slow, with shriveling and drying, with blowing of
            the wind from without that dried Him and pained Him more
            with cold, more than my heart can think.*

And all the other pains, because of which I saw that all I can say is
    too little, for it cannot be told!
That showing of Christ's pains filled me full of pain,
    because I was well-aware that He suffered only once,
    though He wished to show it me,
    and fill me with awareness as I had before desired.

And in all this time of Christ's pains
        I felt no pain except for Christ's pains.
    Then I thought, "I knew but little what pain it was that I asked for,"
        and like a wretch I repented me,
        thinking that if I had known what it would be,
        I would have been loath to have prayed for it,
        for it seemed to me that my pains went beyond any bodily death.

I thought: "Is any pain in hell like this?"
    And I was answered in my reason:
        "Hell is a different pain, for there is despair.
        But of all pains that lead to salvation,
        this is the most pain—
            to see thy Beloved suffer."

How can any pain be more to me than to see Him who is all my life,
    all my bliss, and all my joy, suffer?

Here I felt most truthfully that I loved Christ so much more than myself
    that there was no pain that could be suffered like to that sorrow which
    I had to see Him in pain.

                    ୫ଓ   ୫ଓ   ୫ଓ

   Julian employs every possible comparison to describe the pains of the
body of Christ. It is through such suffering that, intellectually, she can
acknowledge the depth of her one-ing with him. His wounds, the open-
ings into Jesus' mortality, are part of the destruction of his flesh. It is as
if the weight of having that mortality is too heavy: the Christ within is
literally pulled out of shape by the Jesus body. Yet Julian loves that same
human body. Here the nails and the thorns tear the body of Christ to
pieces. This metaphor is extended into the ways in which our faults
wound the body of Christ: not as insults to an abstract God, but as
wrongs to his embodiment in all humanity and the rest of the material
world. Julian writes extensively in the *Showings* about divine love

enfolding human nature like a garment. Here Jesus' flesh is specifically compared to cloth. Love in Christ's flesh is literally torn away rather than safely protecting humanity.

To my knowledge, there is no literary precedent in medieval vernacular piety for the extent of Julian's clinical description of the death of Jesus' body. She writes like an emotional pathologist, chronicling the progress of his mortality and how it felt to him. The several chapters that compose this portion of the *Showings* are extraordinary for their elaboration of the Passion. They are drawn from a strong familiarity with the dying process, tremendous compassion, and an awareness of other physical/chemical phenomena that occur in domestic and public life. Julian fully enters into the work of compassion. Her details draw on an imaginative sympathy that could only come from loving deeply. Of course she loved her God. Writing her text is telling the story, discerning its meaning—how, and what, to express. God said "yes" to Julian: God was willing to show her the pain he suffered. In her relationship with him, Julian's visions allowed him to be her only reality.

Although Julian herself did not suffer, she regrets having asked for this experience. Could she have known suffering and death so intimately and been able to fathom Christ's without loving and being loved in this world? Perhaps given her culture's affective piety it is possible to assert that love for God alone in a devout soul was enough to agitate such pathos. In any case, by this moment in her showings there is no going back. Julian's willful one-ing to God is irrevocable, and whatever human relationships shaped her or remained part of her life, Christ was at the center of her experience. Julian is in mortal illness herself, yet it is God's pain and not her own that she knows. We are all moved to various extents by human suffering. Some of us are so sensitive that we indeed suffer more when a loved one is in pain than when we ourselves are. The Passion is a powerful annual (yet also constant) retelling of the suffering of Jesus the Christ. But what would it feel like to declare, as Julian does, that no pain we experience could be compared to knowing Christ's sufferings? And how might our lives be different after such a showing as Julian had?

⟪ **18** ⟫

Here I saw a part of the compassion of Our Lady Saint Mary,
for Christ and she were so one-ed in love
that the magnitude of her love caused the magnitude of her pain.

In this I saw the essence of natural love, extended by grace, which
creatures have for Him
and this natural love was most fulsomely shown in His sweet Mother,

and even more,
for in so much as she loved Him more than all others,
her pains surpassed all others.

For ever the higher, the mightier, the sweeter that the love is,
the more sorrow it is to the lover to see that body
which is beloved in pain.

And all His disciples and all His true lovers suffered more pains than
their own bodily dying,
for I am certain, by my own experience,
that the least of them loved Him so far above himself that it
surpasses all that I can say.

Here I saw a great one-ing between Christ and us, as I understand it,
for when He was in pain, we were in pain.

And all created things that could suffer pain suffered with Him (that is to say,
all created things that God has made for our service).
The firmament and the earth failed for sorrow in their nature at the
time of Christ's dying,
for it belongs naturally to their character to know Him for their
God in whom all their strength is situated.
When He failed, then it was necessary for them out of nature to
fail with Him as much as they could, out of sorrow for His pains.

And thus they that were His friends suffered pain for love.

And universally, all—that is to say, they that knew Him not—suffered
because of the failing of all manner of comfort, except the
mighty hidden protection of God.

I mean of two manner of folk, as it can be understood by two persons:
the one was Pilate,
the other was Saint Denis of France, who was at that time a pagan;
for when he saw the wonders and marvels,
the sorrows and fears that happened at that time,
he said, "Either the world is now at an end,
or else He that is Maker of nature is suffering."
Wherefore, he did write on an altar: "This is the altar of the unknown God."

God out of His goodness creates the planets and the elements in their nature to
work for both the blessed man and the cursed, and at that time that goodness
was withdrawn from both of them.

It was for that reason that even they who knew Him not were in sorrow at
that time.
Thus was our Lord Jesus given pain because of us,
and we all stand in this kind of pain with Him,
and shall do until we come to His bliss, as I shall say later.

ಐ   ಐ   ಐ

It is not Jesus' death that Julian experiences, but rather his dying. Mary is the source of flesh for the Incarnation. Julian spiritually knows Christ's incarnation in the same bodily sense. Although she does not actually give birth to Jesus, the book of her text bears the Word. Julian's theology throughout the *Showings* demonstrates the degree to which we all bring Christ into the world as part of the ongoing incarnation. That process depends on the "magnitude . . . of love." In Julian it is realized perfectly in this moment: hence her one-to-one correspondence, experiencing fully and completely Jesus' pain. These are the "showings of Divine Love," so it is love that is shown—love embodied even in those moments of pain. The outward reach of the Godself breaks down the barrier between Creator and creature. God-essence infuses all material form; the duality between material nature and God-nature collapses. The trope of mothering makes incarnation manifest. "Mother" becomes emblematic for one-ing; Mary's experience is the epitome of the Godself breaking through.

Hence in the instant of Julian's showings there is no distinction between Mary and Julian. Julian fully experiences divine incarnation just as Mary did. This realization has the potential to sweeten the agony of Jesus' pain that she feels. When we suffer with another, when we know compassion in its highest sense, a one-to-one correspondence, then we know Christ. When we feel another's pain—or joy—we incarnate the Godself into the world. We are literally being Christ for someone.

Julian recognizes that she has a job to do: to teach Christ's one-ing. She does not state that he suffers for us, or that we are responsible for his suffering—rather, it is that one-to-one correspondence, a simultaneous sign of humanity's total one-ing with the incarnate Christ. Julian may have received a particular glimpse of this reality that is deeper than most people get, but the one-ing is with all the broken material world. We find Christ in our suffering. This is not a maudlin glorification of suffering or pain at the expense of realization of joy. Rather, wherever there is suffering in the world, there is Christ. There is no separation or distinction: He is fully one-ed with it. Christ and creation are intimately joined in this dance of suffering and rebirth. Julian inverts the usual image of the crucifixion. It is not that Jesus suffered for us because of his great love; that is a given, but here the relationship is reciprocal. All Created Thing—one-ed in "friendship"—suffered "for love." We need no pious talk about offering up our sufferings to him on the cross. Our sufferings and joys are always already one-ed with his, just as we are all, All Created Thing, always already one-ed to this love.

❧ **19** ❧

At this time I wished to look up from the Cross,
and I dared not,
for I was well-aware that while I gazed on the cross
    I was secure and safe;
therefore I would not agree to put my soul in peril,
    because, aside from the cross,
      there was no protection from the horror of demons.

Then I had a proposal in my reason (as if it were like a friend)
    which said to me, "Look up to heaven to His Father."

And I saw well with the Faith that there was nothing between the
      cross and heaven that could have distressed me.
    Either it was appropriate for me to look up, or else to answer.

I answered inwardly with all the powers of my soul and said,
    "No, I cannot, for Thou art my heaven."
        (This I said because I wished not to look up, for I had rather
          have been
        in that pain until Doomsday than to have come to heaven otherwise
          than
        by Him, for I was well-aware that He who bound me so painfully,
          He would unbind me when He wished.)

So was I taught to choose Jesus for my heaven, whom I saw only in
pain at that time.
    I delighted in no other heaven than Jesus, who shall be my bliss
      when I come there.

And this has ever been a comfort to me: that I chose Jesus for my
    heaven, by His grace, in all this time of suffering and sorrow.
And that had been a learning for me that I should evermore do so,
    choosing only Jesus for my heaven in well and woe.

And although like a sinner I had been sorry
    (I said before that if I had been aware what pain it would be,
       I would have been loath to have asked for it)
    here saw I truly that it was the grouching and cursing of the flesh
      without agreement of the soul
          to which God assigns no blame.

Repenting and willing choice are two opposites which I experienced
    both at once at the same time; and they are two parts:
    the one outward,
    the other inward.

The outward part is our mortal flesh which is now in pain and woe
    (and always shall be in this life) of which I experienced much
      at this time, and that was the part that repented.

The inward part is an exalted, blissful life which is totally in peace
    and love, and this was more secretly experienced;
    and this part is that in which mightily, wisely, and willingly,
    I chose Jesus for my heaven.

And in this I saw truly that
    the inward part is master and ruler of the outward,
    and neither receives orders nor pays heed to the will of the outward,
    but its whole intention and will is endlessly committed to being
      one-ed into our Lord Jesus.
      (That the outward part could turn the inward to agreement
      was not shown to me; but rather that the inward moves the
      outward by grace, and both shall be united in bliss without
      end by the power of Christ, this was shown.)

Julian literally keeps her eyes fixed on the cross. She wants to look up from it, but she cannot. Julian is living out the figurative language that exhorts all Christians to focus on that saving action. We speak of the crux of the matter; the cross is our watershed moment. Yet what does this literally mean for Julian—or for us? She was having a visionary experience the like of which most of us will never know. Nevertheless, the psychological unfolding of her showings is situated right within the text of her own life. This vision sustained her: she had prayed for it. What were the events of Julian's life, even outside of her "mortal illness," that led her to state that she was only safe gazing at the cross? One might say that her interior, as well as exterior vision was focused there. She stared upon a crucifix and thus all of these events came about.

When Julian notes that her reason encouraged her to look up to God the Father, she demonstrates a knee-jerk response from the theology she had been taught. It is a profoundly intellectual, rational gesture: looking from the suffering humanity up to its oneness with God the Father in the Holy Trinity. Creator and Redeemer, Father and Son, are one. Still, she cannot do it. So Julian answers that superego voice with a "no." She defies the thinking in favor of the experiencing. Julian, the epitome of the mystic with a mind, talks back to what her innate divine reason and taught human catechism instruct her to do. Julian finds heaven in the human life of Jesus, even in his suffering on the cross. That one moment of divine compassion is all she needs of heaven, because it makes her aware of her one-ing with God. Soul and body are one, and Julian's suffering and Jesus' are too. She does not need transcendence; it is all there at the cross. Her demons have no power over her because her oneness with God reaches its fullest incarnation in the agony of his crucifixion.

Chapter 19 teaches a deep lesson on human suffering. The important aspect here is choice. Julian could have looked up—at the omnipotent Creator—but she chose not to. She chose to remain in the domain of experience. Whatever Julian suffered before and during her illness, these showings of Jesus' suffering opened her heart to the heaven to be found in human life itself. Julian's language about heaven does not suggest a conversion experience: she does not "find" Jesus in these showings. Rather, she awakens to the fact that she is already fully one-ed with him. Julian is not congratulating herself for "choosing" God over sin. Instead, she celebrates the awareness that this one-ing means that she is fully with him, entirely in "heaven" with him, even in the depths of the greatest human suffering. Julian does not escape the world here; she is not denying pain or living in a dream world of heaven's bliss. On the contrary, she affirms that in all conditions our human experience that is always already one-ed with our God can be known tangibly and transcendentally if we choose to look on Jesus in his humanity, if we keep our eyes on the cross.

So much for "through a glass darkly" here; so much for Julian's earlier half-regret for having asked to see Jesus' pain. The soul is one with God in every circumstance. God is patient with us in our sufferings, in our doubts about what we can endure. God does not ask that we willingly embrace pain for pain's sake; to do so would be inhuman and inhumane.

God does not judge us for our human challenge to reconcile where we are led with where we are. We will always be broken—not split into soul and body, but in need of healing in our human experience. For Julian, the inward life makes this possible; through grace one can make the willful choice to see beyond the brokenness, to look at heaven through the pain. Our outward life may never be able to do this; our human bodies and minds may repent but not fully realize. Yet the human spirit can decide. Julian does not endorse a dualism that enforces subjugation of that inferior creation to the higher soul. Instead, following her focus on Jesus' sufferings, she notes that in Christ they are united. We cannot denigrate one in favor of the other; we cannot scorn our frail flesh. Otherwise, what is the use of gazing on the cross as she does?

❧ **20** ☙

And thus I saw our Lord Jesus lingering a long time
  [for the unity of the Godhead gave strength to the manhood out of
    love to suffer more than all men could suffer].
      (I mean not only more pain than all men could suffer, but also
      that He suffered more pain than all men of salvation who ever
      were from the first beginning until the last day, could measure
      or fully imagine—considering the worthiness of the most exalted,
      honorable King and the shameful, spiteful, painful death—
      because He that is most exalted and most worthy was most fully
      brought to nothing and most utterly despised.)

The most significant point that can be seen in the Passion is to
  comprehend and to understand
    that He who suffered is God—
      seeing beyond this two other points which are lesser
        (the one is what He suffered,
        and the other for whom He suffered).

In this showing He brought partially to mind
    the exaltation and nobility of the glorious Godhead,
    and with that the preciousness and the tenderness of the blessed
      body (which are both united together)
    and also the loathing that is in our nature to suffer pain;
      for as much as He was most tender and pure,
      just so He was most strong and mighty to suffer.

And for the sin of every man that shall be saved He suffered.
And because of every man's sorrow and desolation and anguish,
    He saw and grieved out of kindness and love.
      (In as much as Our Lady grieved for His pains,
        just so much He suffered grief for her sorrow, and more beyond,
          in as much as the sweet Manhood of Him was more noble
            in nature.)

74

As long as He was able to suffer,
  He suffered for us and grieved for us,
  and now He is risen and no more able to suffer,
    yet He suffers with us still (as I shall say later).

And I, gazing upon all this by His grace, saw that the love in Him
  which He has for our soul was so strong that
  willingly He chose the Passion with great desire,
    and humbly He suffered it with great joy, with great satisfaction.

The soul that sees it in this way, when it is touched by grace, shall truly see that the pains of Christ's Passion surpass all pains—that is to say, those pains which shall be changed into everlasting surpassing joys by the power of Christ's Passion.

ஐ ஐ ஐ

Jesus' dying is an ongoing process; His suffering is ongoing; His bliss is equally ongoing. Julian gets the opportunity to witness (in every sense of the "Word"), the continuing process of all that is deemed and done. In her showings Julian experiences God's vision; this is her in-sight. And yet Jesus' "lingering" is so familiar and humbling. While the human mind often favors a swift, easy death, for Julian Jesus' "lingering" is almost heroic. He is not the warrior Christ doing battle, fighting the good fight. If Jesus earns a Purple Heart for his suffering, it is out of love rather than personal glory, valor, or fame. The idea that Jesus suffered is not simply a theological commonplace for the purpose of the elegant rhetorical resolution by resurrection. To say that out of death comes life is a lovely paradox, but for Julian the full embodiment in the Incarnation is what really matters. The mystery of a God who suffers is all we really need to contemplate. How difficult it is! We want our salvific God; we even want one who suffers like us or for us or with us or through us. But how do we approach the simple subject-predicate sentence, "God suffers"? It is at the very heart of Julian's meaning, without which it is difficult to understand her Christianity. That he suffered, that is all there is for Julian. What do we make of a faith in which our one-in-three God suffers?

Christ feels for us in the sympathy we feel for him. Here is the degree of identification Julian experiences both with Mary as representative of all humanity and with Jesus' suffering itself. These showings concern suffering and sorrow, but perhaps most important they call to mind the power and value of compassion. This phenomenon is neither trite nor vague, but in the context of Julian's seeing with the mind of God a complete one-to-one "fellow feeling." She asserts that Christ's grief—God's grief—for our sorrow is greater than anything even Mary might feel at the foot of the cross. Hers is no remote Godhead. Julian teaches that Christ suffered and grieved for our sorrow as long as he was able to suffer. The experience continues in the mind of God and in any aspect of creation's suffering. The God whose bodily suffering is without comparison is a God whose love-longing is equally without peer.

❦ **21** ❧

It is God's will, as I understand it, that we have three ways of looking
   at His blessed Passion.

   The first (which we should view with contrition and compassion)
        is the cruel pain that He suffered; and that one our Lord
            showed at this time and gave me power and grace to see it.

And I looked for the departing of His life with all my might and
   expected to have seen the body entirely dead,
   but I saw Him not so.

And just at the same time that I thought, by appearance,
   that His life could no longer last,
        and the showing of the end properly needed to be near,
        suddenly, as I gazed upon the same cross,
He changed His blessed countenance.
The changing of His blessed countenance changed mine,
   and I was as glad and as merry as possible.

Then brought Our Lord merrily to my mind:
   "Where is now any point to thy pain or to thy distress?"
   And I was completely happy.

I understood that, in our Lord's meaning,
   we are now on His cross with Him
        in our pains and our suffering, dying;
   and if we willingly remain on the same cross with His help and His
        grace until the last moment,
   suddenly He shall change his appearance to us,
   and we shall be with Him in heaven
        (between the one and the other there shall be no passage of time)
   and then shall all be brought to joy.

And so meant He in this showing:
   "Where is now any point to thy pain or thy distress?"
   And we shall be fully blessed.

And here I saw truthfully that if He showed us His most blessed face
   now, there is no pain on earth nor in any other place that would
   distress us, but everything would be to us joy and bliss.
But because He showed to us an expression of suffering as He bore
   in this life His cross,
      therefore we are in distress and labor with Him as our frailty demands.

And the reason why He suffers is because He wishes of His goodness
   to make us heirs with Him in His bliss.

And for this little pain that we suffer here we shall have an exalted, endless
   knowledge in God, which we could never have without that pain.

The crueler our pains have been with Him on His cross, the more
   shall our honor be with Him in His Kingdom.

೮೦   ೮೦   ೮೦

Chapter 21 begins the glorious resolution of the suffering with which these chapters have been concerned. Jesus' suffering ends not in death, but in a change. Julian seeks to describe the very moment of death. Yet she can only speak of Jesus' dying. Her rhetoric signifies the absence of absence. Perhaps it is the greatest mystery and originality (theological and narratological) of the *Showings* that in their telling of the Passion they witness a Jesus who does not die. The secret contained here underscores the poignancy and pregnancy of Julian's revelations. Nothing is as it seems—in narrative or in theology. All creation, seeming to hurdle aimlessly toward certain death, instead contains the lifeblood of the Incarnation. In this Christian theology there is no end. All is, and sustains.

This approach is not a simple, triumphant "Where, death, is thy victory?" conquest through the resurrection. We are challenged by Julian's text to be aware that no aspect of material experience—that ought to be finite, that ought to be limited—is really as our human minds can understand it. We are awakened to look beyond. For Julian there is more than the eyes-on-the-prize of the reward of heaven. Here is a radical epistemology, a counterintuitive means of understanding knowledge and perception. The showings offer a reinterpretation of what she had been taught, or they would not have been necessary. Embedded—indeed, embodied—in that experience is a deeply affective encounter. Julian looks at the expression on Jesus' face. Her Christianity cannot be separated from human feeling: Julian's God is one who intimately shares in what we humans call love. At Jesus' "deathbed," Julian can only speak of her joy because of what she shares with him. Human life places us on the cross with Jesus. Staying there willingly guarantees that in a blink of an eye we are brought to joy. It is difficult to read Julian's severe descriptions of Jesus' dying in the previous chapters. Perhaps it is harder still for us to accept the easy resolution of pie-in-the-sky. But the more valuable message here is that Julian declares that on the cross, in our human suffering, we are never without God's presence. As part of his Incarnation we are merged with his body. Our lives are hanging there with him: there is no difference between him and us.

There is a long history of not seeing the face of God, said to evoke awe. In Julian we are challenged to look God in the eyes ("visionary" indeed) and through that intimate union be transported to paradise. If we could only see—and know, and feel—all our doubts would be resolved. Thus seeing the suffering of Jesus was worth it for Julian; the secret of Julian's showings comes down to being able to look God in the eye. We are joined to God on that cross. We see our pain; we see his; but we are too distracted by it to realize that there is no separation there. We cannot distinguish ourselves in the Passion from him. This is Julian's theological primer, but it is also deeply sound psychologically in terms of the affective response we feel when we witness a suffering God. Julian's ending to this chapter is not trite. It is not that we just get to go to heaven because Jesus suffered for us. Through the Incarnation we share our bodies with him. Through the cross on which we suffer with him we are offered a means to journey into the mind of God as we gaze at his blessed face. We awaken to the fact that our suffering and his are one when we accept the invitation to a deeper understanding. Chapter 21 demonstrates a shift in Julian's text from the suffering body to the loving mind of God. The body of her text likewise moves from description to greater exegesis. In order to do so, here she reads the text of his countenance. Julian is thus prepared to continue the journey. What unfolds from the enfolding love of God's body is the endless theology of love Julian gleans as she looks into the eyes of God.

⁕ **22** ⁖

Then spoke our good Lord Jesus Christ, asking:
   "Art thou well satisfied that I suffered for thee?"
I said: "Yea, good Lord, thanks be to Thee.
   Yea, good Lord, blessed mayest Thou be!"
Then said Jesus, our kind Lord:
   "If thou art satisfied, I am satisfied.
   It is a joy, a bliss, an endless delight to me that ever I suffered the
      Passion for thee;
   and if I could suffer more, I would suffer more."

In this experience my understanding was lifted up into heaven,
         and there I saw three states of bliss,
         by which sight I was greatly amazed.
   (And although I say "three states of bliss," if all are in the blessed
   Manhood of Christ, no one is more, no one is less, no one is higher,
   no one is lower, but equally alike in bliss.)

With respect to the first state,
         Christ showed me his Father
                  (in no bodily likeness, but in His quality and in His actions—
                     that is to say, I saw in Christ what the Father is).
         The action of the Father is this: that He gives recompense to
                  His Son, Jesus Christ. This gift and this recompense is so
                  blessed to Jesus that His Father could have given him no
                  recompense that could have pleased Him better.
         The first state—that is, the pleasing of the Father—appeared to
         me as a heaven,
                  and it was filled with bliss,
                  for the Father is fully pleased with all the deeds that Jesus has
                     done concerning our salvation.

         Wherefore, we are not only His by His paying for us,
                  but also by the gracious gift of His Father

we are His bliss;
we are His recompense;
we are His honor;
we are His crown (and this was a particular wonder and a
wholly delightful vision: that we are His crown).

This that I describe is such great bliss to Jesus that He sets at nought
all His labor
and His hard Passion
and His cruel and shameful death.

And in these words:
"if I could suffer more, I would suffer more,"
I saw truly that as often as He could die, so often He would,
and love would never let Him have rest until He had done it.

And I watched with great diligence in order to know how often He
would die if He could,
and truly, the number passed my understanding and my wits so far
that my reason could not, nor knew how to, contain it or take it in.

And when He had thus often died (or was willing to),
still He would set it at nought for love;
for He considers everything but little in comparison to His love;
for though the sweet Manhood of Christ could suffer but once, the
goodness in Him can never cease from offering;
every day He is prepared for the same, if it could be; for if He
said He would for my love make new heavens and new earth,
that were but little in comparison, for this could be done
every day if He wished, without any labor;
but to die for my love so often that the number passes created reason,
that is the most exalted offer that our Lord God could
make to man's soul, as I see it.

Then He means this:
"How could it then be that I would not do for thy love all that I could?
—this deed does not distress me since I would for thy love
die so often with no regard to my cruel pains."

And here I saw with respect to the second vision in this blessed Passion
that the love that made Him suffer surpassed all His pains
as far as Heaven is above earth;

for the pain was a noble, honorable deed
done at one time
by the action of love;
but the love was without beginning,
is now,
and shall be without ending.

> *It was because of this love He said most sweetly these*
> *words: "If I could suffer more, I would suffer more."*

> *He said not, "If it were necessary to suffer more . . ."for*
> *even though it were not necessary, if He could suffer more,*
> *He would.*

This deed and action concerning our salvation was prepared as well as God
could prepare it.

And here I saw a complete bliss in Christ;
*   for His bliss would not have been complete if it could have been*
*   done any better.*

ɮ೦   ɮ೦   ɮ೦

What does it mean for Christ to ask Julian if she is satisfied by His suffering? Taking the word apart, we are left with the question, "Is it enough?" Literally, has enough been done? The supply, the commodity of exchange, is love. Christ tells her that if it is enough for her, it is enough for him. Plenty, abundance—literally, satisfaction—is a kind of filling, an incarnation. Christ can say to Julian, after she has witnessed his passion, that if she is filled with him—embodying his love—he too is complete. This is not a rhetoric of lack. The love-act of Jesus on the cross is inseparable from the love-acts of creation and incarnation. In all these the human is made fully one-ed with the divine. In all these, it is enough. At the Passover seder there is a long litany of *dayenu's*—"it would have been enough," the various salvific actions of the God of Abraham for the people of Israel. But God has consistently, always and forever, offered more—more salvation than we could ever possibly ask for. Here in Chapter 22 is Julian's *dayenu*. God loved in the creation; God loved in the Incarnation; God loves on the cross. Any of these individually would have been enough to demonstrate God's love. But God cannot be satisfied without loving us more and more. Christ is not glorifying pain by saying that if he could have suffered more, he would have. Rather, in a one-to-one one-ing with human creation, Christ tells Julian that if he could love more, he would. But he could not; this action on the cross is the apex.

We would be God's even without the cross. In his making us, in our embodying him, we have been one-ed to God. Christ told Julian that it was "bliss" to suffer for humanity. Here the process, the outcome, and the humankind one-ed to God are all part of that same bliss. We are what he receives; in us, he is satisfied. Through us, we are enough for him. By us, we make known who he is. We are not the garland of thorns; we are his crown. Our very existence shows forth his glory and honor. We are precious to him. Every day God's love flows out in the sufferings and redemptions experienced and enacted by us, his embodied and one-ed aspects on earth. In living as his crown, we live as his love and in his love. We suffer with him but we also have the capacity, through his grace, to demonstrate his love in the world. Chapter 22 shows the Love that is all that is. Julian rewrites creed, doxology, Gospel: God is simply Infinite Love. In the beginning Love already existed; the form it takes—made manifest in so many different ways in the Incarnation—does not change its eternal essence. Julian cannot keep herself from repeatedly stating God's willingness to love us—join us, save us, claim us, need us—not out of necessity but out of desire. The power of divine love in Julian's theology transforms the acts of the cosmos from a determined, almost reductive, scientific process into a wholly affective action.

23

In these three words: "It is a joy, a bliss, and endless delight to me"
   were shown three states of bliss, in this way:
      in regard to the joy, I interpret the pleasure of the Father; and
      in regard to the bliss, the honor of the Son; and
      in regard to the endless delight, the Holy Spirit.

        The Father is pleased,
        the Son is honored,
        the Holy Spirit delights.

           And here I saw this in relation to the third vision of His
           blessed Passion—that is to say, the joy and the bliss that
           make Him delight in it—for our gracious Lord showed His
           Passion to me in five ways: of which

                the first is the bleeding of the head,
                the second is the discoloring of His blessed face,
                the third is the plenteous bleeding of the body in the slashes
                   of the scourging,
                the fourth is the profound drying (these four regard the
                   pains of the Passion as I said before), and,
                the fifth is what was shown in regard to the joy and the
                   bliss of the Passion.

It is God's will that we have true delight with Him in our salvation,
   and in that He wishes us to be mightily comforted and strengthened,
   and thus He wills that with His grace our soul be happily engaged,
      for we are His bliss,
      for in us He delights without end and
      so shall we in Him with His grace.

All that He has done for us, and does now, and ever shall do,
   was never a cost or burden to Him,
   nor can it be

(*except only what He did in our manhood, beginning at the sweet
incarnation and lasting until the blessed Rising on Easter morning—
only that long did the cost and the burden concerning our
redemption
last in deed—about which deed He rejoices endlessly, as was said
before.*)

Ah, Jesus wishes
that we take heed to the bliss of our salvation that is in the blessed Trinity
and that we desire to have as much spiritual pleasure, with His grace,
as was said before.
(*That is to say, that the pleasure of our salvation be like to the joy
that Christ has about our salvation as much as it can be while we
are here.*)

The whole Trinity acted in the Passion of Christ
(*ministering an abundance of strengths and plenitude of grace
to us by Him*)
but only the Maiden's son suffered
(*about which the whole blessed Trinity endlessly rejoices*).
This was shown in these words: "Art thou well satisfied?"
and by that other word that Christ said, "If thou art satisfied, then
I am satisfied"
(*as if He said: "It is joy and delight enough to me, and I ask nothing
else from thee for my labor except that I can well satisfy thee"*).

In this He reminded me of the quality of a glad giver:
always a glad giver takes but little heed of the thing that he gives,
but all his desire and all his intention is to please him and solace him
to whom he gives it,
and if the receiver accepts the gift gladly and thankfully, then the
gracious giver sets at nought all his cost and all his labor for
the joy and delight that he has because he has pleased and
solaced him whom he loves.
Plenteously and fully was this shown.
Think also wisely of the magnitude of this word "ever";
for that was shown an exalted awareness of the love that He
has in our salvation,
with the manifold joys that result from the Passion of Christ:
one joy is that He rejoices that He has done it in deed, and He
shall suffer no more;

another joy is that He brought us up into heaven and made us to
   be His crown and endless bliss;
another joy is that with the Passion He has redeemed us from
   endless pains of hell.

$$\infty \quad \infty \quad \infty$$

God is joyful because his Son in his humanity said yes to his will. That will is love. In the agony in the garden our human Jesus struggled with his call. Could he say yes? To say that the "bliss" is the Son's "honor" fleshes out this theology. The union between God and humanity comes through that incarnation fully realized on the cross. As the only tangible, visible mundane presence, the body of Jesus as it was known and revered could receive worldly honor in a way that other members of the Trinity could not. He gave his honor in one-ing with us fully. Still, the meaning is not, and never was, about human sacrifice. Christ's death, like the loss of a family member in a warrior culture with "honor prices," was not the compensation. He did not need to be sacrificed for our sins. Rather, like the bereaved family or tribe, we must receive the compensation—of love. That is the Holy Spirit. The Comforter, the "endless delight," works by and through grace in the world. This is our inheritance; this is his honor price. He was one-ed with us; the mortal body he shares with us must by definition die, yet we are left with a different kind of bliss.

The post-crucifixion experience of God's work in the world begins to unfold in Julian's theology. Through the Spirit, lacking his human body on earth, we remain in the dance of intimate communion with God. This is God's will. The Word took flesh and dwelt among us; the humanity of God said yes to the call; and in that moment of dying on the cross, the egg of life broke open to set free the grace-filled Holy Spirit to continue God's work in the world. Throughout the history of creation God has been working in and through the material world by grace. Before Jesus' birth and during his life this presence of Love incarnate was working in and through matter. It was, is, and always will be, as Julian articulated in Chapter 22. Yet once that embodiment and resurrection of a Son occurred, the heightened awareness of the work of grace in the world promised more fully and more deeply the interconnected oneness of spirit and flesh. We were told that the Spirit would be with us always, and so it is. The door has been opened by Jesus' life and death. We are invited to go forward and graciously be guided by the Holy Spirit to do his work in the world.

As much as Julian elaborated the suffering humanity of Jesus the Christ, here she collapses that in favor of the workings of God's grace-filled love. Julian dismisses a cost-benefit analysis of the economics of human sacrifice. There is not an "us" versus "them"; we are not an "us" that needs to be set right with God through Christ. On the human level, Jesus suffered when he partook of what we already were and already knew. Julian acknowledges the human "cost" and "burden" for our redemption—but that joyful act does not signify materially in the mind of God, whose will is to continue the flow of love into the world. Julian's Christ moves our eyes from the cross and directs them to our lives in the world, and the ways God can and does work through us. We must look beyond the suffering to see its purpose: the translation, or carrying over, of love. Julian returns to a discourse of satisfaction, God's filling us up with his love through his actions in the world. The Passion on the cross was one of those actions, but as we see through the Trinity, it is only part of the picture. The ongoing, continuing actions of grace in the world— the creations/incarnations, the passions—these are not singular; they are part of God's plan for bringing Love into the world. Julian needed to start with the suffering body of Jesus on the cross because through it she glimpsed her frail humanity. As she steps back, Jesus' place, and her own, in the divine plan slowly begin to dawn on her. Intimacy with the Son was a way in, but focus on his suffering and death is not the end of the story. It is just the start—the entrance the human mind can claim in attempting to glimpse the unknowable, the mind of God.

God welcomes us through the gift of his body, the gift of his life. In a sense the human Jesus is relieved that his suffering is over. Thus the pleasure of the Father is the completion of the will of God. Instead of "endless pains" we are given "endless delight." Yet as we suffer here on earth, we are not alone. It is not simply a question of contemplation of Jesus' passion, a kind of self-willing to one our pains with his. Rather, without any action of our own—mental, physical, or spiritual—we have the infinite grace of the Comforter, the Holy Spirit, to guide us and save us through our personal hells here on earth. They are Christ's passions as much as his cross is.

❀ **24** ❀

Then, with a glad expression, our Lord looked into His wounded side
and gazed with joy,
    and with His sweet gazing He directed the understanding of His
creature through that same wound into His side within.

There He showed a fair, desirable place, and large enough for all mankind
that shall be saved to rest in peace and love.
    And with that He brought to mind His dearworthy blood and
precious water which He allowed to pour all out for love.

And with the sweet sight He showed His blessed Heart cloven in two.
And with this sweet rejoicing, He showed to my understanding, in part,
        the blessed Godhead, strengthening the pure soul to
        understand (in so far as it can be expressed)
that this Heart is to signify the endless love that was without
beginning, and is, and shall be always.

With this our Good Lord said most blissfully, "Lo, how I love thee"
  (as if He had said:
    "My dear one, behold and see the Lord, thy God,
      who is thy Creator and thine endless Joy.
    See thine own Brother, thy Savior;
    my child, behold and see what delight and bliss I have in thy salvation,
    and for my love, enjoy it now with me.").

Also for further understanding this blessed word was said:
          "Lo, how I love thee.
          Behold and see that I loved thee so much before I died for thee
            that I was willing to die for thee;
          and that now I have died for thee, and suffered willingly
            what I can.
          And now is all my bitter pain and all my cruel labor changed
            to endless joy and bliss for me and for thee.

How should it now be that thou wouldst pray for anything that
pleases me, and I would not most gladly grant it thee?
For my pleasure is thy holiness and thine endless joy and bliss with Me."

This is the understanding, as simply as I can express it, of this blessed word:
"Lo, how I love thee."

This our good Lord showed in order to make us glad and happy.

ɞ ɞ ɞ

There is a whole world inside that wounded side. Mystics throughout
history have focused on the wounds of Jesus' body. For some the penetration has been almost sexual: the "bridal mysticism" with the divine
bridegroom has invited the Beloved into a gender-bending holy womb.
For Julian here the penetration is decidedly intellectual, yet, as everywhere else in her text, dependent on a real physical body. If anything,
this journey into the wound/womb of Christ is the first real entry into
the motherhood of God. Julian's visionary experiences are based on a
return to origins. Here her God gazes at his own physical wounds with
joy. Jesus invited Julian inside of him; God invites Julian to enter in. We
all receive this call, if in different forms. Once again, the physical and
the abstract cannot be separated. It is Julian's "understanding" that God
directs inside himself, yet in God's way of teaching, this process has to
happen by means of his wounds. A rupture, a break, an opening of some
kind is necessary to lead the human mind more deeply inside God. The
metaphor operates beautifully, since it is a willing wound of Jesus' body
that he accepted with full bliss on behalf of creation. In Chapter 24 it is
not so much "by his wounds we are healed" as "by his wounds we enter
in and begin to understand."

It may be a commonplace that Julian refers to herself as "his creature,"
but that word choice certainly underscores our oneness with All Created
Thing he has created, and into which she is moving. Divine reason, the
Logos-mind of God, is associated with the mind of Julian as much as her
body is connected with God's in the Incarnation. God literally looks
inside himself, and through that gaze directs Julian in. The metaphor of
sight—of vision and visionary experience—serves to represent the essential process occurring through language of the tangible. Inside God,
he continues to lead. Heaven is to be inside God. There is room enough
for us all. This, not the Passion, is what Julian really prayed for: greater
intimacy with God. She asked to see the external and instead God shows

her what is inside. Touch is a powerful gesture, as is physical union. Here is the first real physical encounter between Julian's body and God's. She continues to preface her remarks with the clarification that the experience occurs in her understanding. Yet like fantasy, vision constitutes and evokes a real physiological response for the individual subject. Inside God is a place of rest, of peace and love. In the heart of God cloven in two we are literally part of his everlasting love. We are his heart; we are his love; we are his "other half." Nothing can separate us from the love of God. Yet it is in his brokenness, as in ours, that we can fully experience the love of God. We need to know this, as does he. The eternity of God's love is one-ed with a broken creation.

Entering into God is not the end point of Julian's journey. It is only the beginning, for her soul cannot recline forever in this peace and rest. In the sight of divine love, Julian must exercise her understanding to learn all that is humanly possible to know about her God. She is called to share that; hence we read her text today. Consolation is the doorway open to the continuing journey. This is the reason why Julian's text does not end here. God wants us to know his rest; he also wants us to know his "delight" and "bliss." But that does not mean we will ever allow ourselves to stay in it forever—at least not until the end of time, or even the end of our mortal time. There is work to be done; there are questions to pursue.

25

With this same expression of mirth and joy
    our good Lord looked down on His right side
    and brought to my mind where Our Lady stood
    at the time of His Passion;
        and He said, "Dost thou wish to see her?"
            (And in this sweet word, it was as if He had said:
            "I know well thou wouldest see my Blessed Mother,
            for after Myself, she is the highest joy that I could show thee,
            and the most pleasure and honor to me;
            and she is most desired to be seen
            by all my blessed creatures.")
Because of the exalted, wondrous, special love that He has for this sweet
    Maiden,
His Blessed Mother, our Lady Saint Mary,
    He showed her highly rejoicing
        (as in view of the intention of these sweet words)
        as if He said:
            "Dost thou wish to see how I love her, that thou canst rejoice with me
              in the love that I have in her and she in me?"

And also for further understanding, this sweet word our Lord God speaks to all
    mankind
that shall be saved (as it were all to one person) as if He said:
    "Do you wish to see in her how thou art loved?
    Because of thy love I made her so exalted, so noble, and so worthy;
    and this pleases me, and so I wish that it pleaseth thee."
    For after Himself, she is the most blessed sight.

        (But from this I am not taught to yearn to see her bodily
        presence while I am here, but the virtues of her blessed
        soul—her truth, her wisdom, her love—whereby I can learn
        to know myself and reverently fear my God.)

And when our Good Lord had shown this and said this word,
  "Dost thou wish to see her?"
    I answered and said: "Yea, good Lord, thanks be to Thee;
      yea, good Lord, if it be Thy will."

Often I prayed this and I expected to have seen her in bodily
  presence, but I saw her not so,
    but Jesus in that word showed me a spiritual sight of her (in the same
      way as
        I had seen her before—little and simple—so He showed her now
        exalted and noble and glorious and pleasing to Him
        above all created beings).

And so He wishes that it be known that all those that delight in Him should
delight in her and in the delight that He has in her and she in Him.

For further understanding, He showed this example:
  as, if a man loves a creature uniquely above all creatures,
    he would like to make all creatures to love and to delight in that
      creature which he loves so much.

And in this word that Jesus said, "Dost thou wish to see her?" it seemed to me
that it was the most pleasing word He could have given me about her with the
spiritual showing that He gave me of her—because our Lord showed me no one
person in particular except
our Lady Saint Mary—and her He showed three times:
  the first was as she conceived,
  the second was as she was in her sorrows beneath the cross,
  the third was as she is now in delight, honor, and joy.

ഇ   ഇ   ഇ

Chapter 25 continues the implied comparison between Julian, all of human nature, and Mary. Christ's "Dost thou wish to see her?" is really "Dost thou wish to see thyself?" The chapter opens out of the "Lo, how I love thee." The narrative trajectory of what unfolds comes from that divine heart of love in Chapter 24—broken to be one with us, like the bread and body of the Eucharist. In Chapter 25 we meet the source of Jesus' human life, the mother. Christ looks down on his right side before he asks the question: He moves into his own wound/womb to do so. Julian is instantly reminded of Mary at the foot of the cross. His suffering in the Passion is literally a labor of love: there he gives birth to more love for the world. She stands in her human suffering, having known the agony of giving birth and the agony of watching that human life end.

Mary's human sufferings are our sufferings, just as Jesus' are. She exists in a special relationship to Jesus the Christ. As God, he is the source of her life in his role as creator. As human, she is the source of his life. To employ the medieval trope, her womb gave voice to the Word. This is of course the model for Julian's activity: from her bodily suffering emerges a text that seeks to articulate God's love. Julian has asked for and experienced the visions of Jesus' pain. She has identified with him. But how closely, how deeply, can she look at Mary? How closely, how deeply, can she look at herself? Julian must discern. She must go forward and indeed must eventually put her text forward. The invitation to look in the face of what brings Love into the world, what embodies the Word, is a call. It is an invitation to look in the mirror. Mary represents that potentiality in each one of us. We are all that much loved because through each one of us God's love can enter the world. We are all called to give birth to him. We are all the highly favored daughters and sons. His love-suffering is as tangible in his acts of creation that made us as in his acts of salvation that continue one-ing us to him. And while we live on earth, our bodies are called to be vessels of that same divine love flowing out into the world. We are made in his image. The person of Mary is a teacher, but what she has is what each of us may perfect and realize. Her "fear" is not terror as much as it is an awe that ones her to him, enabling his work to spill out into the world.

So we return to the question, "Dost thou wish to see her?" Julian is ready to say yes; she is ready to continue answering God's call. She does not see Mary's bodily presence. Mary is not a human being different and separate from Julian herself. She is a spiritual sight shown in Julian's understanding that allows her to answer the call. When we say yes to God, God rejoices in us. We cannot help but celebrate with and within those who say yes to God. Through Mary's body, she is creator; in her human pain she suffered with the saving Christ; in her essence she is that Spirit's "delight." Are we ready to look at ourselves and accept this reality? Are we willing to receive the love of God that calls us, to let his love flow out of us into the world? Saying yes is not pride or arrogance; it is humility. We acknowledge that we are beloved children of God made in his image and pregnant with his love. Hiding our light is denying God's love, refusing to be vehicles for its release into the world. We are loved; we are one-ed with him. We are all called to give birth to God; only the particular manifestations differ.

26

After this our Lord showed Himself more glorified, as I see it, than I saw Him
*   before,*
*   in which I was taught that our soul shall never rest until it comes to Him*
*   knowing that He is the fullness of joy,*
*   simple and gracious,*
*   blissful and true life.*

Our Lord Jesus often said:
*   "It is I,*
*   it is I;*
*   it is I who am most exalted;*
*   it is I whom thou lovest;*
*   it is I whom thou enjoyest;*
*   it is I whom thou servest;*
*   it is I whom thou yearnst for;*
*   it is I whom thou desirest;*
*   it is I whom thou meanest*
*   it is I who am all;*
*   it is I whom Holy Church preaches and teaches thee;*
*   it is I who showed myself here to thee."*

The number of these words surpasses my wit and all my understanding and all
my abilities, and it is a most high number, as I see it, because therein these words
surpass all that heart can wish and soul can desire. And therefore the words are
not explained here, but every man according to the grace that God gives him in
interpreting and loving, receive them in our Lord's meaning.

ဆ ဆ ဆ

God is our all in all. He is, and is about, our being. The Word is the
ineffable, essential speech act who is beyond human language. He is also
all that Julian hears him say as he describes himself. The articulation of

the Word is constant and ongoing. His voice is the verb "to be." Julian begins her quotation of him with a Trinity of "It is I." God is all there is. He is our being; he is being. This is what Abraham, Moses, and all the prophets heard. He is the great "I AM." In the gospels, Jesus asks, "Who do you say that I am?" The Word calls us to embody his being through ourselves. The speech of the incarnate God reads like a litany, but it is a repeated call to recognition, like his body broken in the sacrament. Here is an invitation to answer, to see him where and how he shows us to be. The Word of God is a wake-up call to Julian, confirming and affirming her experience. It is a continuous reminder of God's active presence in our lives.

This is the God Julian has spent her life hearing about, whom she was told to trust, to pray to, to view as creator of the universe. There is no separation between her experience and the abstract ideas of what God "is" that human language has attempted to articulate. This is the God Julian has been taught to love; this is the God she has loved, however unworthy she may feel. This God is simply Love. Here is the dynamic aspect of God's message, the "beingness" of his state. That which Julian has loved is God. Wherever Julian, as a manifestation of the human incarnation of God working in and through her, has loved, there is God. *Ubi caritas et amor, Deus ibi est*. Where charity and love are, there is God. Julian may very well have enjoyed resting in God—before her illness, and in the midst of her showings. But wherever she has known joy, there has God been. Wherever she takes on the role of servant as he did on earth, there is God. The "I" of yearning and the "I" of desire—this is God. The language, the entire discourse surrounding God—the full development of theological systems—these cannot capture the experiential nature of a God whom one longs for and intimately desires. In the essence of longing, in the embodiment of our God, we have already received him in whatever form he shows himself through the created world.

Julian relies heavily on her "understanding," yet language fundamentally lacks meaning in relation to experience. Reason articulates words and theories for God, arbitrary signifiers compared to the true essence that simply IS, and IS all things—the Presence experienced within Julian herself and within all. The awareness of a God in all things makes human attempts at defining meaning arbitrary. Each soul must hear the "It is I" for itself: it must resound in the human heart as befits the individual journey. The spiritual seeker is challenged to recognize God in the slightest and remotest, the most profane as well as the most sacred. Julian's treatment of the Word, who speaks everywhere and in everything, calls us to recognize the speech acts of the Ineffable wherever they may sound. What God has made holy, let no one call profane; whenever the Word speaks, let whoever has ears to listen pay attention.

⊰ **27** ⊱

After that the Lord brought to my mind the yearning that I had for Him
  in the past,
    and I saw that nothing stood in my way except sin
      (and thus I observed universally in us all).

And it seemed to me that if sin had not been,
  we would all have been pure
  and like to our Lord as He made us,

and thus, in my folly, before this time I often wondered why, by the
  great foreseeing wisdom of God,
the beginning of sin was not prevented,
  for then, it seemed to me, all would have been well.

I ought much to have given up this disturbing wondering, but nevertheless,
  I made mourning and sorrow about it without reason or discretion.

But Jesus (who in this vision informed me of all that I needed)
  answered by this word and said:
    "Sin is inevitable,
      but all shall be well,
      and all shall be well,
      and all manner of thing shall be well."

In this unadorned word "sin," our Lord brought to my mind generally
  all that is not good,
  and the shameful despising
  and the uttermost tribulation that He bore for us in this life,
  and His dying,
  and all the pains and sufferings of all His created things, spiritually
    and bodily

(for we are all in part troubled—and we shall be troubled,
following our Master Jesus, until we are completely purged—
that is to say, until we are fully stripped of our mortal flesh and
of all our inward affections which are not truly good).

And with the beholding of this,
with all pains that ever were or ever shall be,
I understood the Passion of Christ to represent the greatest pain
and even more than that.

And all this pain was shown in one stroke
and quickly passed over into comfort
(for our good Lord does not wish that the soul be made fearful
by this ugly sight).

But I saw not sin;
for I believe it has no manner of essence
nor any portion of being,
nor can it be known except by the pain that is caused by it.
And this pain, it is something for a time, as I see it, because it
purges and forces us to know ourselves and ask for mercy. But
the Passion of our Lord is comfort for us against all this, and so
is His blessed will.

And because of the tender love that our good Lord has to all that
shall be saved, He comforts quickly and sweetly, meaning thus:
"It is true that sin is cause of all this pain,
but all shall be well,
and all shall be well,
and all manner of thing shall be well."

These words were said most tenderly,
showing no manner of blame to me nor to any that shall be saved.

Then it would be a great unkindness to blame God for my sin,
seeing He does not blame me for sin.

In these same words I saw a marvelous, high secret hidden in God,
which secret He shall openly make known to us in heaven.

In this secret knowledge we shall truly see the reason why He
allowed sin to come,
and in this sight we shall endlessly rejoice in our Lord God.

ಶಿ   ಶಿ   ಶಿ

Julian's "all shall be well," repeated many times in the *Showings,* suggests future time: something that takes us out of the present-moment awareness. Chapter 27 is very much concerned with the here and now. Time dissolves; separation dissolves. Intimacy with the divine, the subject of the whole of Julian's text, remains. She laments sin because it separates us from God and wonders why it was not prevented so there would be no separation. When Julian speaks of how "all would have been well" in this case, she means that there would be no separation. Nothing would separate God from the "universal." Julian interrogates the nature of the Incarnation. If divine essence infuses all creation, yet there is some block to God in every part of it, how does true one-ing sustain itself? There is a contradiction here, because we cannot at once be one-ed with God and separated from him. Where is God incarnate in our imperfect world? How is there one-ing if we lack something wanted and have something unwanted?

Even in the timeless world of God, the existence of "sin" is not negotiable. It is not possible to go back and prevent it from coming into the world. Thus it must either be part of some system, be of value, or be neutral. The Godhead intimately knew sin through the experience of the Passion. This is precisely why his suffering was necessary. Sin then is not what separates us from God, but rather what ones us to him. Our experience of suffering, of evil, ones us to him. His is the prototype for all suffering, all experience of evil. The narrative of a divine essence that took material form must necessarily include within it a full experience of who we are. Even here there is active sympathy, shared experience. God did not will to be fully one with us by doing the acts we do that are experienced as "sin" by others, that enact separation in our relationships or cause us pain. Rather, God's one-ing came in the form of experiencing the result of them: knowing our pain. Passion aside, there is a danger in glorifying suffering and victimization in this understanding of the world. We are not called to wallow. Instead, we are called, like Jesus the Christ, to allow the Holy Spirit to work to transform it into our glory. His suffering is ours and ours is his; his resurrection is likewise our redemption. This action occurs not simply on the cross and in heaven, but in the very fabric of our lives. Sin, such as it is, is a good here because even as in itself it is separation, its effects in fact work to remove those sources of separation from us. In our trials and troubles, all that separates us from our God is taken away. In the midst of our pain the Spirit wears away our separation until we are fully and completely one-ed with him. The Incarnation is made complete in each one of us and ultimately in all of creation as the Spirit continues to operate.

Julian writes sin out of existence. It lacks essence; it can only be known in its effects. We do not have to struggle against sin; we need to let go. Through the vacuum sin creates, we turn to God of our free will. Sin strips away the illusions of what we think we are and points us to rejoin our will to God. We look to the cross, and insofar as we are agents of sin we are invited to let go. As much as we are experiencing the effects of sin, we can allow for the purgation, knowing we are led closer, nearer, and deeper into the wounded side of love and grace. Again, this is no glorification of suffering, but a willing release and call to allow the work of grace to enfold us, free us, and one us.

God does not blame humanity for sin. It just is. Through our willing acceptance, its effects can lead to transformation. Sin and suffering are vehicles that allow us to renounce those attachments that separate us from God and freely move forward to loving awareness and Spirit-ed one-ing.

In the creation narrative of Genesis, sin came into the world through desire to know as God knows. Julian's experience has been the desire to know more by God's grace, will, and choice. This is shown in her "understanding." Julian lived in an age in which faith and reason were fiercely disputed. Philosophy fought contemplative spirituality. Julian, a laywoman, sought answers from God, and she wrote her witnessing text. The full story may have to wait until heaven, but the assurance of a God of love whose every action in the dynamism of grace is driven by that love—this is enough for her. It is offered to us for our transformations.

☙ **28** ☞

Thus I saw how Christ has compassion for us because of sin.

And just as
> *I was before filled with pain and compassion*
>> *for the Passion of Christ, similarly,*
> *I was here filled in part with compassion for all my fellow*
>> *Christians for that is to say*
>>> *(even though He full well loves the people that shall be saved),*
> *that God's servants, Holy Church, shall be shaken in sorrows and anguish*
>> *and tribulation in this world as men shake a cloth in the wind.*

And regarding this our Lord answered in this manner:
>> *"A great thing shall I make out of this in heaven,*
>> *of endless honors, and everlasting joys."*

Yea, so much so that our Lord rejoices at the tribulations of His servants
> *(with pity and compassion),*
>> *and upon each person whom He loves (in order to bring him to His bliss)*
>> *He lays upon them something that is no defect from His point of view,*
>> *whereby they are*
>>> *disparaged and despised in this world,*
>>> *scorned and mocked,*
>>> *and cast out.*
> *This He does in order to prevent the harm that they would receive*
>> *from the pomp and*
>> *from the pride and*
>> *from the vainglory of this wretched life,*
>> *and to make their way ready to come to heaven,*
>> *and to exalt them in His bliss everlasting without end.*

For He says:
> *"I shall totally shatter you because of your vain affections and*
>> *your vicious pride;*

*and after that I shall gather you together and make you humble
    and gentle, pure and holy, by one-ing you to myself."*

Then I saw
    *that each kind compassion that man has toward his fellow Christian
            with love, it is Christ in him;*
    that each kind of degradation that He has shown in His Passion,
            *it was shown again here in this compassion in which there
            were two kinds of applications of our Lord's meaning:*
    *the one was the bliss that we are brought to in which
            He wants us to rejoice;*
    the other is for comfort in our pain,
            *because He wants us to be aware that the pain shall all be
                transformed into honor and benefit by virtue of His
                Passion,*
            *and that we be aware that we do not suffer alone, but with
                Him,*
            and that we see Him as our foundation,
            *and that we see His pains and His tribulation surpass so
                far*
                *all that we can suffer that it cannot be fully
                comprehended.*

*And the careful awareness to this intention of His saves us from
grumbling and despair when we experience our own pains
    as long as we see truly that our sin deserves it,
yet His love excuses us,
and of His great graciousness He does away with all our blame,
and He looks upon us with mercy and pity as children,
    innocent and not loathsome.*

⁖ ⁖ ⁖

One feels with the Other in compassion; it is perhaps the most fundamental of Christian experiences. Through the Incarnation our God comes to feel with us; through that same experience of incarnation we come to feel with him as we contemplate his sufferings on the cross that are our own pains. Julian's visionary experience allows her to do this. She has compassion for God in contemplating the Passion; in identifying with him she has compassion for all humanity's sufferings and failings—the sins that separate. Compassion is another way of talking about the "sin" that separates. It is a bridge made out of God's love. We get separated from one another, yet some spark of divinity allows us identification. We are one-ed together in the love of God that is compassion.

When Julian has compassion for the Passion of Jesus she cannot help but have compassion for her fellow Christians, insofar as we are the Body of Christ. As "Holy Church" is "shaken," Julian names the institution, the Body of Christ in pain, as the Suffering Servant. She understands the need for compassion, a love that must conquer the separation that is sin. We can view this individually, in our strivings and sufferings, and collectively, as the church corporeal in jeopardy: the fragile web of connection that is the Incarnation, the fibers that, woven together, make us one in the Body of Christ. When we heal separations—closing up the Christ-wound of sin—we are doing God's work of repairing a broken world. God rejoices in our struggles and tribulations, for through them we find our way back to him. We each have our brokenness. Every break is an invitation into the wound/womb of God. In the (com)passion of our personal cross we are loved. Nothing we bear is shameful. We are called to transform these blessings into sites of compassion. By our wounds we are healed, and through them we are called to heal the world. In our weaknesses or sense of difference we learn compassion for others. Thus the separation that is sin is healed. Brokenness is our means to connect with other manifestations of incarnation. These wounds, like Jesus', are how we reach our God. Who has not felt "shattered" at some time? By grace, that shattering is the break to knowledge of God. None of us comes to God whole. We cannot be one-ed to God unless we offer some opening for him to enter in. We need a pierced side of our own, for this is the substance of one-ing connection by which separation—sin—is healed.

Wherever there is compassion, there is God. What I call my God is contained in those transcendent moments of love and compassion that each and all of us share. Where God's love bridges those separations, the resurrection is happening. To Jesus' Passion, these actions of compassion perform a reversal. These compassions are God's comfort that we do not suffer alone. Grace in the Incarnate Love breaks into human relationships. Through resurrections and redemptions we know what it means to be transformed. God does not want us to dwell on our separations, hurts—sins. He constantly breaks through: not in the abstract, but in the grounded world of Holy Creation where each meeting with the Other offers the possibility of one-ing us. We have the choice to say yes, to open ourselves to compassion. Can we allow ourselves to accept a God who looks on us with pity, not with blame?

ᘓ **29** ᘔ

But in this showing I remained watching generally,
   sorrowful and mourning,
      saying thus to our Lord in my meaning with full great fear:
         "Ah! Good Lord, how can all be well considering the great
         damage that has come by sin to Thy creatures?"
            (And here I desired, as much as I dared, to have some more
            open explanation with which I could be put at ease
            in this matter.)

To this our blessed Lord answered most gently,
   and with most loving expression,
      and showed that Adam's sin was the most harm that ever was done,
         or ever shall be done, until the world's end
            (and also He showed that this is openly acknowledged in all the
            Holy Church on earth).

Furthermore, He taught that I should observe the glorious
         reparation, for making this reparation is more pleasing to the
         blessed Godhead and more valuable for man's salvation, without
         comparison, than ever was the sin of Adam harmful.

Then means our blessed Lord thus in this teaching: that we would take heed
   to this:
      "For since I had made well the worst harm,
      then it is my will that thou knowest from that
      that I shall make well everything that is less bad."

ᘔ   ᘔ   ᘔ

Julian is not the passive recipient of visions awarded to her by the Almighty. Her narrative is an active engagement with her God in a search for answers. Julian asks: "How can all be well?" The brokenness of the world is mirrored in the fragmentation of Julian's reason. There is a vacuum here, a space between the certainty that is God and the lack in Julian's soul. Her longing is for God, for the satisfaction that only God can provide. This God is as willing to fill Julian's inquiring mind as her soul. He tells Julian that any isolated act of separation enacted by individual humanity matters little to a God who has made all things well. We are taught to move our focus from our brokenness to the seamless completion in God. Here even the obsession with original sin is stripped away as "reparation" is celebrated. Julian's narrative operates on an existential level, yet her tone remains in the realm of individual human experience. God righted the wrong of the fall of Adam: through the action of the Incarnation, the rent mortal garment of original sin is mended. But grace in the world, the Incarnation spilling out into all things, assures that every tear in the fabric of our lives will be repaired. So as we gaze at ourselves, look at our broken souls, let us not reenact the crucifixion. It has been done; we are always already healed. We need not crucify ourselves when God has no desire to crucify us.

∾ **30** ∾

He gave me understanding in two parts:

The first part is our Savior and our salvation;
    this blessed part is open and clear and fair and light and plenteous,
    for all mankind that is of good will and shall be is contained in
        this part;
    to this we are bound by God
    and attracted and advised, and taught inwardly by the Holy
        Spirit and outwardly by Holy Church in the same grace;
    in this our Lord wishes us to be engaged, rejoicing in Him
        because He rejoices in us, and
    the more abundantly we accept this with reverence and humility,
    the more favor we earn from Him and
    the more help for ourselves; and thus we can see and rejoice
        that our portion is our Lord.

The second part is hidden and sealed from us
        (that is to say, all except for our salvation),
    for that is our Lord's secret purpose,
    and it is proper to the royal authority of God to hold His secret
        purpose in peace,
    and it is proper for His servants, out of obedience and reverence,
        not to wish to know His purpose.

Our Lord has pity and compassion on us because some creatures
        make themselves so busy about His secrets; and I am certain
        if we were aware of how much we would please Him and
        ease ourselves by abandoning that, we would.

The saints that are in heaven wish to know nothing except what
        our Lord wishes to show them,
and also their love and their desire is ruled according to the will of
        our Lord.

*Thus we ought to wish as they do—then shall we not wish nor desire anything
    except the will of our Lord just as they do, for we are all one in
    God's purpose.*

*And here was I taught that we should trust and rejoice only in our
    blessed Savior Jesus, for everything.*

ଔ   ଔ   ଔ

Julian's intellect is her wounded side, the separation from divine Wisdom. It is the womb God enters into and from which she births the words
of her text. Here the commonplace "Jesus is the answer" can be taken
literally. The Word satisfies all questions. Salvation is the answer to the
separation that is sin in the world. Here the definition of "understanding"
gains greater breadth. We are literally embodied in God, saved and protected in the well-making. That occurs not just *through* the Word but literally *in* the Word, by action of the Incarnation. The divine mind works
with the human so that Julian's form of questioning is the agent for enacting that one-ing. Compassion, the subject of Chapter 28, is understanding.
It fills the gap in the human mind and heals the rift of sin. Understanding
and compassion are embodiments of the Word, the dynamic work of
grace that seals separation. We never step outside this epistemological
system because God has answered the question. The answer of the Word
and its salvific act assure us that we are contained within him. Yet we are
invited to greater awareness. The answer is there for us.

We may be contained in him and he may provide us his Word, but in
the "I and Thou" we remain in a broken world. We depend on the continuous action of grace speaking answers. As long as we live, no matter how
much the Word has spoken, resonating in the fibers of ourselves, we cannot have all the answers. Julian's hunger will never be fully sated in this
world, despite knowledge of the voice of God. She speaks to her intellectual curiosity when she advocates God's will as a letting go. This is the
call to the contemplative life, the lesson of still prayer. It does not exist in
a dialectic; it cannot depend on the question-and-answer format that has
already failed Julian. We can only prostrate ourselves before the answer
of the Word, which must be enough for us as long as we are mortal. Julian
maintains her intellectual curiosity and desire for meaning even as she
has been granted these showings. The God who has one-ed us to the divine
mind through reason—and understanding, compassion that heals the
separation that is sin—listens to us in our language and provides the
answers we need. Will we be still enough to rest in him?

᥈ **31** ᥏

And so our good Lord replied to all the questions and doubts that I could raise,
saying most reassuringly:
> *"I am able to make everything well, and*
> *I know how to make everything well, and*
> *I wish to make everything well, and*
> *I shall make everything well; and*
> *thou shalt see for thyself that all manner of things shall be well."*

Where He says, "I am able," I understand as referring to the Father;
> *and*
where He says, "I know how," I understand as referring to the Son;
> *and*
where He says, "I wish to," I understand as referring to the Holy
> *Spirit; and*
where He says, "I shall," I understand as referring to the unity of
> *the blessed Trinity (three persons and one truth); and*
where He says, "Thou shalt see for thyself," I understand the one-
> *ing of all mankind that shall be saved into the blissful Trinity.*

With these five words God wills that we be enclosed in rest and in
> *peace; and thus shall the spiritual thirst of Christ have an end,*
> *for this is the spiritual thirst of Christ: the love-longing that*
> *lasts and ever shall, until we see that sight on Doomsday.*

[For of us who shall be saved, and shall be Christ's joy and His bliss, some are
still here, and some are to come (and so shall some be until that Day).]

Therefore, this is His thirst:
> *a love-longing to possess us all together wholly within Himself for*
> *His bliss, as I see it*
> > *(for we are not now fully as wholly within Him*
> > *as we shall be then).*

For we know in our Faith
    (and also it was shown in all the revelations)
that Christ Jesus is both God and man.

    Concerning the Godhead, He is Himself highest bliss,
        and was so from without beginning,
        and shall be until without end;
    this endless bliss can never be increased nor decreased in itself.
        (This was plenteously seen in every showing—
        and specifically in the twelfth where He says:
        "It is I who am highest.")

    Concerning Christ's manhood,
        it is known in our Faith, and also shown in the revelation, that
        He, with the strength of Godhead, for the sake of love, endured
        pains and sufferings and died in order to bring us to His bliss.
            And these are the works of Christ's manhood, in which He
                rejoices
            (and that He showed in the ninth revelation where He says:
            "It is a joy, a bliss, an endless delight to me that ever I
            suffered the Passion for thee").
        And this is the joy of Christ's works and this He means where
        He said in the same showing that
            we are His joy,
            we are His recompense,
            we are His honor,
            we are His crown.

    Concerning Christ as our Head,
        He is glorified and beyond suffering, but concerning His
            Body (in which His members are knit),
        He is not yet fully glorified nor all beyond suffering;
            because the same desire and thirst which He had upon
                the cross
            (which desire, longing, and thirst, as I see it, was in Him
                from without beginning),
            the same desire and thirst has He still,
            and shall have until the time that the last soul that shall be
                saved has come up to His bliss.
For as truly as there is a quality in God of compassion and pity, just as truly
there is a quality in God of thirst and yearning.

And because of the strength of this yearning in Christ, we must yearn also
for Him (without which yearning, no soul comes to heaven).

This quality of yearning and thirst comes from the endless goodness
of God (just as the quality of pity also comes from His goodness)
and even though He has both yearning and pity, they are two
different qualities, as I see it.
In this goodness is based the essence of the spiritual thirst, which lasts
in Him as long as we are in need, drawing us up to His bliss.

(All this was seen in the showing forth of His compassion, for
that shall cease on Doomsday.)

Thus He has pity and compassion on us,
and He has a yearning to possess us,
but His wisdom and His love do not permit the end to come
until the best possible time.

ॐ   ॐ   ॐ

God's message and Julian's reading of that text expand out of the
unity of the "all shall be well." God the father is "able to make everything
well": thus explaining God as omnipotent Source. The centrality of the
Incarnation is fleshed out in the "I know how," as the Word is the root
of all knowledge—the literal "understanding" Julian craves. God's op-
timism, Christianity's hope, is not at the foot of the cross or at the empty
tomb alone, but in the "I wish to make everything well." We find it in
those spaces and places that cannot be made well—by us, or on this
earth. God's desire for us to see that all shall be made well is the invitation into the wounded side. He longs for us so that we may long for him.
We are given hope so that we might return to him. We are provided the
desire for knowledge so that we might desire him. This is not a static
process. Rather, it is an ongoing thirst, the active call of God to each of
us in the world, and our individual soul's response—collectively as the
incarnate communion of saints—to this call. The full trajectory of the
"all shall be well" is toward ultimate and final union with God. The
economy of our return to God is one of making all things well; the agency
of this thirst is in the form of knowledge. That active longing of God for
humanity is expressed in the same physiological terms Julian employed
in her description of Jesus' suffering: thirst to fill the pierced, bleeding,
watering side.

God's "bliss" is an Alpha-Omega, an eternal Word. In the divine mind all already is well. There we are all already saved. It is done and over in the infinity of the Word. That is what we are all longing to see, the glimpse of Reason that keeps us searching. But this is not the case in God's body, the body of Christ on earth—the Church, All Created Thing. Jesus' thirst on the cross is his desire for fuller one-ing, the more complete union of us-in-him, in addition to the him-in-us of the Incarnation. Every act has been a wish to make all things well. All material creation has always been on the pathway of being made well. God is able to identify with our sufferings because of the wisdom of the head, but he can also identify with our emptiness through the desire of his own body. Our yearning for him is spiritual thirst—our desire for knowledge, our passion for union with the divine mind. In ourselves we have both the Godself desiring a return to the whole—a sort of Neoplatonism—and the divine spark urging us on to choose of our free will to say yes to the call, to answer the "follow me." Pity—identification, literal sympathy, fellow-feeling—comes from God, but so does yearning—the desire for what one lacks. God lacks us, and God desires us. We desire God, but we don't always realize that. Can we sate our thirst as he seeks to sate his through us? Lack, emptiness, is a blessing—not a curse. God's desire for fulfillment draws us to himself. Might we see our own lack, our longing and yearning and thirsting, as of God—and for God, and from God? All cannot be made well until we are all made well, until we fill him and we are all filled. We cannot be made well until we answer God's call. We are active agents of redemption; God's grace in the world leads us to fill his thirst. Can we fill our own in realizing our desire for him?

ⅽ৪ **32** ৪ɔ

One time our good Lord said: *"All manner of thing shall be well"; and another time He said: "Thou shalt see for thyself that all manner of thing shall be well"; and from these two words the soul received various applications.*

One was this: *that He wishes us to be aware that not only does*
       He take heed to noble and to great things, but also to little
       and small things, to lowly and simple things,
both to one and to the other;
and so means He in that He says
    "All manner of thing shall be well";
for He wills that we be aware that the least little thing shall not
    be forgotten.

Another understanding is this: that, from our point of view,
    there are many deeds evilly done and such great harm given
    that it seems to us that it would be impossible
    that ever it should come to a good end;
    and we look upon this,
    sorrowing and mourning because of it,
    so that we cannot take our ease in the joyful beholding of God
    as we would like to do;
       and the cause is this: that the use of our reason is now so
          blind, so lowly, and so stupid that we cannot know the
          exalted, wondrous Wisdom, the Power, and the Goodness
          of the blessed Trinity;
    and this is what He means when He says,
       "Thou shalt see for thyself that all manner of thing shall be well,"
as if He said,
       "Pay attention to this now, faithfully and trustingly, and at
       the last end thou shalt see it in fullness of joy."

And thus, in these same previous five words:
       "I am able to make everything well, etc.,"

I interpret a mighty comfort about all the works of our Lord God
that are still to come.

There is a Deed which the blessed Trinity shall do on the Last Day, as I see it,
and what the Deed shall be, and how it shall be done, is unknown to all creatures
that are beneath Christ, and shall remain so until when it is done.

The Goodness and the Love of our Lord God wills that we be aware that it
shall be done, but His Power and Wisdom by the same Love wishes to keep
and hide from us what it shall be and how it shall be done.
(And the reason why He wills that we know it in this way is
because He wishes us to be more at ease in our soul and more
peaceful in love, refraining from paying attention to all temptations
that could obstruct us from truth, and rejoicing in Him.)

This is the Great Deed
intended by our Lord God from without beginning,
treasured and hidden in His blessed breast,
known only to Himself,
by which Deed He shall make all things well.

For as the blessed Trinity created all things from nothing, just so the
same blessed Trinity shall make well all that is not well.
At this sight I marveled greatly, and looked at our Faith, marveling
thus: our Faith is based in God's word, and it is part of our Faith
that we believe that God's word shall be preserved in all things,

and one point of our Faith is that many creatures shall be damned
(as were the angels who fell out of heaven because of pride—
who are now demons),
and many on earth who die outside of the Faith of Holy Church
(that is to say, those who are heathen men and also men who
have received Christianity but live Unchristian lives and so die
without love)
all these shall be damned to hell without end, as Holy Church
teaches me to believe.

Given all this, it seemed to me that it was impossible that all manner
of thing would be well as our Lord showed at this time;
and in regard to this, I had no other answer in any showing of our
Lord God except this:
"What is impossible for thee is not impossible for me.

I shall preserve my word in all things,
and I shall make everything well."

Thus I was taught by the grace of God that I should steadfastly keep
myself in the Faith as I had interpreted it before, and also that I
should firmly believe that everything shall be well as our Lord
showed at the same time; because this is the Great Deed that
our Lord shall do, in which Deed He shall preserve His word
in everything and He shall make well all that is not well.
But what the Deed shall be, and how it shall be done, there is no creature
beneath Christ that either knows it or shall know it
until it is done
(according to the understanding that I received of our Lord's
meaning at this time).

ɞ   ɞ   ɞ

Chapter 32 is the invitation from God: will you believe, even if you cannot understand, how I will make all things well? "All manner of thing shall be well" is in God's world; it is an abstract notion that does not engage us or ask anything from us. "Thou shalt see for thyself that all manner of thing shall be well" places all of the makings and workings of the universe on God's stage for the human to observe and perceive. We are issued a ticket to the divine play from a God who wants us to know his deeds. Nothing is separate from God's love; no aspect of the creation stands apart from the Incarnation. The divine permeates every part. We inhabit a loving universe in which divine reason cannot be separated from divine love, one-ed in the Trinity. We cannot understand how good can come in spite of evil; it is illogical. Focusing on what has broken from Christ's body breaks us away from our original oneness in him. We have come to rely on our human reason. God calls to the soul to cling to the "all shall be well." All distractions—fear and questioning—contribute to separation from him. At the end of time the eschatological resolution of the "all shall be well" will become present tense. Christ in the Trinity leads to this validation of knowledge. Whatever Adam's fall, in Christ we are given the fruit of the tree. God is aware of how our human mind can fragment and block us. Julian distinguishes the love from the power and wisdom of the Godhead, those parts charged with the "how" and the "what" of the "all shall be well." If in Christ we are one-ed, the Father Creator and dynamic Spirit both continue to work throughout the universe. All parts of the Trinity are necessary for the resolution.

If Christianity is belief that at the end of time all shall be made well, in Julian's visionary experience God has given her his word that this is true. As she represents every human, God has given his Word in Christ. Faith is based on the Word. Christ in the Incarnation is contained, preserved, and sustained in all things. The "all shall be well" must deal with this question of maintenance. The challenge Julian struggles with is what happens with whatever stands outside the faith: those who are not Christian and those who are Christian but are unfaithful. Julian's showings teach the oneness of the Triune God and the one-ing of all created thing with him. There is no room for separation in this cosmology; there is no outside versus inside to the body of Christ. How can there be exclusion versus inclusion? Julian's crisis here, akin to her desire to understand sin—separation from God—is at that crossroads. How can God be in everything—wherein there is both saved and unsaved—yet all shall be made well? Logic breaks down. Julian is left with contradictions, and in that brokenness she must wait. The Body of Christ remains broken here on earth. There is no separation or exclusion in the love of God. No matter how much the human mind fails to understand, the divine mind never stops loving, seeing, believing. Nothing stands outside of this God, even if we cannot understand the reconciliation of contradictions. The only causes of fracture and rupture are our own doubts.

∽ **33** ∾

*And still in this showing I desired, as far as I dared, that I might have had full
view of hell and purgatory.*

> *(But it was not my intention to undertake to challenge anything that is
> part of the Faith—for I believe truthfully that hell and purgatory are for the
> same purpose that Holy Church teaches—but my intention was that for the
> sake of learning I might have seen everything that is part of my Faith,
> whereby I could live more to God's honor and to my benefit.)*

But in spite of my desire I learned nothing whatsoever about this

> *(except as it was said before in the fifth showing where I saw that the Devil
> was reproached by God and endlessly damned, in which showing I inter-
> preted that all creatures that are of the Devil's character in this life and who
> end that way, there is no more mention made of them before God and all
> His holy ones than of the Devil, notwithstanding that they are of mankind,
> whether they have been baptized or not).*

*Although the revelation of goodness was made in which little mention of evil
was made,*

> *yet in it I was not drawn away from any point of Faith that Holy Church
> teaches me to believe.*

>> *I saw the Passion of Christ in various showings (in the second,
>> in the fifth and in the eighth showings, as I said before)
>> (where I had a partial experience of the sorrow of Our Lady
>> and of His true friends who saw Him in pain, but I did not see
>> as specially described in detail the Jews that did Him to
>> death. Nevertheless, I knew in my Faith that they were
>> accursed and damned without end—except for those that
>> were converted by grace).*

*I was strengthened and taught without exception
to keep myself in every detail in the Faith,
and in all that I had understood before,
hoping that I was in that Faith with the mercy
and the grace of God,*

*desiring and praying in my intentions that I might continue therein
    until my life's end.*

*It is God's will that we have great regard for all His deeds that He has done,
        for He wills thereby that we know, trust, and believe all that He
            shall do,
        and evermore it is necessary for us to leave off involving
            ourselves with what the Deed shall be,
        and desire to be like our brethren who are the saints in heaven
            who wish absolutely nothing but God's will,
    then shall we rejoice only in God and be well satisfied both with
        His hiding and with His showing,*

*for I saw truly in our Lord's meaning that the more we busy ourselves
    to know His secrets in this or any other thing,
    the farther shall we be from the knowledge of them.*

፠   ፠   ፠

Julian's thirst for knowledge cannot be quenched: she hopes to see
hell and purgatory. She grapples with what she has been taught and
what she is shown, to reconcile her experience with what she has been
given. Julian discerns. She states that she learned nothing about hell or
purgatory. She does not say that they do not exist. Appropriate to Julian's
status as author and the way in which she has focused on the Word of
God spoken incarnate to humanity, hell is lack of speech. The Devil and
those of his character remain unspoken before God. Failure to exist in
the incarnational world is, simply, to be unuttered. But will this, too, be
made well?

In Chapter 33 Julian cannot keep from speaking about her fidelity to
the church and orthodoxy. The faith "lacks" evil: evil is of nothing, as
Julian speaks earlier about sin, which exists outside and is of nothing to
God. The Word of God knows evil well, as demonstrated by Julian's
vivid visual experience of the Passion of Christ. Within her text we have
manifold depictions of evil. At the most painful point of this chapter,
indeed among the ugliest in all of the text, the author recites her Church's
teaching on the damnation of Jews responsible for Jesus' death. One does
not need to be a theologian or historian to know the bitter history of
Christian anti-Semitism and anti-Judaism, the rhetorical collapse of
biblical crucifiers with contemporary Jews. The faith was responsible for
crusades and inquisitions; the Church contributed to the thinking that

led to pogroms and the Holocaust. But here Julian's statements are more complicated than they first appear. She does not literally see a clear condemnation of "the Jews." She can only rely on what she was taught by the Church. Whether Julian dissents from this or not, the breadth of salvation, the breadth of the mystery of the "all shall be well" in Chapter 32—known only at the end of time—challenges our speaker. What would it mean to suggest that those who crucified Christ would be made well with God? We cannot argue that this was Julian's intention. She was a medieval Christian. Yet Christianity itself is no guarantee of the absence of evil, since the unspoken, those of the Devil's character, could include the baptized.

Julian was tempest-tossed; she was intellectually "overcome" by the contradictions the showings presented her with. As much as she advanced her revelations, Julian also clung to what she had been taught, fighting to make sense of what she knew through experience versus what she had been told. She backs off from the interrogation she had been pursuing. The "all shall be well" is God's business; trying to tease out its meaning on earth might be potentially so iconoclastic that she cannot even go there. Julian is afraid. Perhaps it is fear that the truth of God might be irreconcilable with the belief system she has been taught. What truths are we unwilling to look at? What contradictions do we see that the people of our day are unable to reconcile? In what ways can we—or can't we—live in those contradictions? What do we need to do in order to be willing vessels—voices of God, like Julian—to speak those utterances, incarnate those words of God, into our world?

❧ **34** ❧

Our Lord God showed two kinds of secrecies:
one is the Great Secret with all the secret details that are part of it,
and these things He wills that we understand are hidden
until the time that He will clearly show them to us;
the other are the secrets which He Himself showed openly in this revelation,
for they are secrets that He wishes to make open and known to us;
for He wants us to be aware that it is His will that we know them.
They are secrets to us not only because He wills they be secrets to us,
but they are secrets to us because of our blindness and our
ignorance.
Concerning those weaknesses He has great pity, and therefore
He wishes to make the secrets more open to us Himself,
by which we can know Him and love Him and cleave to Him.

For all that is advantageous for us to be aware of and to know, full graciously
our good Lord will show us through all the preaching and teaching
of Holy Church.

God showed the very great pleasure that He has in all men and women who
strongly and humbly and willingly receive
the preaching and teaching of Holy Church,
for He is Holy Church—
He is the foundation,
He is the essence,
He is the teaching,
He is the teacher,
He is the goal,
He is the reward for which every natural soul toils.

And this is known and shall be known to every soul to which the Holy Spirit
declares it.

*And I hope truly that He will assist all those who seek in this way, for they
    seek God.*

*All this that I have said now, and more that I shall say later, is reassuring
    against sin;*
        for in the third showing when I saw that God does all that is done,
            I saw no sin,
                and then I saw that all is well.
        But when God showed me as regards sin,
                then He said: "All shall be well."

                    ஜ   ஜ   ஜ

   The mind of God can understand the workings of the making-well.
Julian has spent a great deal of effort wringing her hands at the contradictions, while longing for the time when all will be revealed. As the
Showings continues to unfold, the gradual emergence of divine mind as
divine reason becomes clearer. Can it be enough to say that God has all
the answers—even if God wills that one day we will have them too?
Writing, "translating," requires her to discern the meanings, tease out
the "secrets." Julian's descriptions of sin and the radical well-making—a
radical welcome—God provides articulate a Christianity that puts no
limits on the inclusion of God's love. Sin—separation—is something
only we are capable of creating. The secrets reveal our oneness, our unity,
and our one-ing. Our human hard-heartedness and stubbornness imagine that we—or any aspect of God's creation—could ever be separate
from, sinful to, him. Getting the answers, having our human desire for
knowledge—our hunger for divine reason—satisfied in some way is
receiving God in our midst. This is what the Incarnation permitted, and
this is the stuff of Julian's visionary experience. Being open to revelation
is not only knowing God rationally but also loving and, especially, cleaving to him. This is how separation is healed.
   Julian simultaneously endorses the divine teaching authority of the
Church and repudiates that very power, acknowledging the authority
of God alone rather than that of human institutions. She is a mystic, so
by her very experience, no matter how loyal she may be to the earthly
church of which she is a part, her relationship to God is literally through
the Body of Christ. Her focus moves away from the figurative human
construction to the God whom we encounter directly and who longs for
unmediated perfect union with us. God makes the call; we are chosen

to receive his message in whatever way he sends it. In the "secrecy," or discernment, of glimpsing God's will, as Julian knew in her showings, sin did not exist and all was well. She has the assurance from this experience forevermore. We are called to look beyond the present moment of separation, beyond the brokenness of ourselves—in body, mind, and spirit. We are called to look beyond the brokenness of the Body of Christ on earth, the Church. We are called to know that in divine reason, the mind of God, all is already well. And all shall be made well in the fullness of time, and it is God's will that we might see that. May we be vessels and vehicles for the healing of the world's separation as we discern the oneness of God's message for us, his Body the Church.

✺ **35** ✺

When God Almighty had shown so plentifully and so fully of His goodness,
    I desired to know of a certain creature that I loved if it would
    continue in good living (which I hoped by the grace of
    God was begun).
  And in this particular desire, it seemed that I hindered myself,
  because I was not shown at this time.

  And then I was answered in my reason, as it were by a friendly go-between:
    "Take this generally, and see the graciousness of the Lord God
    as He reveals it to thee; for it is more honor to God for thee to see Him
    in all things than in any special thing."

I agreed, and with that I learned that it is more honor to God to
    understand all things in general than to delight in anything in particular.

And if I would do wisely following this teaching,
    not only would I be glad for nothing in particular,
    but also not greatly disturbed by any manner of thing,
        for "All shall be well."

The fullness of joy is to behold God in all.

    For by the same blessed Power, Wisdom, and Love by which He
      created all things,
    to the same end our good Lord leads those things constantly,
    and thereto shall He Himself bring them,
    and when it is time, we shall see it.

        (The basis of this was shown in the first showing and more
        openly in the third where it says, "I saw God in a point.")

All that our Lord does is rightful,
what he tolerates is honorable,
    and in these two is included both good and evil.

All that is good our Lord does,
and what is evil our Lord tolerates.
　(I say not that any evil is honorable,
　but I say the toleration of our Lord God is honorable,
　　whereby His goodness shall be known without end in His
　　marvelous humility and gentleness,
　　　by the action of mercy and grace.)

Rightfulness is that thing which is so good
　　that it cannot be better than it is,
　for God Himself is true rightfulness,
　and all His works are done rightfully as they are appointed from
　　without beginning
　　　by His high Power,
　　　His high Wisdom,
　　　His high Goodness.

And just as He ordained all for the best,
just so He works constantly and leads it to that same end; and He is ever
　most pleased with Himself and with His works.

The beholding of this blissful agreement is most sweet to the soul that sees
　by grace.
　All the souls that shall be saved in heaven without end are created
　　rightful in the sight of God, and by His own goodness,
　and in this rightfulness we are endlessly and marvelously
　　preserved, more than all other created things.

Mercy is an action that comes from the goodness of God,
　and it shall remain in action as long as sin is permitted to pursue
　　rightful souls,
　and when sin has no longer permission to pursue,
　　then shall the action of mercy cease.

　　And then shall all be brought to rightfulness and remain therein
　　without end.

By His toleration, we fall,
and in His blessed Love with His Power and His Wisdom we are preserved,
and by mercy and grace we are raised to many more joys.

*And thus in rightfulness and in mercy He wishes to be known and
loved now without end. And the soul that wisely holds onto this in
grace is well pleased with both, and endlessly rejoices.*

ജ   ജ   ജ

Chapter 35 deals with what appear to be disparate subjects—our
particular rather than general love, and the problem of evil in a world
where there is a loving God. When we put these two pieces of the chapter
together they both concern the issue of attachment versus detachment;
they share an approach to this question of our separation from a God of
love. However much Julian has embraced a life in the love of God, experiencing the visions of oneness with him that she invited, she is, like
each of us, a person who exists in relationship with others. Julian can no
more sever her attachments to love in this world than we can. Professed
life in her day (more so than in ours) called those given to God to literally
consider themselves dead to the world. Yet how is this possible when
we exist as humans who love, feel pain, hurt, cherish old wounds, and
have unhealed as well as joyous places in our memories?

In Julian's theology there is a certain kind of answer that seems counterintuitive. We want to respond that the Incarnation that infuses all creation means that we love everything, and thus the particular held dear to
us is particularly held dear to God. But incarnation does not work that
way, nor does Julian's theology that sees the ever-rushing flow of divine
love coursing through the veins of material creation, dynamic in its stream.
We find God in the faces of our beloveds, in the places and spaces we hold
dear, in all our familiars. Julian's teaching—one that she first has to learn—
is that God calls us to know his love in all created things, not to privilege
any in particular. Our human nature will always fall short of this goal. It
is always going to be a stretch to see the love where we least want to do
so, and to keep in perspective our great appreciation for those fountains
where we have received God's love best. In his twelfth-century treatise
on God and friendship, Aelred of Rievaulx puts forth a virtually "promis-
cuous" vision of spiritual love wherein more is always more. The greater
opportunities we have for love—rather than focusing that human love on
one particular person, place, or thing—the more fully we experience God's
love. The love banquet means we need the whole menu, not just our fa-
vorite dessert, in order to know the divine.

There is healthy psychological reasoning here, lest attachment to an
aspect of material creation that individually must decay and disappear

disrupt our intimacy with God. If I find God only through my human beloved and my beloved dies, so does my rest in divine love. Julian states that we honor God more through general than particular understanding—knowledge, love. It is the outcome, the fate of that to which she is attached, that she wondered about. If we worry about outcomes and are concerned about those things and people we are attached to, we will dwell on the question of evil. It does not help to fret about the real presence of evil in a world where all shall be made well. The immediate actions we see in front of us are nothing compared to the grace of the redemption—and the nature of toleration whereby the actions of mercy and grace must work in a world where evil is found. We look for the mundane rightfulness, but we are not going to see that. If we imagine that "all shall be well" means that each of our particular hopes, desires, and loves will work out as we wish, we will never know God. When things do not go as planned, when all is not well, it looks as if God is absent. We take no comfort if our belief is solely dependent on specific worldly outcomes. It does us no good to set our hopes on the particular, because we will always be disappointed in some way. Since we are the means through which God's mercy and grace must work in the world, if we are paralyzed by depression or discouragement, evil blocks the Spirit. The "soul that sees by grace" and not by sight knows the bliss of God while in this world of more brokenness than wholeness. We are called to remember that all things are working toward the good, that all shall be well—and we shall see it happen. If we are weighed down instead by the idols we love—even those we are bound by duty to nurture—our spiritual growth is thwarted. We are called to more fully realize God's purpose in us because God has greater needs for us beyond those teachers of divine love that are our relationships here on earth. We learn from them, we live them, we love them, and ultimately we must let those attachments go lest their very brokenness distract us from the wholeness we hope for in our God who calls us according to his purpose.

Chapter 35 is that call to let go. The action toward God is always moving us forward despite the distractions of the failures of our lives. When we see ourselves collectively as a community wherein divine love is grounded and founded—not here or there in particular, but wholly and fully one-ed with the One—we glimpse the end point. We see what He is and where we are heading, even as we cherish the means of getting there—the dynamic action of grace working in the world, known and revealed to us in our experiences and relationships.

⚛ **36** ⚓

Our Lord God showed me that a deed shall be done
  and He Himself shall do it;
    and it shall be honorable and marvelous and fruitful,
⎧ *and through me it shall be done,*
⎩ *and He Himself shall do it.*

And this is the highest joy that the soul recognized:
    that God Himself shall do it,
    and I shall do nothing at all except sin,
    and my sin shall not hinder His goodness from working.

And I say that the beholding of this is a heavenly joy in a reverent
soul which evermore naturally by grace desires God's will.

This deed shall be begun here,
and it shall be honorable to God
and plentifully beneficial to His lovers on earth,
    and ever as we come to heaven we shall see it in marvelous joy,
and it shall last thus in operation until the Last Day,
and the honor and the bliss of it shall continue in heaven before God
    and all His holy ones without end.

In this way was this deed seen and interpreted in our Lord's intention,
    and the reason why He showed it
    is to cause us to rejoice in Him and all His works.

When I saw His showing continued, I understood that it was shown as a
great event which was to come (which God showed that He Himself would
do). This deed has these qualities which I mentioned before. This He showed
most blissfully, intending that I should accept it wisely, faithfully, and
trustingly.

But what this deed would be, that was kept secret from me.
　And in this I saw that He wills not that we fear to know the things
　that He shows—
　　　He shows them because He wishes us to know them and by this
　　　knowledge He wills that we love Him
　　　　and delight in Him
　　　　and endlessly rejoice in Him.

Because of the great love that He has for us,
　He shows us all that is honorable and beneficial for the present.
The things that He wills to have secret now, still of His great goodness,
　He shows them concealed,
　　　in which showing He wills that we believe and recognize that
　　　we shall see them truly in His endless bliss.

Then we ought to rejoice in Him both for all that He shows,
　and for all that He hides;
　　and if we willingly and humbly do this,
　　　we shall find therein great ease,
　　　and we shall have endless favor from Him for that.

Thus is the interpretation of this word: that it shall be done through me
　　　(that is, the general man, this is to say, all
　　　　that shall be saved).

It shall be honorable and marvelous and fruitful and God Himself shall do it.
　And this shall be the highest joy that can be, to behold the deed
　　　that God Himself shall do,
　and man shall do absolutely nothing except sin.

Then means our Lord God thus: as if He said:
　"Behold and see.
　Here thou hast cause for humility;
　here thou hast cause for love;
　here thou hast cause to know thyself;
　here thou hast cause to rejoice in me; and because of my love, do
　　　rejoice in me, for of all things, with that thou canst most
　　　please me."

And as long as we are in this life, whenever we by our folly turn to
paying attention to the Reprobate, tenderly our Lord God touches us
and blessedly calls us, saying in our soul:

*"Let me be all thy love, my dearworthy child. Occupy thyself with me, for
I am enough for thee, and rejoice in thy Savior and in thy salvation."*

And I am certain that this is our Lord's action in us.
    The soul that is pierced with it by grace shall see it
        and experience it.

*And though it is so that this deed be truly understood for the general
man, yet it does not exclude the particular;*
    for what our good Lord wishes to do through His poor creatures,
        is now unknown to me.

*This deed and the other I mentioned before, they are not both one,
but two different ones.*
    However this deed shall be done sooner,
    and that other one shall be when we come to heaven.
And to whom our Lord gives it, this deed can be known in part,
    but the Great Deed mentioned before shall neither be
        known in heaven nor earth until it is done.

*Besides this, He gave special understanding and teaching about the
working of miracles, thus:*
    "It is known that I have done miracles here before, many and very
        exalted and astounding, honorable and great;
    and just as I have done in the past, so I do now constantly,
    and shall do in the course of time."

It is known that before miracles come sorrow and anguish and
        tribulation; and that is so that we would know our own
        feebleness and our misfortune that we have fallen into by sin
    in order to humble us,
    and cause us to fear God,
    crying for help and grace.

And great miracles come after that,
    and they come from the exalted Power, Wisdom, and Goodness of God,
        showing His strength and the joys of heaven (in so far as that
            can be in this passing life),
        and that in order to strengthen our faith and to increase our
            hope, in love.

For that reason it pleases Him to be known and honored in miracles.
Then He means thus: He wills that we be not carried overly low
because of sorrows and temptations that befall us, for it has ever
been this way before the coming of miracles.

ᙡ ᙡ ᙡ

Julian speaks as herself and as every person, the human. Through humanity, through materiality, through all created things, God is ever working. We are the means by which grace speaks the Word in the world. In and of ourselves we are agents of separation. This is not so much an Augustinian distortion, that we are perversely pulling away from God. Rather, it is a splitting of the oneness. God operates in us and through us; nothing that we do can prevent that from occurring. Collectively, God is working through all material creation, and if there are rifts, splits, breaks somewhere—separations or "sins" due to the presence of evil in the world—they do not prevent the God-force of grace from operating. However much I sin, fall short of the mark, and contribute to separation rather than one-ing union, the power of grace will still continue to work through me personally; God will never cease using me as a vector of divine action in the world. The God-verb activity of divine love working in the world thwarts the conclusion that any single divine act ever could or would happen in isolation. The deed is incarnation, inseparable from creation. It is the birthing of grace into the world, wherein the power of God is never separable from materiality. To repeat: regardless of how fallible, broken, and separate matter may be, this cannot stop the continuous flow of divine action in the world, in us and through us. God wants us to know and see that.

Knowledge of this creative force is not antithetical to God's will. Concealment is both an invitation to trust in God—an assurance that he one day wants us fully one-ed in his divine reason—and an invitation to our inquiring minds to discern the ways and deeds of God. Secrecy and concealment are not denial. Instead, they pose a question that invites desire, nurturing our relationship with God as thirst seeking satisfaction. The Word as *Logos* taking flesh, redeeming all created things, is embodiment, the sanctification of life in materiality whereby nothing is excluded. God continues to answer Julian's question, how all could be made well. God is ever working through all created things, regardless of separation and for the purpose of healing, in the operation of incarnation and the work of grace in the world. The full realization of the union of matter and Godself is always "to be." It happened in the creation; it happened in the Incarnation; it happens in each act of new creation. It will no longer need to happen anew when there will be no separation, when sin is no more and when one-ing union has been fully realized. Created things create rifts, but the power of God is greater. God keeps drawing us back like a loving parent to a child. He fills us and makes us whole; we need no more than him to fill those gaps of separation. Thus we are called, invited to witness his love in the world: to be actively, consciously aware of the flow of grace through us and to partner with him in that process. This is what vocation means. This exists not only at the cosmic level but also in each atom. Here, there, and everywhere is a new incarnation; here, there, and everywhere is an opportunity for redemption, for healing the separation that is sin. The grace-filled action of God in the world never stops. Julian distinguishes between what can be known here on earth and what we will never know until we cross over. There are moments for each of us when we may be given an awareness of the dynamic Real Presence of the divine in our midst, a sacramental taste of Incarnation. Yet we will never know how all can be made well. If we did, we would be at journey's end. Narrative poses that question, like a mystery novel. We are invited to walk the road; we cannot bypass its struggles and turn to the end of the book. Once we have arrived, we will know all the answers. It is the author God's will that we might know his Word— here in part, and in full at the end of the story.

From time to time we will be presented with occurrences that defy our reason. We are challenged to see those as evidence of God's work in the world, but also as reminders of the power of God. God is not limited as we are in action, any more than divine reason is limited as is our reason. Here is another invitation to trust and an assurance that we will not be disappointed. We are called to see these opportunities for radical God-action as testaments to what God can do that we cannot with our own minds and bodies. Miracles are not meant to crush our pride but, rather, to inspire us to trust that we are not expected to do it all by our limited resources. God can make whole what we cannot heal; God can mend separations we cannot. God wants to—to complete material creation as well as to call forth our desire for him. When we are thus called, we long for the God who can do what we cannot and we intellectually thirst for the understanding of his divine reason. At the microcosmic level, even if the "all shall be well" speaks to the end of time, we are left with a God who loves us enough that we are enough for him and he is enough for us.

☙ **37** ❧

God reminded me that I would sin;
>and because of the delight that I had in gazing upon Him, I did not
>pay heed quickly to that showing.

>And our Lord most mercifully waited and gave me grace to listen.
>(And this showing I received particularly to myself, but by all
>the gracious comfort that follows, as you shall see, I was taught
>to accept it on behalf of all my fellow Christians—all in general,
>and nothing in particular.)

Though our Lord showed me that I would sin, by "me alone" is meant "all."

And in this I perceived a gentle anxiety, and to this our Lord answered:
>"I keep thee full safely."

This word was said with more love and steadiness and spiritual
>protection than I know how or am able to tell.

As it was shown that I would sin,
in just the same way was the comfort shown—safety and protection
>for all fellow Christians.

What can make me love my fellow Christians more than to see in
God that He loves all that shall be saved as if they were all one soul?
>>For in every soul that shall be saved is a divine will that never
>>consented to sin nor ever shall;
>just as there is a savage will in the lower part of man which can
>will no good,
>so, too, there is a divine will in the higher part of man which will
>is so good that it can never will evil, but always good,

and because of that we are what He loves,
and endlessly we do what delights Him.

131

And thus our Lord showed the completeness of love in which we stand
in His sight—

{ yea, that He loves us now as well while we are here as He shall
when we are there before His blessed face.

So because of the falling away from love on our part,
from that is all our difficulty.

ЄͰ   ЄͰ   ЄͰ

Unity is found through the mystery of the Trinity. In our human manifestation on earth, that Godself is as part of us as it is of God the Father. Yet still there is separation: distinctness, but also rupture. Chapter 37's opening—"God reminded me that I would sin"—fractures the unity of Julian's spiritual rest in God. It is a theological pronouncement of the separation found in a broken world. It is not so much microcosm representing macrocosm. Rather, within God's world there is a will to bring all things together. The powers in the universe that lead and return to this unity could not operate if there were no gap to be filled—if the wounded side were not opened. Julian wants to rest in God, not to face the reality of this splitting energy in the material world, which she cannot help but participate in. God's awakening is not a punishment; it is a gift. Every awareness of the rending of the garment of incarnation is a simultaneous awareness of the work of good, the work of God, in the world—always one-ing us back together in him. Sin is a reminder of grace, a reminder of God's will that the rift be healed. No one, no single person is meant to take responsibility for that division; no single act of "sin" is in and of itself the separation from God for that person. We collectively repent—work together for the healing of our divisions (from one another and from God)—rather than blame others or ourselves for any specific breaks.

"Sin" is neither individual nor particular, but we are one in the unity of the God inside us each. We cannot be separated. The collective sin that grace and our will work to repair does not remove us from that body of God in which we reside. We are all on the inside of creation, and we are all part of the healing as much as we are all part of the brokenness. Our real self is the God in us, not that unalienable share we all have in that wound. Julian posits a new metaphor apart from the inside/outside separation of the wounded body. No matter the wound draining life-blood, no matter the opening affected by and affecting separation, we stand always in the completeness of love. Her visual metaphor is important, given Julian's "visionary" experience. God's "vision"—what he desires, longs for, indeed even prays for—is us: the completeness of love, the completeness of him. His love never waxes or wanes. God is staring as deeply into our hearts now as he ever will when all shall be made well. The making-well at the end of time does not depend on our resolution of a false separation in this world. We are one-ed with him now in love as we shall be forevermore. Surely it is only our own sense of separation that causes us pain and grief. God's love for us is the same yesterday, today, and always. Sin, that open wound, is only a gulf between God and ourselves if we imagine it to be so. The love of God remains constant for us—on the other side and in the now.

❦ **38** ❧

Also God showed that sin shall not be shame, but honor to man—for just as
      for every sin there is a corresponding pain in reality, just so,
      for every sin, to the same soul is given a blessing by love.

Just as various sins are punished with various pains according to
      how grievous they are,
just so shall they be rewarded with different joys in heaven for
      their victories after the sins have been painful and sorrowful
      to the soul on earth.

For the soul that shall come to heaven is so precious to God and the place so
   honor-filled
    that the goodness of God never permits the soul that shall finally
      come there to sin
    unless those sinners of that sort are to be rewarded
      and made known in Holy Church on earth
      and also in heaven without end,
      and blessedly made good by exceeding honors.

In this vision my understanding was lifted up into heaven;
   and then God brought cheerfully to my mind
     David and others in the Old Law with him without number,
   and in the New Law He brought to my mind first
     Mary Magdalen,
     Peter and Paul,
     and Thomas and Jude
     and Saint John of Beverly
     and others also without number
       and how they are recognized in the Church on earth along
        with their sins,
       and it is to them no shame, but all of the sins have been
        changed to honor.

Because of that our gracious Lord shows about sins
   here in part
   like what it is there in fullness,
      for there the sign of sin is turned to honor.

In comfort to us because of his familiarity
   our Lord showed Saint John of Beverly,
      very exalted,
and brought to my mind how he is a neighbor at hand
      and of our acquaintance.

And God called him "Saint John of Beverly" as clearly as we do, and
      did so with a very glad, sweet expression showing that he is a
      most exalted saint in heaven in His sight, and a blessed one.

With this He made mention that in Saint John's youth and in his tender time
   of life,
he was a dearworthy servant of God, much loving and fearing God,
   and nevertheless God allowed him to fall,
      mercifully protecting him so that he did not perish
      nor lose any time.

And afterward, God raised him to many times more grace,
   and by the contrition and humility that He showed in his living,
      God has given him in heaven manifold joys exceeding what he
      would have had if he had not fallen.

And God shows that this is true on earth by the working of plenteous miracles
around Saint John's body constantly.

And all this was to make us glad and cheerful in love.

⁊ ⁊ ⁊

Julian uses dualities rather than "dualism" to put forth a profoundly positive view of hope for humanity, for imperfect creation. She operates within a universe wherein sin is never final. While Christianity teaches that Christ is the redeemer, Julian teaches that the particularity of redemption occurs not just personally for the individual, but specific to any single act of sin that is simultaneously the one and only separation from divine love. The separation from divine reason (the real "sin") has

tangible material manifestations—"pains." Every instance of separation
is a "blessing" in its opportunity for healing, the mending of the wound.
Every particular healing is part of the great, singular healing. The "honor"
is the invitation to return: the voice of divine love that cries, "Come
home." This process does not so much engage a cerebral act of will as it
describes and defines the dynamism of grace working through All Created Thing that leads everyone to the "all shall be well." Julian's articulation of the process takes into account the twists and turns of our spiritual
growth. Her theology does not promise salvation in the abstract, but the
healing of separation. Righting of sin in Julian is the one-ing that seals
up all our wounds. This cosmic process of grace working in the world
affects each one of us in our specific circumstances. Julian's notion of sin
and redemption is thus both general and particular. She strongly emphasizes the teaching value of our sins. We don't win the prize for slaying
the dragon and finding the grail in and for ourselves. Rather, the cosmic
closure of the gap that is sin is likewise both general and particular. Just
as it exists in both philosophical abstraction and the particularity of sin
in the world, this healing has implications for ourselves and for the entire
community.

Sin is given meaning through the stories of our lives: the ways in
which our personal narratives have the power to lead others to wholeness that is both individual and cosmic. The blessing to which Julian
alludes, the repair of the world, happens as each of us participates in the
one-ing, answering the call that heals our wounds of separation. Sin has
value in its teaching capacity: in Julian not with fire and brimstone, hell
and damnation. Instead, Julian's notion of sin offers countless moments
for personal transformation through the experience of others' testimo-
nies. She recites a litany of the righteous whose struggles to turn and
return to the One continue to teach us. Julian understands the visions
she is receiving as neither personal, individual, nor prophetically intended for the present and future. Rather, what God has shown her
provides a way of reading the long narrative of creation. Sin is no shame,
and here the very sins are teachers to countless people. Julian concludes
Chapter 38 with a rather homiletic hagiography of St. John of Beverly
that illustrates this process in praxis through the trope of miracles. In
our modern world we are less likely to associate changes with direct
physical contact. Yet transformations, metaphorical and otherwise, do
occur. Jesus the Christ was one whose presence alone effected dramatic
change. The wisdom of Jesus catalyzed the actions of those who encountered him in their lives. We might say the same about inspiring stories

we hear. Coming into contact with the body of a "saint," even more than her or his story, has the power to remind us that the person shares our humanity. In our most dramatic moments of transformation we recall that we all share in creation's brokenness and we all have the opportunity to participate in the one-ing to wholeness offered by God. Our sins are always already forgiven; our journeys lead us to an awareness of the God Who waits for our unfolding realization. The body of Julian's text calls us to witness this reality, to reach forth to touch the fringes of his garment and be healed. Such healing is only possible in community, where the one and the whole are individually and collectively one-ed to the Whole. Herein the wound is healed; here our sins are forgiven.

⚛ **39** ⚛

Sin is the harshest scourge that any chosen soul can be struck with.
> *This scourge chastises a man and woman terribly*
> *and damages him in his own eyes to such an extent that sometimes*
>> *he thinks of himself as not worthy except to sink into hell—*
> *until contrition seizes him by the touching of the Holy Spirit*
> *and changes the bitterness into hopes for God's mercy.*

Then his wounds begin to heal
> *and the soul, directed into the life of Holy Church, begins to revive.*
>> *The Holy Spirit leads him to confession,*
>> *willingly to confess his sins, nakedly and honestly,*
>> *with great sorrow and great shame that he has so befouled the*
>>> *fair image of God.*

Then he undertakes penance for every sin, imposed by his confessor
>> *(which is instructed in Holy Church by the teaching of the Holy*
>>> *Spirit).*
> *And this is one humiliation that much pleases God;*
> *and also humbly bearing bodily sickness sent from God;*
> *and also sorrow and shame from without,*
> *and reproof and despising from the world*
> *with all kinds of grievance and temptations which we are thrown*
>> *into, bodily and spiritually.*

Most preciously our good Lord protects us when it seems to us that we are nearly forsaken and cast away because of our sin and because we see that we have deserved it.

And because of the humility that we gain in these troubles, we are raised very high in God's sight, by His grace.

Also our Lord visits whom He will with particular grace with so great contrition (also with compassion and true yearning for God) that they are suddenly released from sin and pain and taken up to bliss and made equal with the exalted saints.

> *By contrition we are made pure,*
> *by compassion we are made ready,*
> *and by true yearning for God we are made worthy.*

These are three means, as I understand, by which all souls come to heaven—that is to say, those who have been sinners on earth and shall be saved.

By these remedies it would be fitting for every soul to be healed.

And even though the soul is healed, its wounds are seen before God,
> *not as wounds, but as awards.*

> *And so contrariwise,*
>> *as we are punished here with sorrow and with penance,*
>> *we shall be rewarded in heaven by the gracious love of our*
>>> *Lord God almighty who wills that no one who comes*
>>> *there lose his efforts in any degree,*
>>>> *for He considers sin as sorrow and pain for His lovers to*
>>>> *whom because of love He allots no blame.*

The recompense that we shall receive shall not be little, but it shall
> *be exalted, glorious, and full of honor.*

And in this way shall all shame be transformed to honor and more joy.

Our gracious Lord does not wish His servants to despair because of
> *frequent or grievous falling,*
>> *because our falling does not prevent Him from loving us.*

Peace and love are always in us, existing and working, but we are not always
> *in peace and in love.*

However, He wills that we take heed in this way—
> *that He is the ground of all our whole life in love, and,*
> *furthermore, that He is our everlasting protector*
>> *and mightily defends us against all our enemies*
>> *who are most terrible and fierce against us*
>>> *(and our need is so much the more because we give those*
>>> *enemies opportunity by our falling).*

છ્ર   છ્ર   છ્ર

The sentence that opens Chapter 39 articulates an action that comes from without rather than within. It is neither the action nor the fault of the soul that it should be struck by sin. Being chosen to experience sin is a grace and blessing rather than a curse. Indeed, where there has been sin, there is greater strength. The God-essence ever working in the world works upon us to seek to repair the separation. As Jesus' wound operates as a way in for Julian, an invitation to us to heal the separation that is sin and join in the fuller one-ing, so our own wound draws us more deeply into ourselves, into a greater experience of the Godself that is always already there. The wound is not just an invitation to healing; it is the call to realize the God in us. We are never saved unless we are all saved. The healing from the wound that is sin can only take place in community, where our wounds are revealed. They serve as invitations to others to recognize the experience of separation and to likewise hear the call of God nearer. It is not sin as much as the awareness of sin (separation) that is the first step to this greater one-ing. Thus we are purified of the filth of sin itself. We feel our pain and the pains of others, including the wounds of Jesus Christ. This is the com-passion, the experience of separation known by his wounds and in our wounds. It can only occur in the context of lived experience, sharing with All Created Thing, rational nature aware of pain and separation. We cannot know God unless we desire God. We must journey through our wounds to the Godself inside leading us to pursue our true selves. In this sense the separation that is sin is the wound of separation from who we are. The quest for healing and wholeness always leads us there, away from false illusions. This is heaven.

We have all known satisfaction in achieving goals we had never thought we could. The majority of the time we acknowledge that the process itself was of value for what we learned. In Julian's theology we get to have our cake and eat it too. The journey teaches us the lessons we need to learn. We make the accomplishment that earns us the award. But we cannot forget that the starting point was a wound. Every wound has this potential, through grace, to lead us to a heaven, to greater wholeness. Every wound is God's invitation nearer. There is no fault or blame here, just a call to grow in the way God needs us to grow. Sin is no more than this: the potential for realization of growth toward God put forth as an awareness of lack in wholeness. That wholeness is God. God leads us on the way to our individual wholeness. Sin is not our fault. Peace and love are the essence of the divine we all share at the root of our being and to which we are called to return: not despite but by means of our outer separations and wounds. God protects us, but not as we might think. God's protection is not outside, preventing the separations from happening. Rather, God's protection is always working from the inside, using every wound to draw us nearer and raise our awareness. We finally look within . . . and discover that all there is inside is peace and love. The sin, the separation, the pain, the wounds—all those are outside. All there is inside is God.

⚘ **40** ⚘

It is a supreme friendship of our gracious Lord
  that He protects us so tenderly while we are in our sin.
Furthermore, He touches us most secretly
  and shows us our sin by the sweet light of mercy and grace.
    But when we see ourselves so foul,
    then we imagine that God is angry with us for our sin,
    and then by the Holy Spirit we are guided by contrition to prayer
      and to the desire to amend our life with all our might,
    in order to abate the anger of God,
        until the time that we discover a rest in soul and a quietness in
        conscience.
Then we hope that God has forgiven us our sins—and it is true.

And then our gracious Lord shows Himself to the soul, all merrily
    and with glad countenance, with friendly greeting, as if the soul
      had been in pain and in prison, saying sweetly thus:
        "My dearly beloved, I am glad thou has come to me.
        In all thy woe, I have always been with thee,
        and now thou seest my loving and we are one-ed in bliss."

In this way are sins forgiven by mercy and grace
        and our soul honorably received in joy
              (just as it shall be when it comes to heaven)
        as often as it comes
            by the gracious working of the Holy Spirit
        and the virtue of Christ's Passion.

Here I understand truly that everything is prepared for us by the great goodness of God to such an extent that whenever we are ourselves in peace and
love, we are truly safe.

But because we cannot have this in fullness while we are here,
    therefore it is right for us evermore to believe in sweet prayer

*and in love-filled yearning with our Lord Jesus. He yearns
ever to bring us to the fullness of joy (as it was said before
where He shows the spiritual thirst).*

*But now, because of all this spiritual comfort that is spoken of above,
if any man or woman is led by folly*
 *to say or to think: "If this is true, then it would be good to sin in order to
have more reward,"*
  or else to place less weight on sin,
 *beware of this leading, for truly, if it comes, it is untrue and from
the enemy.*
*Because the same true love that touches us all by His blessed comfort,
 that same blessed love teaches us that we should
  hate sin for the sake of love alone.*

*And I am certain, from my own experience, that the more every
natural soul sees this in the gracious love of our Lord God,*
 the more loath it will be to sin,
 and the more it will be ashamed.

*For if before us were laid all the pains in hell and in purgatory and
  on earth, death and all the rest, over against sin,
 we ought rather to choose all that pain than sin,
 because sin is so vile and so much to be hated,
 that it cannot be compared to any pain—if that pain is not sin.*

*To me was shown no more cruel hell than sin,
 for a natural soul has no pain except sin,
 and all is good except sin,
 and nothing is evil except sin.*

*And when we direct our attention to love and humility, by the working
 of mercy and grace, we are made all fair and pure.*

*As powerful and as wise as God is to save man, also He is just as willing
 to do so.*

*Christ Himself is the ground of all the customs of Christian men, and
  He taught us to do good against evil.
Here we can see that He is Himself this love,
 and He does to us as He teaches us to do,
 for He wills that we be like Him in wholeness of endless love*

for ourselves and
for our fellow Christians.

No more than His love for us is broken off because of our sin,
so no more does He will that our love for ourselves and for our fellow
      Christians be broken off.

But unashamedly hate sin and endlessly love the soul as God loves it.
Then would we hate sin just as God hates it,
and love the soul just as God loves it,
for this word that God said is an endless comfort:
      "I keep thee full safely."

ဆ   ဆ   ဆ

Julian models human relationships on the love between the soul and
God as much as she likens the bond between the divine and the human
to connections between people. The central metaphor in Julian is the
healing of wounds—the closing of gaps, the resolution of separation.
Forgiveness is the model for how we stand in relation to the transcendent.
Our separation from God is not his separation from us. It is impossible,
even in a state of sin, for God ever to be separate from us. Julian's chi-
valric motifs are useful: this comrade, this ally, will always stand by us
as our guardian. However, the alliance is internal rather than external,
for the Friend touches within, going to the very place where that separation exists. With our awareness comes our forgiveness. Our God guides
us to our wounds. When we look God in the face, we are always already
forgiven. God has pointed the way for us; we only need to look at him.
Our recognition of his love is the willful gesture on our part that ones
us to him. He leads us; we choose to come. Intentionality and willfulness
are operative. To deliberately avoid God, to separate oneself from him
simply so that one can be received back, deserves no praise. That would
be as if the Prodigal Son were testing his father's love rather than acting
out of our childish human ignorance. As Julian subtly repeats, our falling
into sin—experiencing separation—is not calculated perversion but is
the natural state of our existence. We wait in our incompletion so that
we may be completed in him. The dynamic actions of mercy and grace
are active to effect this return. Forgiveness is nothing more than being
completed in God. Thus is the separation resolved, in and through all
and each, yet without individual blame. Our desire for God and God's
desire for us are the workings of mercy and grace to singly and fully

make all things well: closing our wounds, enacting forgiveness. The awakened consciousness, the aware soul, is better able to recognize separation—sin—and avoid it. This is our journey.

Friendship is forgiveness. It is healing the wounds between aspects of God's creation. It is our work in the world that ones us to one another just as we are one-ed to him. We are not called to withdraw from interactions where there is brokenness and separation. Rather, in filling the gap between our broken selves we effect the work of mercy and grace here on earth. We embody God through our healing. The ideal of friendship is a perfect fellow human who can bear all that we cannot and can forgive us; but friendship also exists in the communion between pieces of God's creation. There is God. We are called to forgive as we have been forgiven. This forgiveness is and is not the challenging literality of forgiving a friend or asking God's forgiveness. We must move into our own wounds and seek to heal our share in others' brokenness. Forgiveness in Julian is the realization that all the actions of the universe are working to heal the separation that is "sin"; we are called to be part of that divine mercy and grace through awareness and response. Forgiveness is God working in us and through us here on earth.

ↀ **41** ↁ

After this our Lord showed regarding prayer
     and in this showing two applications of our Lord's meaning:
   one is rightful prayer,
   the other is sure trust.

And yet frequently our trust is not complete,
    for we are not certain that God hears us,
       because of our unworthiness (as it seems to us)
       and because we feel absolutely nothing
    (for we are frequently as barren and dry after our prayers as
      we were before).

And thus it is in our feeling, our foolishness, that the cause of our
    weakness lies (for this have I experienced in myself).

And all this brought our Lord suddenly to my mind and He showed
    these words and said:
   "I am the ground of thy praying—
      first, it is my will that thou have something,
      and next I make thee to want it,
      and afterwards I cause thee to pray for it.
         If thou prayest for it,
         how, then, could it be that thou wouldst not get what thou
           askest for?"

And thus in the first proposition, with the three that follow, our good Lord
    shows a powerful encouragement, as can be seen in the above words.

In that first statement, where He says: "if thou prayest for it, etc.,"
      there He shows the very great pleasure and endless reward that
      He will give us because of our praying.

In the second statement, where He says: "How then, could it be? etc.,"
      this was said as an impossible thing,

Because it is the most impossible thing that can be that we
     should pray for mercy and grace and not get it.
Because everything that our good Lord causes us to pray for,
He himself has already appointed to us from without beginning.

Here can we see, then,
    that it is not our praying that is the cause of the goodness and
      grace that He does for us,
        but God's own characteristic goodness.

And that He showed truthfully in all those sweet words when He says,
 "I am ground . . ."

   And our good Lord wills that this be recognized by His lovers on earth

   and the more that we recognize this,
   the more we shall pray (if it is wisely accepted)
   and this is our Lord's intention.

Praying is
   a true, gracious, lasting intention of the soul
   one-ed and made fast to the will of our Lord
   by the sweet, secret working of the Holy Spirit.

Our Lord Himself,
   He is the first receiver of our prayer, as I see it,
   and He accepts it most favorably,
   and, highly rejoicing,
   He sends the prayer up above
   and places it in a Treasury where it shall never perish.

   It is there before God with all His holy saints,
      constantly acceptable,
       always assisting our needs;
         and when we shall receive our bliss,
         our prayer shall be given to us as an award of joy
         with endless honor-filled favor from Him.

Most glad and happy is our Lord about our prayer,
   and He watches for it
   and He wishes to enjoy it,
   because with His grace
      it makes us like Himself in character as we are in nature.

And this is His blessed will, for He says this:
> *"Pray inwardly even though it seems to give thee no pleasure, for*
> *it is beneficial enough though thou perceivest it not.*

Pray inwardly,
> *though thou sensest nothing,*
> *though thou seest nothing, yea,*
> *though thou thinkest thou canst achieve nothing,*
>> *for in dryness and barrenness,*
>> *in sickness and in feebleness,*
>> *then is thy prayer completely pleasing to me,*
> *though it seems to give thee but little pleasure.*

~~And thus all thy living is prayer in my eyes."~~

Because of the reward and the endless favor that He wishes to give
us for it, He desires to have us pray constantly in His sight.
> *God accepts the good intention and the toil of His servants, no*
> *matter how we feel,*
wherefore it pleases Him that we work both in our prayer and in
> *good living by His help and His grace,*

>> *reasonably with good sense,*
>> *keeping our strength for Him*
>> *until we have Him whom we seek in fullness of joy,*
>> *that is, Jesus.*

>> *(He showed this word before in the fifteenth revelation:*
>> *"Thou shalt have Me for thy reward.")*

And thanksgiving is also part of prayer.
Thanksgiving is
> *a true, inner awareness,*
> *with great reverence and loving awe*
> *turning ourselves with all our might towards the actions our good*
> *Lord guides us to,*
> *rejoicing and thanking Him inwardly.*

And sometimes, because of its abundance, thanksgiving breaks out with voice
and says:
> *"Good Lord, thanks be to Thee; blessed mayest Thou be!"*

And sometimes when the heart is dry and feels nothing
   (or else by temptation of our Enemy)
   then the heart is driven by reason and by grace
   to call upon our Lord with voice,
      recounting His blessed Passion and His great goodness.

And the strength of our Lord's word
   is directed into the soul,
   and enlivens the heart,
   and introduces it by His grace into true practices,
   and causes it to pray most blessedly,
   and truly to delight in our Lord.

That is a most blessed, loving thanksgiving in His sight.

Both prayer and trust pertain to the wholeness that the separation of sin thwarts. When we are in "sure trust," there is no separation. Our prayer is that desire to heal the wound. We are not conscious of it. It is not deliberate, and in fact our outward perceiving minds and bodies may feel the very opposite. Our trust is our rest in God wherein nothing separates us from His loving arms. Our prayer is what is always working to get us to that place. Chapter 41 warns against reliance on a mood or feeling. We are praying even when we least feel ourselves doing so. Trusting what seems, what we can outwardly perceive, is the mistake. This is not how God works—particularly a God whose best logic is that we receive life through death! Julian admits that she has put too much trust in feeling, even in her own limited judgment. Her experience of the showings depends on a suspension of disbelief. It seems "special," but this level of revelation is working in and through every one of us. We are just too grounded in appearances to recognize it. Praying is simply drawing the soul nearer. That is not done by us; it is done by God. We may think we are choosing to pray, but in fact it is the God-in-us that is always, constantly praying. God "grounded" in us is forever working toward union. At times it just keeps occurring in the dynamic whirl of the universe, like all the other physical, chemical processes we never notice. At other moments we do it deliberately, like our breath. In those instants when we will ourselves to "choose prayer" we should not invest too much in how we feel. If conscious prayer is just a fraction of our lives, how much is accomplished in unconscious prayer! What we are always asking for in our prayer—whether we are aware of it or not—is deeper, fuller union, the completion of the one-ing. It would be impossible for us to pray for mercy and grace and not get it. That is all we are ever praying for. It is the action of the Spirit in the world healing our wounds. We make too much of prayer, trying to get it "right," when prayer is really God in us working through us to join us more fully with him—effortlessly. Every moment and molecule of our lives is prayer, so grounded are we in God. Thus prayer is letting go, losing the distraction of what it feels like, the attention on what we may consciously be praying for. This is hard for us to hear, especially the accomplished "pray-ers" among us who take intentions to heart. It is the willingness to turn them over to God that matters, to acknowledge that we are always already praying. Our hearts are turned toward God; the intentions we cherish are sites within which God's mercy and grace are working. It comforts us to pray "for" people or outcomes or even things. But the Spirit is there from "before the beginning," and surely before we ask for God's attention.

This does not mean we should fail to cultivate deliberate prayer. A conscious time spent in awareness—like an awareness of our breath— reminds us of this working. Our decision to be conscious of this one-ing acting in and through us is our willingness to partner with God in healing our wounds and our world's brokenness. Saying "yes" opens us to those intuitive moments when we awaken to God's call, as when Julian saw his showings and teachings. We are no longer trying to figure it all out by ourselves based on our limited perceptions. We can receive the guidance God wants to give us so that we can release the Spirit in our lives and into the world. Our outer layers are peeled away, like Jesus' mortal body shed for his glory. We no longer need to trust appearances: we can be all mercy and all grace. God calls Julian repeatedly to "pray inwardly." Here is our call; herein is God's command. We must disregard the outer brokenness of our lives, the imperfections and failures, the impossibilities and limitations. Instead, we are invited to trust that none of it matters compared with this drawing out of Godliness into the world so the Spirit might operate. The forms, the deliberations, the sweetness or bitterness—they mean nothing if we allow ourselves to be vessels pouring God out into the world. We will be one-ed in the end, no matter what. The cultivation of awareness helps us to listen more carefully to what we are needed for here.

Julian writes of thanksgiving: as with prayer, just by living we are thankful. Through us God releases his potential for mercy and grace into his creation; the work of the Spirit in the world is always a thanksgiving.

We are drawn to this awareness called "prayer" because it is the way we are consciously thankful. It is the acknowledgment of something working in us and through us. By such means we say "thank you" in living. That thanksgiving guides us to what God needs us to do. We are always thankful, but only at times can our rational mind articulate it as so. When we feel sorrow, pain, or suffering we are experiencing Jesus' Passion. We are not failing to be thankful then; rather, our very suffering is in itself a kind of thanksgiving. It ones us to him in our eucharist—thanksgiving, communion—of pain. The Word is in us: this word is our prayer, this word is our act of one-ing. Whether we glimpse conscious awareness of it or not, whether we deliberately cultivate its love-meaning through what we arbitrarily call prayer, it is always praying in us. We are always, through mercy and grace, in the process of one-ing with our God; we are always in prayer.

❦ **42** ❧

Our Lord God wishes for us to have true understanding,
  and especially in three matters which are related to our prayer.

  The first is by whom and how our prayer originates;
    "by whom" He shows when He says, "I am ground. . ."
    and "how" is by His goodness, for He says, "First, it is my will . . ."
  For the second, in what manner and how we should practice our
        prayers; and that is that our will be transformed into the will
        of our Lord, rejoicing; and this He means when He says, "I
        make thee to will it . . ."
  For the third, that we understand the fruit and the end of our
        prayer: that is, to be one-ed to and like our Lord in everything.

And for this meaning and for this end was all this loving lesson shown;
  and He wishes to help us,
  if we will make our prayer just as He says Himself—
  blessed may He be!

This is our Lord's will:
  that our prayer
  and our trust
    be both equally great.

For if we do not trust as much as we pray,
  we do incomplete honor to our Lord in our prayer,
  and also we delay and pain ourselves;
  and the reason is, as I believe, because
        we do not truly acknowledge that our Lord is the ground on
              which our prayer grows,
  and also that we do not recognize that prayer is given us by the grace
      of His love.

*For if we knew this, it would make us trust that we would
receive, by our Lord's gift, all that we desire.*

*For I am certain that no man asks mercy and grace with a true intention,
unless that mercy and that grace have been first given to him.*

*But sometime it comes to our mind
that we have prayed a long time,
and yet, we believe that we have not received our request.*

*However because of this we should not be sad,
for I am certain, in keeping with our Lord's purpose, that either we are
to await
a better time,
or more grace,
or a better gift.*

*He wills we have true knowledge that in Himself He is Existence
itself; and in this knowledge He wills that our understanding be
grounded with all our might and all our purpose
and all our intention.
And on this foundation He wills that we take our place
and make our dwelling.*

*By the gracious light of Himself, He wills that we have understanding
of three things that follow:
The first is our noble and excellent creation;
the second, our precious and dearworthy redemption;
the third, everything that He has made beneath us to serve us and
which, for love of us, He protects.*

*What He means is thus, as if He said:
"Behold and see that I have done all this before thy prayer,
and now thou art and thou prayest to Me."
Thus He intends that it is right for us to know that the greatest deeds are done
as Holy Church teaches.*

*And in contemplating this we ought to pray with gratitude for the deed
that is now being done—
and that is to pray
that He rule us and guide us to His honor in this life,
and bring us to His bliss—
and for that He has done everything.*

What He intends is this:
>   *that we understand that He does everything,*
>   *and that we pray for that.*

>>   *For the one is not enough,*
>>>>   *for if we pray and do not understand that He does it, it makes*
>>>>   *us sad and doubtful, and that is not His honor,*
>>>   *and if we understand what He does, and we do not pray, we*
>>>>   *do not our duty. And that way it cannot be, that is to say,*
>>>>   *that is not the way He sees it,*
>>   *but rather to understand that He does it and to pray also,*
>>>   *in that way is He honored*
>>>   *and we are helped.*

Everything that our Lord has already appointed to do, it is His will
>   *that we pray for that, either in particular or in general.*

And the joy and the bliss that that is to Him,
and the gratitude and honor that we shall have from that,
>   *it surpasses the understanding of all creatures in this life,*
>>   *as I see it.*

Prayer is
>   *a right understanding of that fullness of joy that is to come,*
>   *with true yearning and certain trust.*

In prayer,
>   *the tasting of our bliss (that we are naturally appointed to)*
>>   *naturally makes us to yearn;*
>   *true understanding and love (with sweet remembrance of our Savior)*
>>   *graciously makes us trust.*

And thus by nature do we yearn,
and by grace do we trust.
>   *And in these two actions, our Lord watches us constantly,*
>   *for it is our duty,*
>   *and His goodness can assign no less to us.*

Therefore, it is proper for us to give our best effort thereto;
and when we have done it,
>   *then shall we still think that it is nothing—*
>   *and truly it is nothing.*

But we do what we can,
and humbly ask mercy and grace,
and all that we fall short, we shall find in Him.

Thus He means where He says: "I am the ground of thy praying."
And thus in this blessed word, along with the showing, I saw a
complete victory against all our weakness and all our doubtful fears.

   ⁎ ⁎ ⁎

We pray well because it is the response to God's call to acknowledge the one-ing that grace is enacting in all creation. We share in divine reason. We have Jesus' example of the Incarnation. Prayer is *imitatio Christi*. Jesus' life was a perfect prayer. As we are open to healing our separation, we more fully live out our call. The process is dynamic; it is our prayer—conscious and unconscious, mindfulness and "prayer in action." Divine love draws us to itself. The events of our lives, watching and waiting, fail to demonstrate the effects. We never have a constant awareness of the grace one-ing us to God. In Julian's extraordinary experience of the showings she receives a narrative of what is taking place. If we are lucky—or if we really need it, or if we really practice mindfulness—we might get a glimpse. Our lives lack awareness of the Spirit operating in the realm of the unseen. The rational mind must cultivate trust in the "all shall be well" regardless of our feelings of the moment and the outward events of our lives. The more cultivated our reason, the harder this is to maintain. When we are on our knees, we are most desperate. We are on our "needs." We ask for mercy and grace because this is when we remember them. In those moments God coddles us, reminding us of who we are and what we need. As we grow and continue to pray, we forget. We become frustrated when we cannot see outcomes. We are called to progress in awareness beyond our imagined separation from God to a fuller sight of our "grounding" in him. There are we, there is he; action is infused with the dynamic meaning that is mercy and grace—Love.

In choosing to pray we are realizing the Incarnation of divine reason in us. Divine wisdom rests in us; the desire for "understanding" is no more than the want of one-ing. Activating our rational minds, saying yes to the call, is part of our return. In the creation and Incarnation, God poured out; as we live, as we consciously move toward spiritual union with our Source, we participate with the Spirit of mercy and grace. We are always already one-ed when we decide to pray because we are willing to merge our wills with God's as the Spirit works out Love's meaning. We participate in the ongoing trajectory of creation toward the "all shall be well." God wills that we understand that he does everything and that we pray for that. This is trust; this is faith. If the mind grasps God's action but we do not say yes to the call, we fail to do our part. God wills that we pray that his will be done because by this means we partner in the acts of creation and redemption.

We cannot live our particular experience of creation without mindfulness of all we cannot understand, nor can divine Mind that longs for our understanding keep us in Love without making us yearn for completion—the healing of separation, the desire for wholeness in both head and heart. Thus trust mediates between the two in this existence where we have neither complete understanding nor full experience of the object of our longing. We hold on to the belief that our grounding is in God; all our experience is this prayer. Prayer, if in our experiential praxis a journey to a deeper union we might "feel," in the mind of God is the ongoing process of one-ing: the "all shall be well" becoming rather than being. By nature we yearn but by grace we trust. The one cannot help but happen as it is God's will; the other is the working of the Spirit in the world.

43

Prayer ones the soul to God;
> for though the soul is ever like God in nature and essence
> > (restored by grace),
> it is often unlike God in its external state by sin on man's part.

Then is prayer a witness that the soul wills as God wills,
and it comforts the conscience and inclines man to grace.

In this way He teaches us to pray and
mightily to trust that we shall have what we pray for;
> for He looks upon us in love
> and wishes to make us partners in His good will and deed,
> and therefore He moves us to pray for that which it delights Him to do.

For these prayers and good will (which we have as His gift), He will
> reward us and give us endless recompense.
> > (And this was shown in this word: "If thou prayest for it . . .")
> In this word, God showed as great pleasure and as great delight
> as if He were much beholden to us for every good deed that we do—
> > (and yet it is He who does it)
> and for the fact that we pray to Him mightily to do everything that pleases
> Him,
> > as if He said:
> > > "How couldst thou please me more than to pray to me
> > > mightily, wisely, and willingly to do the thing that I am
> > > going to do?"

And thus the soul by prayer comes to agree with God.

When our gracious Lord by His particular grace shows Himself to
> our soul, we have what we desire,
> > and then we do not see for that time what more we should pray for,
> > > but all our purpose with all our might is fixed wholly upon the
> > > contemplation of Him.

This is an exalted incomprehensible prayer, as I see it,
  for the whole cause for which we pray
    is to be one-ed to the vision and the contemplation
  of Him to whom we pray,
      marvelously rejoicing with reverent fear
      and such great sweetness and delight in Him
        that for the time being we can pray absolutely nothing
        except as He moves us.

I am well aware that the more the soul sees of God,
    the more it desires Him by His grace.
But when we do not see Him in this way,
    then we sense a need and cause to pray—
        because of our falling short,
        because of the unfitness of ourselves for Jesus.

For when the soul is tempted, troubled, and left to itself by its unrest,
    then it is time to pray to make that soul pliant and obedient to God.
        (But by no kind of prayer does one make God pliant to himself,
          for He is always the same in love.)

Thus I saw that whenever we see needs for which we pray,
    then our good Lord follows us,
    helping our desire.

And when we by His special grace plainly gaze upon Him,
    seeing no other,
    then we need to follow Him
    and He draws us into Him by love.

Then I saw that His constant working in all manner of things
        is done so well,
        so wisely,
        and so powerfully
    that it surpasses all our imagining,
    and all that we can suppose and comprehend.

        And then we can do nothing more than to gaze at Him
        and rejoice with a high mighty desire to be wholly one-ed to Him,
            and to pay attention to His prompting,
            and rejoice in His loving,
            and delight in His goodness.

Then shall we, with His sweet grace, in our own humble constant
> *prayer, come unto Him now in this life by many secret touchings*
> *of sweet spiritual sights and experiences, meted out to us as our*
> *simplicity can bear it.*

And this is wrought, and shall be, by the grace of the Holy Spirit,
> *until we shall die in yearning for love.*

And then shall we all come unto the Lord,
> *knowing ourselves clearly,*
> *and possessing God fully,*
> *and we being eternally completely hidden in God,*

>> *seeing Him truly*
>> *touching Him fully,*
>> *hearing Him spiritually,*
>> *and delectably smelling Him,*
>> *and sweetly tasting Him.*

Then we shall see God face to face, simply and most fully—
> *the creature that is created shall see and eternally contemplate*
> *God who is the Creator.*

(For no man can see God in this way and live afterwards—that is to say,
in this mortal life—
> *however, when He of His particular grace wishes to show Himself here,*
> *He strengthens the creature beyond itself, and He moderates the show-*
> *ing according to His own will, so that it does good at the time.)*

ℛ ℛ ℛ

Julian calls prayer a witness to the like-willedness of the soul and God. In conscious prayer we are always and only saying, "Thy will be done." To assert that God teaches us to pray and trust, and thus we shall have what we pray for, is really stating that as we are one-ed to God we come into communion with God's will and know what God wants for us. Our distractions fall away and we become "partners" with God in both "will and deed." That partnership is important, because action cannot be separated from intention. This is as true in making prayer conscious as it is in making our work in the world tangible. When we are one-ed with God, we are also called to be—with him and in him, in mindful prayer. When we are consciously one-ed with God we are aware of what we are called to do. God is behind it all. We know that kind of poking and prodding; we know when we feel led to something, to some desired outcome we may not even understand. Yet we feel ourselves strangely moving ahead, both into the darkness and out of it. Here we go forward from an unconscious state of grace working in us and through us into a mindful state of awareness of God's needs for us in our world. This is discernment; this is spiritual growth—the awakening to and realization of God's call. We think we are praying for outcomes; we believe we are discerning God's will. But in truth we are always, already, and only being led. God is ready to accomplish all through grace; one-ing prayer is nothing more than a conscious partnership with the "Thy will" that will be done.

When God shows himself to us in contemplative prayer we feel there is nothing more we can ask for. We are as wholly and totally one-ed with him as we mortals can be. Yet this is the exception, not the rule. If we always basked in the presence of God, we would have no conscious desire for active prayer, for we would already be "there." Instead, the absence leads us on, from the memory of some bliss, taste, or invitation. That is prayer: the search for what we know as home. We thank God for this lack, because it is what moves us to conscious awareness of our one-ing prayer, renewed focus and purpose for what we need to do. We live in a broken, unhealed world, a place of gaping wounds. It is our job to repair, and our memories of perfect oneness move us forward to accomplish God's will. The desire for figuring out what we desire—the longing for God—makes us work. We are pulled along by God to answer our questions, and in the process we end by doing what God needs us to do. We become aware that God is calling us to do something and we had better listen. We trust that what we are drawn to is what God is drawing us to for a reason. When we find God in that place, we choose to accomplish what he is asking of us there.

This is how we come to know God. We follow what seeks us, we look for God there, and we do what we need to do. Here is the Holy Spirit at work in the world through grace. Julian awaits the day when we shall see God face-to-face but acknowledges that God picks times to come to us for particular reasons. The meaning of her text is to record that reason—love; thus is her theology, her glimpse of God, shown to us.

❧ **44** ❧

God showed frequently in all the revelations that man continually
  performs His will and His honor everlastingly,
   without any ceasing.
  (And what this action is was shown in the first revelation, and
  that on a wonderful basis: for it was shown in the operation of
  the soul of Our Blessed Lady Saint Mary, by truth and wisdom.)
  But I hope, however, by the grace of the Holy Spirit, that I shall
  say what I saw.

Truth perceives God,
and wisdom contemplates God,
  and from these two comes the third,
and that is a holy, wonderful delight in God, which is love.

   Where truth and wisdom are, in truth there is love,
   truly coming from them both,
   and all are of God's creation.

For He is eternal supreme Truth,
  eternal supreme Wisdom,
  eternal supreme Love uncreated;
  and man's soul is a created thing in God,
  which has the same divine qualities except created.

And continually the soul does what it was made for:
  it perceives God,
  it contemplates God,
  and it loves God.

Because of this God rejoices in the creature and the creature in God,
endlessly marveling.

In this marveling the creature sees his God, his Lord, his Creator,
so high, so great, and so good in reference to himself who is created,
that scarcely does the creature seem anything at all by himself;
but the clarity and the purity of truth and wisdom cause him to
see and to recognize that he is created because of love
and in this love God endlessly keeps him.

ર૦   ર૦   ર૦

In Chapter 44 the union between God and Created Thing is expressed as harmony rather than dissonance. At the soul level there is no separation. There is no struggle or striving. The whole universe operating toward making all things well does not mean that in our essence we are separated from God. Rather, it is on account of the fact that interiorly our souls are always in union with the divine will that the exterior workings toward reunion are possible. God will make all things well so that at the surface level all shall be as well as it already is on the more "substantial" plane, literally in our substance. Mary is cited as an example of interior and exterior in harmony. In all the rest of us, interior grace is working to bring the exterior into sync with it. This is true and constant prayer. Our souls are in harmony with God: therein is our struggle. The more the outward contradicts our true inner nature, the more we will suffer. Of course, the greater the suffering to reconcile surface with substance, the more that grace is working in our lives. In our most heart-wrenching times, when we feel most divided, God's grace—prayer—is more active than ever. Our souls and our bodies are making all things well. Such work can be messy and painful.

Julian articulates a trinity of our soul's reality: truth perceiving God, wisdom contemplating God, love delighting in God. That truth is what Julian knew when she realized and acknowledged God's showings to her. Wisdom worked within her as she discerned God's meaning. Of course, love has been the meaning and end point of the process. But they are as united and inseparable as the doctrine of the Trinity. In Julian's theology it is impossible to know God's love without also having understanding, and seeing the truth also means experiencing that love. This interdependence/indistinguishability also applies to our "inner/outer" struggle. Even if we know perfection in our souls, the Incarnation means that we can never rest until the external is transformed. And in the midst of our greatest transubstantiations on the material plane, when all lacks order and meaning, there is perfect love, truth, and wisdom to be found in our souls, and "we" are never separate from "he." In Julian's theology heart is addressed with head. Love is not only found where there is truth and wisdom: love indeed comes from both of these. So we are neither blinded by divine reason nor asked to renounce our reason insofar as they are one and the same. In the substance of things they all are creations of God. Here we have not simply "where charity and love are, there is God," but where truth and wisdom are, there is love, and there is God. The only difference between these qualities in humanity and these qualities in God is that in us they are created by him, in him they have ever been. We reside in him: the human "soul is a created thing in God." So God contains all creation, and we are nothing if not of him.

Thus we know what to do at heart. We perceive, contemplate, and love. This trinity explains Julian's articulation of how she experienced her visions in body, mind, and soul. But this reality is in itself a cause of divine bliss. The divine rejoices in this creation. God is glad that there is more truth, wisdom, and love. God celebrates having created that which is drawn to truth, wisdom, and love. Our very existence is a subject for God's rejoicing, and we exist for the very purpose that God might rejoice. At our soul level we also rejoice in him. Just as we are constantly in prayer, so our souls are ever rejoicing in him. When we cannot feel this joy, and especially in those moments when we feel most blocked or most distressed, the grace of God is working to make all things well. Our lives are out of harmony with this inner rejoicing; from here our healing begins. We are nothing of ourselves. We can see only our brokenness and broken world. But in our souls this is not so. The soul perceives, contemplates, and loves. We cannot experience this completion without God's active work of mercy and grace. We awaken to truth, we glimpse wisdom, we know love. Through these means—truth in its clarity, wisdom in its purity—our outer selves reach the inner reality: the greatest of these, which is love. When we look up at God, our souls see that we are he; on the external level, we only know separation and difference, the "I and Thou." In the interior space, we are always one-ed in love.

❧ **45** ❧

God judges us based on the essence of our human nature
      which is always kept constantly in Him,
      whole and safe without end;
and this judgment comes from His rightfulness.
But man judges based on our changeable fleshliness
      which seems now one thing, now another,
      according to what it picks from among the parts
      and expresses publicly.
  And this human judgment is muddled,
      for sometimes it is good and gentle,
      and sometimes it is cruel and oppressive.
          Insofar as it is good and gentle, it is part of rightfulness;
          and insofar as it is cruel and oppressive, our good Lord Jesus
            reforms it by mercy and grace through the virtue of His
            Blessed Passion and so brings it into rightfulness.

And though these two are thus reconciled and one-ed,
still both shall be acknowledged in heaven without end.

The first judgment is of God's rightfulness, and that is from His high
  endless love.

    This is that fair, sweet judgment that was shown in the whole fair
    revelation in which I saw Him assign to us no kind of blame.
        And although this was sweet and delightful,
            yet in the observing of this alone
            I was unable to be fully comforted, because of the judgment
              of Holy Church which I had understood before and was
              constantly in my sight.

    And therefore by this Church judgment it seemed to me that it
      was necessary for me to acknowledge myself as a sinner.

And by the same judgment,
> *I acknowledged that sinners are sometimes deserving of blame*
> *and anger,*
but these two things—blame and anger—I could not find in God.

Therefore my deliberation and desire was more than I know or can tell,
> *because God Himself showed the higher judgment at the same*
>> *time, and therefore it was necessary for me to accept that—*
> *but the lower judgment was taught me previously in Holy Church,*
>> *and therefore I could in no way give up that lower judgment.*

Then this was my desire:
> *that I could see in God*
> *in what way the judgment of Holy Church here on earth is true in His*
>> *sight,*
> *and how it is proper for me truly to understand it.*
>> *(By this both judgments could be saved, in so far as it would be*
>> *honorable to God and the morally right way for me.)*

To all this I had no other response except an amazing example of a
lord and of a servant (as I shall tell later)—and that most mystically shown.

And yet I remained in my desire
> *(and I will until my end)*
> *that I could by grace distinguish these two judgments as is proper for me—*

for all heavenly and all earthly things that belong to heaven
> *are contained in these two judgments,*
> *and the more knowledge and understanding*
> *that we have of these two judgments*
> *by the gracious guiding of the Holy Spirit,*
> *the more we shall see and understand our failures, and ever the more*
>> *that we see our failings, the more naturally by grace we*
>> *shall yearn to be filled full of endless joy and bliss,*
> *for we are created for that,*
> *and the essence of our human nature*
>> *is now blissful in God,*
>> *and has been since it was made,*
>> *and shall be, without end.*

ଊ ଊ ଊ

"Judge not that ye be not judged" is easier said than done. The human mind is always assigning praise or blame to actions or intentions. In Chapter 45 we remain in the inseparability between our true selves and our God. God cannot condemn our "essence," because God of all goodness cannot condemn Godself. Our essence is always one-ed, no matter the outward appearance. Julian contrasts God's judgment with human judgment, which changes based on outer circumstances and is public. But even when and where human judgment is "cruel and oppressive," God reforms it. By the Passion we are not simply *taught* compassion; it literally *effects* it. For some, knowledge of the Passion and its implications will make them kinder; for others, the harshness may beget violence in the world. It is not this human perspective that the Passion corrects. The lesson of forgiveness, wholeness, integration—one-ing—can only take place through God's judgment, not humanity's. That message is intended for our treatment of others as well as how we look at ourselves. If God does not blame us, why should we blame ourselves? If God does not blame others, what right do we have to blame?

Julian struggles with God's law and human law, divine punishment and retribution versus the mundane equivalent. They are not the same, even within those institutions that claim divine authority. God's "judgment" is not judgment *per se*; it is love. His judging is not binary, dichotomous, black and white. It is seeing us as we truly are, part of him in our essence. This perspective (and it is that) is the work of the scientist who wonders at the depth of complexity when examining the simplest result of her experiment under the microscope. God saw it, and it was good. This is God's "judgment" of us, seeing us as we really are. Julian uses language that underscores her certainty when she observes that God does not blame us. This can only be understood if we remember that God is not looking at our "externalness." God is only and always seeing us from within, viewing our substance as of himself.

These showings challenge Julian's "understanding." She is forced to acknowledge that outward appearances do not represent interior essence. This awareness may sound trite, but it is more complex. Julian learns a different way of experiencing God that does not simply say that the external is false as opposed to the internal. Rather, the outward—the Church, human judgment—has its rules and laws and means of working. The inward is of a totally different epistemology and essence. This is not "black or white" thinking, making the interior right and the external wrong. They operate on different planes. The grace and mercy of the internal is always operating through the external to lead toward the "all shall be well," the great one-ing. Yet there is no way we can ever perceive that with our outer sight alone. If we try, we will be frustrated.

Julian maintains her orthodoxy when she states that by "church judgment" she is a sinner, sometimes deserving of "blame and anger." But she could never find those qualities in God. The external is the way of brokenness and wounds in need of healing; from the inside out, the work of mercy and grace are always making all things well. Julian's understanding remains restless. She is compelled to accept the "higher judgment"—God's judgment. She must embrace the notion that in our essence we are always of God; we do not deserve blame or anger. She keeps the "lower judgment" that blames in its place. Julian is not just paying lip service to the Church of her day. On the contrary, she is implicated in the same rhetoric. In her essence she knows how God sees us: this is the gift of her showings. But as long as she is human she will participate in the discourse of blame and anger. In our brokenness we can live no other way. We may glimpse compassionate perfection. The more conscious awareness we have of this part of ourselves, the more we are freed to be willing hands for the repair of the world. Nevertheless, we humans will judge by human standards. God will not judge us or blame us for judging in this way since it is our human nature to do so.

Julian wishes to live without the capacity to blame or judge. She also wants to be able to see the workings of God's judgment through the Church, but it is difficult for her to do so. This is not a condemnation as much as it is an acknowledgment both of the humanness of the institution and of the reality that it practices human judgment while claiming God's authority. Julian needs spiritual sight while experiencing the mundane. She submits herself to the Church while maintaining her belief in the superiority of "God's judgment" to human judgment. In some way the one must work through the other. There is both "no blame" and the working toward "no blame" in the broken world. Human judgment has the potential to participate in mercy and grace. This operates in the Passion, wherein contemplation of suffering and forgiveness can teach us to renounce blame and anger. It remains the task of the human to claim authority for the blame and no-blame. An awareness of God's love for us and our essence in him makes us bold to see those outer wounds (and blame, and judgment) as the road toward the "all shall be well." He who was blameless teaches us not to blame. Through reflection on his Passion we can glimpse God's true judgment of our essence within us. From a culture obsessed with self-blame and blame of others for the murder of God, Julian calls upon us to revise our indictments—or at least use them as windows of one-ing into the essence of our soul. When the finger is pointed at us we can go within and know our true life in God and look without to right our wrongs.

☞ **46** ☜

But the passing life that we have here in our fleshliness does not
know what our self is, except in our Faith.
> *And when we know and see truly and clearly what our self is, then*
> *shall we truly and clearly see and know our Lord God in fullness of joy.*
> > *And therefore it is essential*
> > > *that the nearer we are to our bliss,*
> > > *the more we shall yearn—*
> > > > *and that both by nature and by grace.*

We can have knowledge of our self in this life by the continual help
> *and strength of our own noble human nature.*
In this knowledge, we can increase and grow by the furthering and
> *aiding of mercy and grace,*
> > *but we can never fully know our self,*
> > *until the last point,*
> > > *and at that point this passing life*
> > > > *and all manner of pain and woe shall have an end.*

And therefore, it belongs properly to us, both by nature and grace,
> *to yearn and desire with all our might to know our self*
> *and in this full knowledge we shall truly and clearly know our God*
> > *in fullness of endless joy.*

And yet, during all this time from the beginning to the end of the revelation,
> *I had two kinds of observations:*
> > *the one was of endless continuing love, with a security of protection*
> > > *and blissful salvation (for the whole showing was about this);*
> > *the other was the common teaching of Holy Church, in which*
> > > *teaching I was previously formed and grounded, and was*
> > > *willingly keeping it in practice and in understanding.*

169

And the beholding of all this came not from me,
> *because I was not by the showing moved nor led from the Church*
> *teaching in any kind of point,*
>> *but in the showing I was rather taught to love that teaching,*
>> *to delight in it, for by it I could (with the help of our Lord and*
>>> *His grace)*
>> *grow and rise to more heavenly knowledge and nobler loving.*

And thus, in all this beholding it seemed to me to be necessary to see
> *and to know that we are sinners,*
> *and we do many evils that we ought to stop,*
> *and we leave many good deeds undone that we ought to do.*
> *And for this we deserve pain and blame and wrath.*

But notwithstanding all this, I saw truthfully that our Lord was never
angry, nor ever shall be,
> *for He is God:*
> *He is good,*
> *He is life,*
> *He is truth,*
> *He is love,*
> *He is peace;*
> *and His power, His wisdom, His Love, and His Unity do not*
>> *allow Him to be angry.*
> *(For I saw truly that it is against the character of His Power*
>> *to be angry,*
> *and against the character of His Wisdom,*
> *and against the character of His Goodness.)*

God is the goodness that cannot be angry, for He is nothing but goodness.
> *Our soul is one-ed to Him, who is unchangeable goodness,*
> *and between God and our soul is neither anger nor forgiveness,*
>> *as He sees it.*
> *For our soul is so completely one-ed to God by His own goodness,*
> *that there can be absolutely nothing at all separating God and soul.*

To this understanding the soul was led by love and drawn by power
in every showing. That it is thus—and how it is thus—our good Lord
showed truly by His great goodness, and also that He wills that we
desire to comprehend it (that is to say, in so far as it is proper for
His creature to comprehend it).

Everything that this simple soul understood, God wills that it be
*   shown and known,*
for those things which He wishes to keep secret, He Himself
*   mightily and wisely hides out of love*
*   (for I saw in the same showing that much that is secret is hidden*
*   which can never be known until the time that God of His*
*   goodness has made us worthy to see it).*
With this I am well satisfied,
*   awaiting our Lord's will in this high wonder.*

And now I yield myself to my mother, Holy Church,
as a simple child ought.

ᛒ   ᛒ   ᛒ

In our human experience we know ourself by our "faith." Julian champions and validates the contemplative life, but she also maintains the power of our reason. We cannot fully know God in our human experience unless we undertake a long, hard look at ourselves. We are not going to find God outside ourselves, but only within. We see God, we are shown God, inside ourselves—for that is where he is to be found. The realization of bliss, the "fullness of joy," is unfolded in that process. The experience of coming to self-knowledge is coming to intimacy with God. That takes place in our minds, with the help of our reason that is God's reason dwelling within us, as much as it is spiritual and corporeal. The fewer the obstacles in our way, the more we want that knowledge of God. It is literally natural for us, as part of God's creation, to desire full union with him. Our humanity is not despicable: through our God-given reason, as well as through our wounds, faults, and failings, we journey to our true oneness with the God for whom we long, who is ever moving us closer to him. We will only completely know ourselves at the end of time. The imperfection of our judging selves that is part of our human nature must await ultimate perfection: making whole, clean, and pure, stripping away the foul to expose the fair.

Julian's preoccupation with the indivisibility between God and the self has implications for the unfolding of her text. She spent decades discerning God's meaning in the showings. It has been an experience of coming to know herself as well as coming to know her God. Nevertheless, in those places and spaces where her understanding is frustrated, Julian must turn it over to God and trust that she will "get it" at the end of time. However limited reason may be, love is never restricted. Julian relies on the Church's teaching as a window for the progress of her soul. She views her "self" as part of that Church, the Christian believers on earth. The first place to look for God, to grow in her movement forward on the journey, is the institutional Church: in all its humanity, struggling along just as she is, toward the final one-ing. Yet Julian cannot abandon the teachings of her revelations. God is described as good, life, truth, love, and peace.

God's unity is Julian's ever-present theme. We are his unity. It is impossible for God in his unity to be angry, because that would require God to be angry at Godself. If knowing ourselves allows us to know God, and if at our center there is nothing but God in us, then there can be no anger. Forgiveness would imply that some repair is necessary. As we are kept in God, that too is impossible. At our soul/self level there is no need to make amends, for we are already one. On the outer level there may be all sorts of necessity for healing, just as even judgment, in the world's eyes, must have its place. Despite confusion, despite lack, despite intellectual thirst and spiritual hunger for God, there is always only love: Unity. The journeying soul requires understanding. We cannot grow without the use of our reason that is part of the divine mind. These are not secrets, mysteries of our God, privileged to a certain individual to whom they might be shown. Far from it—this is the purpose of Julian's showings: to translate God's message, through her understanding, for all people.

⋈ **47** ⋈

Two objectives belong to our soul by obligation:
> one is that we reverently marvel,
> the other is that we meekly suffer, ever rejoicing in God.

For He wants us to know that we shall in a short time see clearly
within Himself all that we desire.

Notwithstanding all this, I beheld and marveled greatly at the mercy
and forgiveness of God,
> for by the teaching that I had beforehand, I understood that the
> mercy of God was supposed to be the remission of His wrath after
> the time that we have sinned.

>> (It seemed to me that to a soul whose intention and desire is to
>> love, the wrath of God would be more severe than any other
>> pain, and therefore I accepted that the remission of His wrath
>> would be one of the principal objectives of His mercy.)

But in spite of anything that I might behold and desire, I could not
see this point in the entire showing.

But how I saw and understood concerning the works of mercy, I shall
say somewhat, in so far as God wishes to give me grace.
> I understood thus:
>> man is changeable in this life,
>> and by frailty
>> and by simplicity
>> and lack of cunning,
>>> being overcome, he falls into sin.

He is impotent and unwise by himself,
> and also his will is overwhelmed during this time he is in
> temptation and in sorrow and woe.

And the cause is blindness, for he sees not God —
  because if he saw God constantly,
  he would have no harmful experience,
  nor disturbance of any kind,
  nor the distress that is a servant to sin.

This I saw and felt at the same time,
  and it seemed to me that the sight and the feeling was noble and
    plenteous and gracious in comparison to what our ordinary
    experience is in this life,
  but yet I thought it was only small and lowly in comparison to the
    great desire that the soul has to see God.

I perceived in me five kinds of operations which are these:
  rejoicing,
  mourning,
  desire,
  fear,
  and certain hope:
    "rejoicing" because God gave me understanding and knowledge
      that it was Himself that I saw;
    "mourning," and that was because of failing;
    "desire," and that was that I might see Him ever more and
      more, understanding and acknowledging that we shall
      never have full rest till we see Him truly and clearly in heaven;
    "fear" was because it seemed to me in all that time that that
      vision would fail and I would be left to myself;
    "certain hope" was in the endless love, that I saw I would be
      protected by His mercy and brought to His bliss, and
      rejoicing in His sight with this certain hope of His merciful
      protection gave me understanding and comfort so that
      mourning and fear were not greatly painful.

And yet in all this I beheld in the showing of God that this kind of
vision of Him cannot be constant in this life—and that for His own
honor and for increase of our endless joy.

And therefore we are frequently without the sight of Him,
  and at once we fall into ourselves,
  and then we discover no sense of rightness—nothing but the
    contrariness that is within ourselves

(and that from the ancient root of our First Sin with all that
follows after from our own contrivance)
and in this we are troubled and tempted with a sense of sins and
of pains in many different ways, spiritually and bodily, as it is
familiar to us in this life.

ဢ   ဢ   ဢ

God cannot be angry. Mercy cannot simply be "the remission of his wrath." Julian was taught that mercy was just that, but she does not see it this way in the showing. She discusses mercy through the metaphor of sight. Soon we shall see clearly. The cause of sin is blindness, not seeing God. We come to this through our weakness, not malice. Separation, sin, is the absence of the constant awareness of God. Since that is impossible for us to have, the human cannot be blamed. We cannot be held responsible for what it is our nature to do. God is not angry with us for acting without the abilities we lack. Julian says she both saw and felt this teaching. Her glimpse is much more than an ordinary experience of God. Still, it is not enough. This kind of sight eludes us. It is merciful. The sight of Godself in Julian's understanding is a merciful act because through it she became more fully aware of her one-ing with Divine Reason. Our humanity cannot see as God sees. We make mistakes. We see our separation, so we experience sin. The outer and inner differ. The interior sight of God considers us, mindful of our limitations. We view ourselves through that glimpse of divinity we know. The very memory of God in our essence makes us conscious of imperfections, where we need mercy. God can look at the glass half full because he sees all of us in his sight. We view the glass as half empty because that is the most we can see from our human perspective. Consciousness, the recall of Godself in us, is God's mercy working in and through us. Mercy is the awareness of the dissonance between what we are and what we could be. If we had no sight of ourselves, if we could not stand back from where we are and glimpse our faults and failings, we would lack the memory of our oneness with him. That is the true perfection of our essence: the one-ing to be finished when the outward is reconciled with the inward, the realization of our need for mercy.

Mercy causes us to rejoice that we can be still and know that God is God. Mercy awakens us to the rupture between what we are and what we could be. We mourn our lack of oneness. Mercy is awareness that salvation is the sight of God, where there is no separation. We long for that constant vision that in God's eyes is ever present, that for us is always "to-be." Mercy is the adrenaline rush that keeps us moving toward God with our eyes on the prize, holding on to what we know to be the truth of our being despite outward events. Mercy is the hope that we need not fear, that we are always in him and can never be separated. We do not maintain this knowledge at all times—we cannot feel mercy always as we operate out of our brokenness. When we do not see God we return to our forgetting. Yet no matter how little we see, how infrequently we glimpse, the inner work of mercy continues on in spite of the circumstances of our lives. How might we remember? In what ways do we need to embody divine mercy—be merciful?

❧ **48** ❧

But our good Lord, the Holy Spirit
    (who is endless life dwelling in our soul)
  full safely keeps us,
  and makes a peace in the soul,
  and brings it to rest by grace,
  and makes it submissive,
  and reconciles it to God.
And this is the mercy and the way in which our Lord constantly leads
us as long as we are here in this changeable life.

I saw no wrath except on man's part, and that He forgives in us.
  For wrath is nothing else but a departure from and an opposition
  to peace and to love,
    and either it comes from the failure of power
    or from the failure of wisdom,
    or from the failure of goodness
      (which failure is not in God but it is on our part — for we,
      because of sin and miserableness, have in us a wrath and a
      continuing opposition to peace and to love—and that He
      showed very often in His loving demeanor
      of compassion and pity).

The basis of mercy is love,
and the action of mercy is our protection in love;
  and this was shown in such manner
  that I could not conceive of the property of mercy
  in any other way than as if it were all love in love.

That is to say,
  mercy is a sweet, gracious working in love mingled with plenteous
    pity, as I see it.

Mercy works, protecting us,
        and mercy works transforming everything into good for us.

Mercy, out of love, allows us to fail to a limited extent,
and in so far as we fail, in so much we fall;
and in so far as we fall, so much we die;
        for it is necessary that we die
        in as much as we fall short of the sight and sense of God,
        who is our life.
        Our failing is frightful,
        our falling is shameful,
        and our dying is sorrowful;
                but still in all this, the sweet eye of pity and of love never
                        departs from us,
                and the working of mercy ceases not.

For I observed the attribute of mercy and I observed the attribute of grace,
which are two kinds of action in one love;
mercy is a pity-filled attribute which belongs to Motherhood in tender love,
and grace is a dignified attribute which belongs to royal Lordship in the
        same love.

Mercy works:
        protecting,
        enduring,
        bringing life, and healing,
        and all is from the tenderness of love;
and grace works:
        building up,
        rewarding, and
        endlessly going beyond what our loving and our labor deserves,
        spreading out widely
        and showing the noble, plenteous largess of God's royal
                Lordship in His marvelous courtesy.

And this is from the abundance of love,
        for grace converts our frightful failing into plenteous endless solace,
        and grace converts our shameful falling into noble, honorable rising,
        and grace converts our sorrowful dying into holy, blissful life.

I saw full certainly that
> *ever as our contrariness makes pain, shame, and sorrow for us*
>> *here on earth,*
> *just so on the contrary, grace makes solace, honor, and bliss for us*
>> *in heaven,*
> *exceeding the earthly to such an extent*
>> *that when we come up and receive the sweet reward which*
>>> *grace has created for us,*
> *then we shall thank and bless our Lord, endlessly rejoicing that*
>> *ever we suffered woe.*

And that shall be because of an attribute of blessed love that we shall discover in God—which we might never have known without woe going before.

And when I saw all this, it was necessary to agree that the mercy of God and the forgiveness is in order to abate and consume our wrath, not His.

৪৩ ৪৩ ৪৩

Julian calls the third member of the Trinity the "endless life dwelling in our soul." It resolves the dissonance of our brokenness. It is mercy. This is not God saying he accepts our apology. Rather, it is the active work of healing the fragmentation of ourselves and our world. When Julian says that God forgives us our wrath, she observes how God heals our wounds. Peace and love are oneness; anger is our collective open wound. Julian names a trinity of failures that produce wrath. They are repaired through the work-in-progress of our external one-ing with God: in the power of the Creator, the wisdom of incarnate Understanding, and the goodness of dynamic grace. The outward reality of our separation moves toward the harmony of our inner oneness. Mercy is grounded in love. Its effect, its application, is protecting and enclosing us. Our rough edges, our abrasions, are sealed by this love. Thus God works for transformation. We experience his dynamic love. Our separation and lack of full sight of God require us to depend on mercy. We would not be connected to God through this tangible means were we complete in and of ourselves. Our one-ing God who is always in process uses our outer brokenness to join us to himself. When mercy accomplishes its task, that one-ing will be fully realized. The "eye of pity and of love"— the sight of God—is always with us, moving us toward ultimate completion. Can we trust this working where God's sight is not our sight, in those places where we most need mercy and healing?

ℭ **49** ℬ

To the soul this was a mighty wonder
  (which was continually shown in all showings,
  and with great diligence observed)
  that our Lord God, as far as He is concerned, cannot forgive—
    because He cannot be angry—it would be impossible.

For this was shown:
  that our life is all based and rooted in love,
  and without love we cannot live.

And therefore to the soul
  (which by His special grace sees so obviously the exalted
  marvelous goodness of God, and that we are endlessly one-ed to
  Him in love)

it is the most impossible thing that can be that God would be angry,
  for wrath and friendship are two opposites.

He who lays waste and destroys our wrath and makes us humble and
    gentle, it is essential for us to believe that He is always clothed
    in that same love, humble and gentle—which is opposite to wrath.

I saw full certainly that where our Lord appears,
  peace comes to pass
  and wrath has no place.

I saw no kind of wrath in God,
    neither for a short time
    nor for long.
      (For truly, as I see it, if God were to be angry even a hint,
      we would never have life nor place nor being.)

  As truly as we have our being from the endless Power of God
    and from the endless Wisdom
    and from the endless Goodness,

just as truly we have our protection in the endless Power of God,
in the endless Wisdom
and in the endless Goodness.

Although we feel miseries,
disputes
and strifes in ourselves,
yet are we all mercifully enwrapped
in the mildness of God and in His humility,
in His kindliness and in His gentleness

I saw full certainly that all our endless friendship,
our place,
our life, and
our being is in God,
because that same endless goodness that keeps us that we perish
not when we sin,
that same endless goodness continually negotiates in us a peace
against our wrath and our contrary falling,
and with a true fear makes us see our need strongly to seek
unto God in order to have forgiveness with a grace-filled
desire for our salvation.

We may not be blissfully saved until we are truly in peace and in love,
for that is our salvation.

Although we
(by the wrath and the contrariness that is in us)
are now in tribulation, uneasiness, and woe
(as it falls to our blindness and frailty)
yet are we sure and safe by the merciful protection of God
so that we perish not.

But we are not blissfully safe in possessing our endless joy until we
are wholly in peace and in love—that is to say,
fully gratified with God
and with all His works
and with all His judgments,
and loving and peaceable with ourselves
and with our fellow Christians
and with all that God loves, as love pleases.

And this God's goodness carries out in us.
  Thus I saw that God is our true peace
  and He is our sure keeper when we are ourselves unpeaceful,
  and He continually works to bring us into endless peace.

And thus, when we, by the action of mercy and grace, are made
humble and gentle, we are completely safe. When it is truly at peace
in itself, suddenly the soul is one-ed to God,
because in Him is found no wrath.

Thus I saw that when we are wholly in peace and in love, we find no
contrariness nor any kind of hindrance.
  And that contrariness which is now in us,
  our Lord God of His goodness makes most profitable for us,
  because that contrariness is the cause of our tribulations and all our woe,
    and our Lord Jesus takes those
    and sends them up to heaven,
    and there are they made more sweet and delectable than heart
      can think or tongue can tell,
    and when we come there, we shall find them ready,
      all transformed into truly beautiful and endless honors.

Thus is God our steadfast foundation here,
  and He shall be our complete bliss
  and make us unchangeable as He is, when we are there.

ಔ   ಔ   ಔ

It is our anger, not God's. It is God's mercy, not ours. All mercy comes from God. All human acts of mercy have their source in God. All this is shown continually to Julian in every showing. How can we who get angry understand a rational mind who cannot and therefore does not need to forgive? The impossibility of God's anger is because God is our friend. This is not sentimental piety. In the Incarnation we are forever one-ed with God. God as love is the opposite of anger. Wrath, sin, and separation are fragmentation. God is the antithesis of brokenness: God and anger are mutually exclusive. If God were angry—broken rather than whole—we could not exist. Creation depends on the one-ness of Created Thing with God. The Incarnation could not have occurred if God were angry. Godself could not have spilled out into the material world. While outward perception suggests that the diversity of the mate-

rial world defies the Oneness of God, the inner reality is the intercon-
nection of the One. We are grounded in the Love that is God. In the
Incarnation God heals us of His nature as he loves us of His Love. We
exist by His Trinity and we are sustained by that same trinity of mercy—
power, wisdom, and love.

We feel miseries, disputes, and strife as sorrow, fights, and disequi-
librium. The Incarnation, our endless friendship with God, locates our
place, life, and being in him. Goodness, the mercy and grace acting in
the world, keeps us. That same work negotiates a peace of wholeness
against our wrath of separation. Forgiveness is this making whole: it is
God's healing of our divided self. Fear is the separation from God that
pushes us to seek Him so that we might be healed. We desire the salvation of the completed one-ing. Salvation, heaven, is the peace and love
that is God. The work of mercy and grace in the world will be accomplished only when this is accomplished. The soul is one-ed to God when
it is at peace with itself, when brokenness is mended. For this to happen,
the inward reality of our one-ing must be in total harmony with our
outward selves. We humans get occasional glimpses of this sight of God
as Julian experienced it. Our "contrariness," the imbalance of ourselves,
keeps the dynamic action moving forward. The future is at hand, through
the completion of the work of our healing. What can we have here; what
must we wait for? We are impatient creatures. God is our true peace, our
sure keeper when we are not at peace. We are made humble and gentle.
Safety and security are the peace that the world cannot give, what is
necessary for the soul to be one-ed to God. Once anger, unrest, is gone,
the soul can be united with God, who is only peace, no wrath. When we
have really arrived, nothing tears us away or blocks us. Contrariness
now is for good, for through its instigation our troubles and grief are
transformed. Where do we need to forgive? How do we need to forgive?
Who do we need to forgive . . . starting with ourselves?

03 **50** 80

*In this mortal life mercy and forgiveness is our way and evermore
leads us to grace.*

*By the temptation and the sorrow that we fall into on our part
we are often dead, according to man's judgment on earth,
but in the sight of God the soul that shall be saved was never
dead and never shall be.*

*And yet here I wondered and marveled with all the diligence of my
soul, meaning thus:*

*"Good Lord, I see Thee who are very truth
and I know truly that we sin grievously all day and are much
blameworthy;
and I can neither relinquish the knowledge of this truth,
nor can I see Thee showing to us any manner of blame.
How can this be?"*

> *(For I knew by the common teaching of Holy Church and by my
> own sense that the guilt of our sin continually hangs upon us,
> from the First Man unto the time that we come up into heaven.)*

Then was this a miracle to me:

*that I saw our Lord God showing to us no more blame
than as if we were as pure and as holy as angels are in heaven.*

*Between these two opposites my reason was greatly troubled by my blindness,
and could have no rest for fear that His blessed Presence would
pass from my sight and I be left in ignorance of how He looks
on us in our sin.*

> *(For either it was necessary for me to see in God that sin was
> all done away,
> or else it was necessary for me to see in God how He looks at it—
> whereby I could truly recognize how I ought to look at sin and
> the manner of our guilt.)*

184

My yearning went on, continually gazing on Him,
>*and yet I could have no patience because of great dread and*
>*perplexity, thinking:*
>>*"If I take it thus—that we are not sinners and not blameworthy—*
>>>*it seems likely I would err and fall short of knowledge of this*
>>>*truth.*
>>*But if it is so that we are sinners and blameworthy, good Lord,*
>>>*how can it then be that I cannot see this verity in Thee,*
>>>*who are my God, my Creator, in whom I desire to see all truths?"*

[Three points make me brave to ask this:
>*the first is because it is so lowly a thing*
>>*(for if it were a lofty thing, I would be terrified);*
>*the second is that it is so ordinary*
>>*(for if it were special and secret, also I would be terrified);*
>*the third is that it is necessary for me to be aware of it, as it seems to me, if*
>*I shall live here*
>>*(for the sake of the knowledge of good and evil, by which I can,*
>>*by reason and grace, the more separate the good from the evil,*
>>*and love goodness and hate evil,*
>>>*as Holy Church teaches).]*

I wept inwardly with all my might,
>*searching in God for help, meaning thus:*
>*"Ah, Lord Jesus, King of bliss, how shall I be comforted?*
>*Who is it that shall teach me and tell me what I need to know, if I*
>*cannot at this time see it in Thee?"*

ဆ ဆ ဆ

Julian continues to struggle over the apparent reality of our blame-worthiness versus the lack of blame God casts upon us. External observation is supported by the teaching of her Church as well as by her so-called common sense. Julian is afraid that her connection with God will pass before she gets the answers she needs. However much we might struggle, most religious people reach a point at which we accept that some things we call the workings of God do not make rational sense. This does not mean we will, or should, stop asking questions. They are the means for our one-ing; they are the work of mercy and grace in the world, the action of the Spirit. Julian has no way of rationally explaining how and why a contradiction exists. We have all wrestled with some intellectual problem, trying to systematically figure it all out. When a question is intimately connected with faith, it can be a torment. Julian puts her cards on the table. She needs either to know that sin was done away with or to learn how God looks at it. Julian says that the emperor has no clothes: she points out the logical impossibility of what she has been shown. The depth of her rational mind, the extent of her intellect, makes it unfeasible for her to swallow whole the irreconcilable differences between her reason and God's. She justifies her questioning by saying that the answers will help her to lead a better life. If any of us received the kind of visions Julian knew, we would be demanding lots of explanations. At the same time, she is truly overwrought by the question she is asking. She wants to believe that her visionary experience is true. Julian also wants to affirm the enormously attractive theology of no-blame that she has been shown. She is desperate, and prepared to doubt. Clinging with all her strength to a belief that God will give her the answers—and that no one but him could ever address such contradictions—she intellectually prostrates herself before a God who is her teacher. Unknowing is longing for God. Desire for understanding is part of what leads us to divine reason. We are all frustrated in being unable to discern the mind or will of God. The questions we ask—the work of our reason, our doubts—draw us to him.

❧ **51** ❧

*Then our gracious Lord answered in showing very mysteriously a
wonderful illustration of a lord who has a servant, and He gave
insight to my understanding of both of them.*
*(This insight was shown twice in the lord,
and the insight was shown twice in the servant;
then one part was shown spiritually in bodily form,
and the other part was shown more spiritually,
without bodily form.)*

*For the first was thus: I saw two persons in bodily form, that is to
say, a lord and a servant;*
and with this God gave me spiritual understanding.

*The lord sits solemnly in repose and in peace, the servant stands
near, before his lord reverently, ready to do his lord's will. The lord
looks upon his servant most lovingly and sweetly, and humbly he
sends him to a certain place to do his will.*

*The servant not only goes, but he suddenly leaps up and runs in
great haste because of his love to do his lord's will. And immediately
he falls into a deep pit and receives very great injury. Then he groans
and moans and wails and writhes, but he cannot rise up nor help
himself in any way.*

*In all this, the greatest misfortune that I saw him in was the lack
of reassurance, for he could not turn his face to look back upon his
loving lord (who was very near to him and in whom there is complete
comfort), but like a man who was feeble and witless for the moment,
he was intent on his suffering, and waited in woe.*

In this woe he endured seven great pains.
*The first was the painful bruising which he received in his falling,
which was very painful to him.*

The second was the sluggishness of his body.

The third was the weakness resulting from these two.

The fourth, that he was deluded in his reason and stunned in his
  mind to such an extent that he had almost forgotten his own
  love to do his lord's will.

The fifth was that he could not rise up.

The sixth was a most amazing pain to me and that was that he lay
  alone—I looked all about and watched, and neither far nor
  near, high nor low, did I see any help for him.

The seventh was that the place in which he lay was a huge, hard,
  and painful one.

I wondered how this servant could humbly endure there all this
woe. And I watched deliberately to see if I could discover any failure
in him, or if the lord would allot him any blame, and truly there was
none seen—for only his good will and his great desire were the cause
of his falling, and he was as willing and as good inwardly as when he
stood before his lord ready to do his will.

And in the same way his loving lord constantly watched him most
tenderly;
  and now with a twofold attitude:
    one outward, most humbly and gently with great
      compassion and pity
      (and this was from the first level of the showing);
    another inward, more spiritual, and this was shown with a
      guiding of my understanding to the lord, and by this guiding,
      I saw him greatly rejoice, because of the honorable repose
      and nobility that he wills and shall bring his servant to by
      his plenteous grace
    (and this was from that other level of the showing)
  and now my understanding led back to the first part of the
    showing, keeping both in mind.

Then says this gracious lord in his meaning: "Behold, behold, my
beloved servant! What harm and distress he has received in my service
for my love, yea, and because of his good will! Is it not reasonable
that I reward him for his fright and his dread, his hurt and his wounds
and all his woe? And not only this, but does it not fall to me to give a gift
that is to him better and more honorable than his own health would have been?
Otherwise it seems to me I would be doing him no favor."

*In this an inward, spiritual showing of the lord's meaning settled
into my soul, in which I saw that it was fitting and necessary—
seeing his great goodness and his own honor—that his dearworthy
servant whom he loved so much would be truly and blessedly
rewarded without end beyond what he would have been if he had
not fallen. Yea, and to such an extent that his falling and all the
woe that he had received from it would be transformed into high
and surpassing honor and endless bliss.*

*At this point the showing of this illustration vanished, and our good Lord
directed my understanding onwards in vision and in showing
the rest of the revelations to the end.*

*But notwithstanding all this diversion, the wonder of the illustration
never went from me; for it seemed to me it was given me as an answer
to my desire, and yet I could not perceive in it a full interpretation
for my comfort at that time.*
*In the servant (who symbolized Adam, as I shall say) I saw
many varied characteristics which could by no means be
attributed to individual Adam.*

*And so at that time I remained much in ignorance, because the full
interpretation of this wondrous illustration was not given me at that
time. In this mysterious illustration the secrets of the revelation are
still much hidden, and nevertheless I saw and understood that every
showing is full of secrets, and therefore it behooves me now to tell
three aspects by which I am somewhat eased.*
*The first is the beginning of the teaching which I understood in the
showing at that original time;*
the second is the inner teaching which I have understood in it since then;
*the third, all the whole revelation from the beginning to the end
(that is to say, concerning this book)
which our Lord God of His goodness frequently brings freely to
the sight of my understanding.*

*And these three are so united, as I understand it, that I do not know
how to, nor am I able to divide them.*
*From this three-in-one I gain teaching by which I ought to believe
and trust in our Lord God:
that of the same goodness with which He showed it and for the
same purpose,*

just so of that same goodness and for that same purpose He will
explain it to us when that is His will.

Twenty years after the time of the showing (short three months) I
received inner teaching, as I shall say:
"It is right for thee to take heed to all the qualities and conditions
that were shown in the illustration even though thou thinkest that
they are obscure and uninteresting to your sight."
I assented willingly with great desire, looking inwardly with deliberation
at all the points and aspects that were shown at the previous time,
to as great an extent as my wit and understanding would serve—
beginning with my looking at the lord and at the servant,
and the lord's manner of sitting,
and the place that he sat on,
and the color of his clothing and the kind of style,
and his outward expression,
and his nobility and his goodness within;

at the servant's manner of standing
and the place where and how,
at his manner of clothing, the color and the style,
at his outward behavior
and at his inward goodness and his willingness.

The lord that sat solemnly in repose and in peace,
I interpreted that he is God.
The servant that stood before the lord,
I interpreted that he symbolized Adam
(that is to say, one man was shown at that time, and his falling,
to make it thereby to be understood how God looks upon a man
and his falling, for in the sight of God all mankind is one man
and one man is all mankind).
This man was damaged in his strength, and made completely feeble,
and he was stunned in his understanding, for he turned away
from the gaze of his lord.
But his will was kept wholly in God's sight—for I saw our Lord
commend and approve his will
(however, he himself was prevented and blinded from the
knowledge of this will, and this is great sorrow and painful upset
to him;

for he neither sees clearly his loving lord [who is most humble
and gentle to him] nor sees truly what he himself is in the
sight of that loving lord).

And well I knew,
  when these two elements—the knowledge of self and the knowledge
          of our Lord—are wisely and truly perceived,
  we shall get rest and peace here in part,
  and the fullness of the bliss of heaven, by His plenteous grace.

(This was a beginning of teaching which I saw at that same time
by which I could come to recognize how He looks upon us in our
sin. And at that time I saw
  that pain alone blames and punishes,
  but our gracious Lord comforts and succors,
  and He is always of glad disposition to the soul,
  loving and yearning to bring us to bliss.)

The place that our Lord sat on was humble, on the barren and
desert earth, alone in wilderness. His clothing was wide and long,
and most befitting as becomes a lord. The color of his clothing was
blue as azure, most grave and fair. His countenance was merciful,
the color of his face was light brown with well-shaped features. His
eyes were black, most fair and fitting, showing full of loving pity.
And within him was a lofty sanctuary, long and broad, all full of
eternal heavenliness. And the loving gaze with which he looked upon
his servant constantly (and especially when he fell) it seemed to me
could melt our hearts for love, and burst them in two for joy.

This beautiful gazing appeared a fitting mixture which was wondrous
to see:
  one part was compassion and pity,
  the other was joy and bliss.
      (The joy and bliss surpassed as far the compassion and pity as
      heaven is above earth.)
      The pity was earthly and the bliss was heavenly.

  The compassion and the pity of the Father was for the falling of Adam,
      who is His most beloved creation.

  The joy and bliss were for the falling of His dearworthy Son,
      who is equal with the Father.

(The merciful vision of His lovely face filled all earth and
descended down with Adam into hell,
and with this constant pity Adam was preserved from
endless death.
And this mercy and pity dwell with mankind until the time
we come up into heaven.)

But Man is blinded in this life,
and therefore we cannot see our Father God as He is.

And whenever He of His goodness wills to show Himself to Man,
He shows Himself humbly as man.
(notwithstanding that, I understood truly we ought to know and
believe that the Father is not man).

And His sitting on the bare earth and desert is to mean this—
He made Man's soul to be His own City and His dwelling place
(which is the most pleasing to Him of all His works),
and whenever man had fallen into sorrow and pain he was not
wholly fit to serve in that noble position;
and therefore our kind Father rather than give Himself any other
space, sits upon the earth, awaiting mankind
(who are muddled with earth)
until whenever by His grace His dearworthy Son had brought
again His City into its noble beauty with His harsh labor.

The blueness of His clothing symbolizes His steadfastness.
The brownness of His fair face with the fitting blackness of the
eyes was most agreeable to show His holy gravity.
The breadth of His clothing which was beautiful and flamboyant,
symbolizes that He has enclosed within Himself all heavens
and all joy and bliss.

(And this was shown in one stroke where I say "my understanding
was guided to the Lord." In this guiding I saw Him highly
rejoicing because of the honorable restoration that He wills and
shall bring His servant to by His plenteous grace.)

And still I wondered, examining the lord and the servant as I said before.
I saw the lord sit solemnly and the servant standing reverently before his lord.

In the servant there is a double meaning:

one outward,
another inward.

>*Outwardly, he was clad humbly as a workman who was used to hard*
>>*labor, and he stood very near the lord (not right in front*
>>*of him, but partly aside on the left). His clothing was a*
>>*white tunic, thin, old and all soiled, stained with sweat of*
>>*his body, tight fitting for him and short, as it were but a*
>>*hand's width below the knee, undecorated, seeming as if it*
>>*would soon be worn out, about to be turned to rags*
>>*and torn.*

>>*And in this I marveled greatly, thinking: "This is now*
>>*unfitting clothing for the servant that is so highly loved to*
>>*stand before so dignified a lord."*

>*But inwardly, in the servant was shown a foundation of love*
>>*which he had for the lord which was equal to the love that*
>>*the lord had for him. The wisdom of the servant saw*
>>*inwardly that there was one thing to do which would be to*
>>*the honor of the lord. And the servant, for love, having no*
>>*regard for himself nor to anything that might befall him,*
>>*hastily leaped up and ran at the bidding of his lord to do*
>>*that thing which was the lord's will and his honor.*

For it seemed by his outward clothing that he had been a regular
>*workman for a long time;*

and by the insight that I had (both in the lord and in the servant), it
>*seemed that he was new, that is to say, newly beginning to*
>*labor—as a servant who had never been sent out before.*

There was a treasure in the earth which the lord loved. I marveled
and imagined what it could be.

>*And I was answered in my understanding: "It is a good which is*
>*lovely and pleasant to the lord."*

>>*(For I saw the lord sit as a man, but I saw neither food nor*
>>*drink wherewith to serve him; that was a wonder.*
>>*Another wonder was that this solemn lord had no servant but*
>>*one, and him he sent out.)*

I watched,
>*wondering what kind of work it might be*
>*that the servant would do.*

Then I understood that he would do the greatest work and hardest
toil that is—he would be a gardener;
digging and ditching,
straining and sweating,
and turning over the earth,
and seeking the depths,
and watering the plants on time.
And in this he would continue his labor
and make sweet streams to run,
and noble and plenteous fruits to spring, which he would bring
before the lord and serve him therewith to his delight.

And he would never return until he had prepared this food all ready
as he knew that it delighted the lord, and then he would take this
food with the drink, and bear it most honorably before the lord.

And all this time the lord would sit in the same place awaiting his
servant whom he sent out.

(I still wondered from whence the servant came, for I saw that
the lord had within himself endless life and all kinds of goodness,
except that treasure that was on the earth—and that was grounded
in the lord in wondrous depth of endless love [but it was not wholly
to his honor until this servant had dug it thus nobly and brought it
before him, in himself present]. And except for the lord there was
nothing but wilderness. And I did not understand all that this
illustration meant, and therefore I wondered whence the servant came.)

In the servant is included the Second Person in the Trinity,
and also in the servant is included Adam, that is to say, all men.
(And therefore, when I say "the Son," it means the Godhead
which is equal with the Father, and when I say "the servant," it
means Christ's manhood which is true Adam.)

By the nearness of the servant is understood the Son, and by the
standing on the left side is understood Adam.

The lord is the Father, God.
The servant is the Son, Christ Jesus.
The Holy Spirit is equal Love who is in Them both.

When Adam fell, God's Son fell—

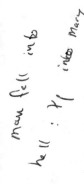

because of the true union which was made in heaven,
God's Son could not be separated from Adam
  (for by "Adam" I understand "all men").
Adam fell from life to death into the pit of this miserable world
  and after that into hell.
God's Son fell with Adam into the pit of the womb of the Maiden
  (who was the fairest daughter of Adam) and that in order
    to obtain for Adam exemption from guilt in heaven and on
    earth. And he mightily fetched Adam out of hell.

By the wisdom and goodness that was in the servant is understood
  God's Son.
By the poor clothing as a workman standing near the left side is
  understood the manhood of Adam, with all the misfortune and
  weakness that follow from that—
    for in all this our Good Lord showed His own Son and Adam as
    but one man.

The virtue and the goodness that we have is from Jesus Christ, the
weakness and the blindness that we have is from Adam—both of
which were shown in the servant.

And thus has our good Lord Jesus taken upon Himself all our guilt;
and therefore our Father can, and will, no more assign blame to us
than to
  His own Son, dearworthy Christ.

In this way He was the servant before His coming onto the earth,
    standing ready before the Father intentionally until whatever
    time the Father would send Him to do that honorable deed by
    which mankind was brought again into heaven—that is to say,
    notwithstanding that He is God (equal with the Father as
    concerns the Godhead) in His foreseeing purpose He was
    willing to be man to save man by fulfilling His Father's will.

So He stood before His Father as a servant, willingly taking upon
  Himself all our burden.
And then He leaped up wholly ready at the Father's will,
and soon He fell most lowly into the Maiden's womb, having no
  regard for Himself nor for His harsh pains.

The white tunic is His flesh;
> *its thinness is that there was absolutely nothing separating the*
>> *Godhead and manhood;*
> *the tightness of the tunic is poverty;*
> *the age is from Adam's wearing it;*
> *the staining of sweat, from Adam's toil;*
> *the shortness shows the servant's work.*

And thus I saw the Son standing, saying in His meaning,
> *"Behold, my dear Father, I stand before Thee in Adam's tunic all*
> *ready to jump up and to run. I am willing to be on the earth to do Thine*
> *honor when it is Thy will to send me. How long shall I wish for it?"*
>> *(Most truly was the Son aware when it was the Father's will*
>> *and how long He would wish for it—that is to say, from the*
>> *point of view of His Godhead, for He is the Wisdom of the Father.)*

Therefore this meaning was shown in understanding about the manhood
> *of Christ:*
>> *all mankind that shall be saved by the sweet incarnation and*
>>> *blissful Passion of Christ, all is the manhood of Christ,*
>> *for He is the Head*
>> *and we are His members*
>>> *(to which members the day and the time is unknown when*
>>> *every passing woe and sorrow shall have an end, and the*
>>> *everlasting joy and bliss shall be fulfilled—which day and*
>>> *time, all the company of heaven yearns to see).*

All who are under heaven who shall come to heaven, their way is by
yearning and desire.
> *This desire and yearning was shown in the servant standing before the lord*
> *(or else thus, in the Son's standing before the Father in Adam's tunic),*
for the yearning and desire of all mankind that shall be saved was
manifested in Jesus
> *(for Jesus is all that shall be saved*
> *and all that shall be saved is Jesus),*
and all from the love of God, with obedience, meekness and patience,
and virtues that belong to us.

Also in this marvelous illustration I receive a teaching within me
> *(as it were the beginning of an ABC)*
> *whereby I can have some understanding of our Lord's meaning,*

> because the secrets of the revelation are hidden in this
> illustration (notwithstanding that all the showings are full of
> secrets).

The sitting of the Father symbolizes His Godhead
> *(that is to say, in order to show repose and peace,*
> *for in the Godhead can be no toil).*
And that He showed Himself as lord symbolizes our manhood.
The standing of the servant symbolizes labor.
That he stands on the side and on the left symbolizes that he was not
> *fully worthy to stand directly before the lord.*
His leaping up was the Godhead,
> *and the running was the manhood*
>> *(for the Godhead leaps from the Father into the Maiden's womb,*
>> *descending into the taking of our human nature; and in this*
>> *falling He received great injury; the injury that He received was*
>> *our flesh in which He also soon had powerful experiences of*
>> *mortal pains).*

By the fact that He stood fearfully before the lord, and not directly so,
>> *indicates that His clothing was not respectable enough to*
>> *stand directly before the lord, and that could not, or would not,*
>> *be His position while He was a workman.*
> *And also He could not sit in repose and peace with the lord until*
> *He had won His peace properly with His harsh toil.*
By the left side symbolizes that the Father left His own Son willingly
>> *in the manhood to suffer all man's pains without sparing Himself.*
By the fact that His tunic was at the point of being turned to rags
>> *and torn is understood the stripes and the scourges,*
> *the thorns and the nails,*
> *the pulling and the dragging,*
> *His tender flesh tearing*
>> *(as I saw to some degree, the flesh was torn from the skull,*
>> *falling in shreds until the time the bleeding stopped; and then*
>> *the flesh began to dry again, clinging to the bone).*

And by the wallowing and writhing, groaning and moaning, is understood
>> *that He could never rise omnipotently from the time that He was*
>> *fallen into the Maiden's womb until His body was slain and dead,*
>> *He yielding His soul into the Father's hands along with all*
>> *mankind for whom He was sent.*

And at this point of rising He began first to show His power, for
He went into hell, and when He was there He raised up out of the
deep darkness the Great Root of Jesse which properly was knit to
Him in high heaven.

The body was in the grave until Easter morning, and from that
time on He lay down never more.

Then was rightfully ended the wallowing and the writhing, the
groaning and the moaning; and our foul mortal flesh that God's
Son took upon Himself

    (which was Adam's old tunic, tight, bare, and short)

then by our Savior was made fair, new, white, and bright, and of
endless purity, wide and long, fairer and richer than was then the
clothing which I saw on the Father,

    for that clothing was blue,
    and Christ's clothing is now of a light, becoming
    mixture which is so wonderful that I cannot
    describe it, for it is all of true glory.

No longer does the Lord sit on the ground in wilderness, but now He sits on His
    noblest throne which He made in heaven most to His pleasure.

No longer stands the Son before the Father as a servant fearfully
    plainly clad, in part naked, but now He stands before the Father
    directly, richly clad in blessed ampleness, with a crown upon His
    Head of precious richness

(for it was shown that we are His crown,
which crown is the Father's joy,
    the Son's honor,
    the Holy Spirit's pleasure,
    and endless marvelous bliss to all that are in heaven).

Now the Son does not stand before the Father on the left side as a workman,
    but He sits on His Father's right hand in endless repose and peace.
    (But it is not meant that the Son sits on the right hand, side by side,
    as one man sits by another in this life; for there is no such sitting,
    as to my sight, in the Trinity for He sits on His Father's right hand,
    that is to say, in the highest nobility of the Father's joys.)

Now is the Spouse, God's Son, in peace with His beloved Wife,
    which is Holy Church, the Fair Maiden of endless joy.

Now sits the Son, true God and Man, in repose and peace in His City,
which His Father has devoted to Him out of His endless purpose,
and the Father is in the Son,
and the Holy Spirit in the Father and in the Son.

Julian gets the answers she is looking for. God says yes, and she receives a showing. Julian recounts a parable of the fall of Adam, who loses sight of God. Humanity fell for the desire for knowledge—what Julian seeks in her understanding. After the fall, humanity is no worse inwardly than ever. God rejoices in being able to return humanity to the harmony of inward and outward wholeness. God celebrates being able to give a gift greater than what humanity knew before the fall. Julian goes on to articulate a trinity of knowledge: what she literally knew at the time of her showings, the meaning that unfolded in her twenty years of reflection on them, and the overall significance of her entire experience, "concerning this book." They are as united rhetorically in her experience as the Trinity is in her understanding of God. At that later date something moved Julian to consider more deeply the details of what she had been shown. The rest of Chapter 51 proceeds with a detailed parsing of that single showing. Here Adam is described as "stunned in his understanding," his gaze turned away from God. Adam, like Julian years hence, can no longer see as clearly as at the moment of experience. Julian receives a wake-up call to return, to revisit the insight she had known. As she recalls the showing, she chronicles God's compassion and pity for humanity, his joy and bliss for his incarnate self in Christ. God is with us through all our falling, at both the individual and archetypal, cosmic levels. We are blocked from this awareness in our limited vision.

God is ever in the midst of us, in the material of earth. The creator is distinct from the creature, but the creator dwells in all Created Thing. God the creator chooses to dwell in all creation, not separate from it. God awaits us in our flesh. The service of God to matter, and matter to God, is joyous to both. This occurs not at the highest but in the humblest, most concrete manifestations of creation. Creation loves the creator as the creator loves creation. That is the inward reality, no matter the outer appearances. Creation serves the creator; creation nourishes the creator. Creation is always a new creation, ever unfolding new life and being out of its self. All is set before the creator for his delight. Creation includes

Jesus the Christ as much as all of humanity. Jesus cannot be separated from Adam. By this act of creation God can no more blame Adam, or us for our sins, than he can blame himself—his Son, Jesus the Christ. In the Incarnation the distinctions between creator and creation are blurred. All humanity is the humanity of Christ. Desire for union is manifested in Jesus: He is our longing for oneness with the creator.

Julian is at peace here in a way she was not at the time of the events of Chapter 50. Julian can say with confidence that with the same goodness that God gave her the showings, she trusts that God explains them at the right time. Julian was awakened two decades after her visions to pay attention to their meaning, even the parts that might seem obscure and uninteresting. She performed the difficult task of listening. What do we need to examine in our lives, no matter how long ago? What do we need to look for? How has God acted there, in what ways has God moved? We should not pass anything over because it seems minor or lacking an easy explanation. We must leave no stone unturned in self-reflection. Often this means going into the hurt places, the forgotten spaces, to see what they have to teach us. God wants to bring us there.

⚛ **52** ☙

Thus I saw that
　God rejoices that He is our Father,
　God rejoices that He is our Mother, and
　God rejoices that He is our true Spouse and that our soul is His
　　beloved wife.
　And Christ rejoices that He is our Brother,
　and Jesus rejoices that He is our Savior.

These are five high joys, as I understand, in which He wishes that we rejoice:
praising Him, thanking Him, loving Him, endlessly blessing Him.

All we who shall be saved, for the period of this life, have in us a
wondrous mixture both of well and woe:
　we have in us our Lord Jesus arisen;
　we have in us the misery of the misfortune of Adam's falling.

　Dying, we are steadfastly protected by Christ, and by His gracious
　　　　touching we are raised in certain trust of salvation.
　And by Adam's falling we are so fragmented in our feeling in
　　　　differing ways (by sins and by various pains, in which we are
　　　　made sad and blind as well) that scarcely do we know how to
　　　　obtain any comfort.

　But in our intention we await God and faithfully trust to receive
　　mercy and grace;
　and this is His own working in us.

Of His goodness He opens the eye of our understanding by which we have in-
sight—sometime more and sometime less—as God gives us ability to receive it.

And now we are raised into one, and again we are allowed to fall into the other.

And thus is this mixture so wondrous in us that scarcely do we know
about ourselves or about our fellow Christians how we hold out,
because of the wonderment of these different feelings—

> *except for that same holy assent that we consent to God when we*
> *sense Him, truly willing to be with Him with all our heart, with all*
> *our soul, and with all our strength.*

> *And then we hate and despise our evil stirrings and all that might*
> *be occasion of sin, spiritually and bodily.*

> *And yet nevertheless when this sweetness is hidden, we fall again*
> *into blindness, and so into woe and tribulation in diverse ways.*

But then this is our comfort:

> *that we know in our faith that by the strength of Christ, who is our*
> *protector, we never consent to sin, but we rail against it, and*
> *endure in pain and woe, praying until that time when He shows*
> *Himself again to us.*

And thus we remain in this muddle all the days of our lives.

But He wills that we trust that He is everlastingly with us, and that
in three ways:

> *He is with us in heaven, true man in His own Person drawing us*
> *upward (and that was shown in the spiritual thirst);*
> *and He is with us on earth, leading us (and that was shown in the*
> *third showing, where I saw God in a point);*
> *and He is with us in our soul eternally dwelling, ruling and taking care*
> *of us*
> > *(and that was shown in the sixteenth showing, as I shall say).*

Thus in the servant was shown the misfortune and blindness of Adam's falling,
and in the servant was also shown the wisdom and goodness of God's Son.

In the lord was shown the compassion and pity for Adam's woe;
and in the lord was also shown the high nobility and the endless
> *honor that mankind has come to by virtue of the Passion and the*
> *death of His dearworthy Son.*

> *Therefore He powerfully rejoices in Adam's falling, because of the*
> *noble raising and fullness of bliss that mankind has come to,*
> *surpassing what we would have had if Adam had not fallen.*

*And thus in order to see this surpassing nobility my understanding
was led to God at the same time that I saw the servant fall.*

And so we have now cause for mourning,
　　　for our sin is the cause of Christ's pains;
and we have everlastingly cause for joy,
　　　for endless love caused Him to suffer.

*Therefore the creature who sees and senses the working of love by
grace hates nothing but sin;*
　　　*for of all things, as I see it, love and hate are the most unyielding
　　　and most immoderate opposites.*

*Notwithstanding all this, I saw and understood in our Lord's purpose
　　　　　that we cannot in this life keep us from sin as totally in complete
　　　　　purity as we shall in heaven.*
　　*But by grace we can well keep ourselves from the sins which
　　　　　　would lead us to endless pain (as Holy Church teaches us) and
　　　　　　avoid the venial ones, reasonably within our power;*
　　and, if at any time we fall by our blindness and our misery,
　　　　that we can readily arise,
　　　　knowing the sweet touching of grace, and
　　　　*willingly amend ourselves following the teaching of Holy Church
　　　　　　according to the sin's gravity,*
　　　　and go forthwith to God in love.

*Neither on the one hand fall overly low, inclining to despair,
nor on the other hand be over reckless as if we gave no heed,*
　　but humbly knowing our weakness,
　　*aware that we cannot stand even a twinkling of an eye except by
　　　　the protection of grace,*
　　and reverently cleaving to God,
　　trusting in Him alone.

*For one way is God's point of view,
and the other way is man's point of view;*
　　for it belongs to man humbly to accuse himself,
　　*and it belongs to the excellent goodness of our Lord God graciously
　　　　to forgive man.*

*These are two parts that were shown in the double attitude in which
the lord viewed the falling of his beloved servant.*

*The one was shown outward, very humbly and gently, with great
     compassion and pity,
and the other of inward endless love.*
*And just so wills our Lord that we accuse ourselves,
     willingly and truly seeing and recognizing
     our falling and all the harms that come therefrom,
          understanding and being aware that we can never
          reinstate it,
     and along with that that we also willingly and truly recognize and
     acknowledge
          His everlasting love that He has for us, and His plenteous mercy.*

*Thus graciously to recognize and acknowledge both together is the gentle self-
accusing that our Lord asks of us, and He Himself does it wherever it happens.*

*This is the lower part of man's life and it was shown in the outward
expression, in which showing I saw two parts:
     the one is the pitiful falling man,
     the other is the honorable amends that our Lord has made for man.*

*The other expression was shown inwardly, and that was more exalted
and all the same;
     for the life and the strength that we have in the lower part is from
     the higher, and it comes down to us from the self's natural love by grace.*

*There is absolutely nothing separating the one and the other, for it is all one
     love.*

*This blessed love has now in us a double action:
     for in the lower part are
          pains and sufferings,
          compassions and pities,
          mercies and forgiveness
          and such other things that are beneficial,
     but in the higher part are none of these, except the same high love
               and overwhelming joy, in which overwhelming joy all pains
               are wholly destroyed.*

*In this our good Lord showed not only our excusing, but also the honorable
     nobility
               that He shall bring us to, transforming all our guilt into endless honor.*

ဢ   ဢ   ဢ

Julian rejoices wholeheartedly at what God has to offer and grieves at the fact that it is not available all the time. We project our human understanding onto God, our desire for relationship, which is only fitting, given how we know him. Our outer selves seek the completion we cannot achieve in this world. Our inner selves rest in him, but we rarely glimpse that peace. It is natural that Julian articulates God's joy in his relationship with us using human paradigms: father, mother, beloved spouse, brother, savior. It would be limiting to understand God through the metaphor of any one of those relationships. It can be limiting to attempt to describe him through all those human ways of knowing the Other. Julian's litany of the range of ways we know God creates the permutations of our experience of him. They could expand into the infinite, which is exactly what she wishes to convey. The advantage of speaking of God's joy in us through an array of human relationships is that it teaches us to seek him in those same relationships we have with our fellow human beings. God wants us to rejoice in them. They are the source of our healing—the closure of the wounds that separate us from God and from one another—and they are also the means for us to know God.

We vacillate and suffer when we are limited in our knowledge of God. We may seek him in our understanding, as Julian does through questions, but we may not always find him there. When we apply that same dialectic of desire to our human relationships—where might we find him, what "questions" need "answers"—we find ourselves on the journey. Sometimes our separation is healed by abstractions; other times we need to move into our experience of relating to creation around us to heal the rift between creator and creature. While we await God, he "opens the eye of our understanding by which we have insight—sometimes more and sometimes less." We don't have outward control of what we receive from God. We rarely see our own blocks to him and "we remain in this muddle all the days of our lives." Julian's human images of God's love can help us out of that mud. They remind us that God is always with us, if not in one form then in another. When we cannot discern God's will we have to look for it in another human being, not in the abstraction of our solitary journey with God. When we cannot see our way to God, we need to let others see us as we are and be our eyes. The same trust applies to our relationship with God. God wills that we both recognize his joy in us and turn our outer ways toward him. To say we are without blame does not mean we are perfect. Rather, we acknowledge that we are being perfected. We are part of all being made well. Our best human relationships guide us to healing wounds—our own and those of others. The relationships that awaken us as Julian was awakened to the work of mercy and grace outside and inside ourselves are vehicles for the repair of the world.

⚝ **53** ⚝

I saw that He wishes us to be aware that He does not take the falling of any
  creature
that shall be saved more severely than He took the falling of Adam
      (who we know was endlessly loved and safely protected in the
      time of all his need, and now is blissfully restored in high,
      surpassing joys)
for our Lord God is so good, so gentle, and so gracious that He can
never assign fault to those in whom He shall ever be blessed and praised.

And in this that I have now said my desire was in part answered, and
my great fear somewhat eased by the loving, gracious showing of our
Good Lord.
    In this showing I saw and understood full certainly that in every
    soul that shall be saved is a divine will that never consents to sin,
    nor ever will.

      This will is so good that it can never will evil, but evermore
      continually it wills good and does good in the sight of God.

Therefore our Lord wishes that we recognize this
    in the Faith and the Belief of the Church
    and specifically and truly that we have all this blessed will whole
        and safe in our Lord Jesus Christ,
    for that kind of human nature with which heaven shall be filled
    ought properly, by God's righteousness, to be so knit and one-ed to
    Him that in that human nature is guarded an essence which can
    never be (nor should be) parted from Him—and that through His
    own good will in His endless foreseeing purpose.

Notwithstanding this rightful knitting and this eternal one-ing, still
    the redemption and the buying back of mankind is necessary and
    beneficial in every instance,

since it is done for the same intention and to the same end that
Holy Church in our Faith teaches us.

I saw that God never started to love mankind,
   for just as mankind shall be in endless bliss fulfilling the joy of God
     as regards His works,
   just so the same mankind has been, in the foresight of God, known
     and loved from without beginning in His rightful intention.

By the endless intention and consent of the full agreement of all the Trinity,
   the Mid-Person wished to be ground and head of this fair human nature,
     out of Whom we are all come,
     in Whom we are all enclosed,
     into Whom we shall all go,
     in Him finding our full heaven in everlasting joy
       by the foreseeing purpose of all the blessed Trinity
       from without beginning.

Before ever He made us, He loved us,
and when we were created we loved Him.
   And this is a love created
     by the natural essential Goodness of the Holy Spirit,
     mighty by reason of the Power of the Father,
     and wise in reminder of the Wisdom of the Son,
       and thus is man's soul made by God
       and at the same moment knit to God.

Thus I understand that man's soul is created out of nothing—that is to say
   it is created, but out of nothing that has been created, like this:
when God wished to create man's body,
   He took the slime of earth
     (which is material mixed and gathered for all physical creatures)
   and out of that He created man's body.
But for the creating of man's soul,
   He willed to take absolutely nothing,
   but He created it.

And thus is the human nature created rightfully one-ed to the Creator—
   who is Essential Nature uncreated:
   that is, God.
And therefore it is that there can, and will be, absolutely nothing
separating God and man's soul.

In this endless love man's soul is kept whole
* as the matter of the revelations means and shows;*
In this endless love we are led and protected by God
*   and never shall be lost,*
*   for He wishes us to be aware*
*   that our soul has a life which*
*   of His goodness and His grace,*
*   shall last in heaven without end,*
*   loving Him,*
*   thanking Him,*
*   praising Him.*
And just as we shall exist without end,
so too we were treasured in God,
*   and hidden,*
*   known,*
*   and loved from without beginning.*

Wherefore He wishes us to be aware
*   that the noblest being that ever He made is mankind*
*   (and the fullest essence*
*   and the highest virtue*
*   is the blessed soul of Christ).*

Furthermore He wishes us to be aware that mankind's dearworthy
soul was preciously knit to Him in the creation—
*   and this knot is delicate and so powerful that it is one-ed into God.*
*   In this one-ing it is made endlessly holy.*

Furthermore, He wishes us to be aware that all the souls that shall
be saved in heaven without end
*   are knit and one-ed in this one-ing,*
*   and made holy in this holiness.*

ɞ ɞ ɞ

God takes no human fall any more seriously than the fall of Adam. We rarely think of our personal falls from grace in the same league as that. Just as Jesus' saving action set right Adam's fall, so too is every act of salvation accomplished by Christ as singular and significant for each human being as it was for Adam. All life matters. We are all Adams. The subject of inclusion and radical welcome infuses Chapter 53. Julian's glimpse of salvation allows her to assert that in every soul to be saved there is a divine will that never consents to sin. The outer self may experience separation, "sin." The inner self, the soul, is so joined with God that it can never be separated from Him. Nothing can separate us from the love of God. God never started to love humankind: there is no beginning of God's love for humanity. Julian calls God "essential nature uncreated"— we humans are knit (a sensory verb to describe an immaterial process) to God because God made our souls out of nothing material. Despite Julian's focus on soul, the body does not go missing. Chapter 53 celebrates individual humans' and collective humanity's union with the divine from whom it is impossible to be separate. At the same time, Julian suggests that some humans are separate; not everyone will be saved. If nothing can separate us from the love of God, what might be the stumbling blocks to our salvation? We could belabor the limits to God's salvation according to the historical Julian and her theology. Earlier chapters suggest that there is no outside to God: all creation is enclosed in him. How "all shall be well" in this phenomenon puzzles Julian. It is one of the secrets she must wait to learn in heaven.

What are the blocks to our salvation? What sorts of things get in the way of our relationship between soul and God? These could be among the holiest and most dutiful of our priorities. What are the limits to our inclusion? Who do we think ought to be in our own personal kingdom of God? This can be literal, in the sense of the people we expect to see in heaven, as well as figurative—what are the limits to our welcome? The knitted garment of one-ing is God's hospitality. Are our limitations to who is welcome in our personal kingdom blocking our salvation—are they unraveling the knot of our individual soul's one-ness with God? Are our blind spots really our falls requiring redemption and healing?

∞ **54** ∞

Because of the great endless love that God has toward all mankind,
He makes no distinction in love between
the blessed soul of Christ
and the least souls that shall be saved.

It is very easy to believe and to trust that the dwelling of the blessed
soul of Christ is utterly high in the glorious Godhead,
but truly, as I understand in our Lord's meaning,
where the blessed soul of Christ is,
there is the essence of all the souls
that shall be saved within Christ.

We ought highly to rejoice that God dwells in our soul, and much
more highly to rejoice that our soul dwells in God.
Our soul is created to be God's dwelling place, and the dwelling
place of the soul is God, who is uncreated.

It is an exalted understanding inwardly to see and to know
that God who is our Creator dwells in our soul,
and it is a more exalted understanding inwardly to see and to know
that our soul, which is created,
dwells in God's essence—
from which essence, by God,
we are what we are.

I saw no difference between God and our essence,
but just as if it were all God,
and yet my understanding accepted that our essence is in God—that
is to say, that God is God, and our essence is a creation of God.

The all Powerful truth of the Trinity is our Father, for He created us
and keeps us within Him;

and the deep Wisdom of the Trinity is our Mother in whom we are
      all enclosed;
the exalted Goodness of the Trinity is our Lord and in Him we are
      enclosed and He in us.
    We are enclosed in the Father,
    we are enclosed in the Son,
    and we are enclosed in the Holy Spirit;
      and the Father is enclosed in us,
      and the Son is enclosed in us,
      and the Holy Spirit is enclosed in us:
        all Power,
        all Wisdom,
        all Goodness,
        one God,
        one Lord.

And our faith is a virtue that comes
    from our natural essence
    into our fleshly soul by the Holy Spirit,
and within this virtue all our virtues come to us
    (for without that no man may receive virtue).

Faith is nothing else but a right understanding (with true belief and
      certain trust) of our being—
    that we are in God,
    and God in us—
which we do not see.

And this virtue of faith
    (with all others that God has ordained to us coming within it)
works great things in us,
    for Christ's merciful working is in us
      (and we graciously reconciling to Him through the gifts and the
      virtues of the Holy Spirit),
and this working causes us to be Christ's children
and Christian in living.

              ଞ   ଞ   ଞ

There is no distinction between our particular soul and Christ's. This is the work of the Incarnation: God-in-us. All souls are contained in

Christ's soul, in God. We dwell in him as he dwells in us. We have our created being in the essence that is uncreated. There is no difference between our essence and God's. As we are enclosed in him, he is also enclosed in us, in our souls. This is the inner self. This metaphor of enclosure answers Julian's questions. We are enclosed in the Trinity as the Trinity is enclosed in us. Here is unity. Julian describes faith as a virtue coming from natural essence to fleshly soul. These are oxymorons, contradictions in terms. They suit the paradox of enclosure that Julian dwells in and upon. God's essence is to create; it is that which is natural. Faith comes from the Creator as source. Creation is ever enclosed in the Creator; the potentiality of creating resides in him. That essence becomes enclosed in us: it is the soul contained in our material bodies. All material creation, All Created Thing, contains this essence as God contains that potentiality for all creation. Thus divine mind encloses all there is and Julian can assert that faith is "right understanding"—reason. All questions have an answer, even if they cannot be glimpsed easily in this life. We are in God and God is in us even though we cannot see this. The external appearance challenges the interior reality. The Incarnation, Christ's humanity and ours, is the answer to a divine question. We are called to doubt outside circumstances and trust a logic we cannot see. Christ's merciful working—the action of grace—is in us. The Incarnation is contained there as we are the vessels of that potential. Faith is literally working in us; it is dynamic, not static. The body-soul can only be bisected, "crossed," in the Spirit, mercy and grace. In birth, the soul of God gives more life.

We wait in our embodiment for God to answer our questions. Julian's ecstasy—a joy in creation, a celebration of the dialectic—is tangible in her text, as she ones faith and her understanding in the mind of a God who is nothing but Answer. This is prayer: the ongoing dialogue between body and soul, self and God, Incarnation and *Logos*.

⸂ 55 ⸃

Thus Christ is our Way,
  safely leading us in His laws,
and Christ in His Body powerfully bears us up to heaven.

I saw that Christ,
  having in Him all of us who shall be saved by Him,
graciously presents his Father in heaven with us.

And this present most thankfully His Father receives and courteously
gives it to His Son, Jesus Christ.

  This gift and action is joy to the Father
  and bliss to the Son
  and delight to the Holy Spirit.

And of everything that is proper to us,
  it is most delight to our Lord that we rejoice in this joy which is in
  the blessed Trinity because of our salvation.

    (This was seen in the ninth showing
    where it speaks more of this matter.)

Notwithstanding all our feeling, woe or well, God wills that we understand
and believe that we exist more truly in heaven than on earth.

  Our faith comes
    from the natural love of our soul
    and from the clear light of our reason
    and from the steadfast remembrance
      which we have of God in our first creation.

At the time that our soul is breathed into our body (at which time we
    are made fleshly)
also quickly mercy and grace begin to work,
having charge of us and protecting us with pity and love.

In this action the Holy Spirit forms in our faith the hope
> *that we shall come again up to our essence,*
> *into the strength of Christ,*
> *increased and fulfilled through the Holy Spirit.*

Thus I understand that the fleshliness is based in nature,
> *in mercy,*
> *and in grace,*

and this basis enables us to receive gifts which lead us to endless life.

*For I saw most certainly that our essence is in God, and also I saw
that God is in our fleshliness,*
> *for at the self-same moment that our soul is made fleshly,*
> *at the same moment is the City of God established in our soul from
> without beginning.*

Into that City He comes and never shall remove it,
> *for God is never out of the soul*
> *in which He dwells blissfully without end.*

> *(This was seen in the sixteenth showing where it says: "The
> place that Jesus takes in our soul, He shall never remove it.")*

*All the gifts that God can give to creatures He has given to His Son Jesus
for us.*
> *These gifts He, dwelling in us, has enclosed in Himself until the
> time that we are grown and matured,*
> > *our soul with our body*
> > *and our body with our soul*
> > > *(either of them taking help from the other),*
> *until we are brought up in stature as nature works, and then, on
> the basis of human nature*
> > *with the action of mercy,*
> *the Holy Spirit graciously breathes into us the gifts leading to endless
> life.*

Thus was my understanding led by God
> *to perceive in Him and to understand,*
> *to be aware and to know,*
> *that our soul is a "created trinity,"*
> *like to the uncreated blessed Trinity*
> *(known and loved from without beginning)*
> *and in its creation it is joined to the Creator as it is aforesaid.*

This sight was most sweet and wondrous to behold,
            peaceable and restful,
            safe and delightful.

And because of the honorable one-ing that was thus brought about
by God between the soul and body,
        it is inevitable that mankind should be brought back
                from double death.

This bringing back could never be until the time that the Second
                Person in the Trinity had taken the lower part of mankind
                (He to whom the highest part was one-ed in the first creation) and
                        these two parts were in Christ
                        —the higher and the lower—
                        which is but one soul.

            In Christ,
                    the higher part was one in peace with God
                            in full joy and bliss;
                    the lower part, which is fleshly, suffered for
                            the salvation of mankind.

(These two parts were seen and experienced in the eighth
showing, in which my body was filled with the experience
and memory of Christ's passion and His death—and furthermore, with this
was an ethereal feeling and secret
inward vision of the high part that I was shown at that
same time [when I could not on account of the intermediary's suggestion look
up into heaven],
and that was because of the powerful vision of the inner
life, and this inner life is that exalted essence, that
precious soul, which is endlessly rejoicing in the Godhead.)

ಐ   ಐ   ಐ

The Incarnation leads created things back to God. We are contained
in him. Our soul may be enclosed in his soul, but our bodies are also
enclosed in his body. Our true selves, our souls, rest in God. Faith is like
attracting like: the essence that is God-in-us called to oneness. Our reason
is one-ed with divine reason, for in him our understanding knows the
answer. We literally remember God, because he is our origin. The po-

tentiality of creation made manifest in us and one-ed with him in the Incarnation is never forgotten on the soul level, despite the outward circumstances of our lives. In him we have our first creation: that singular experience of oneness that unites All Created Thing. Mercy and grace—the work of the Spirit—operate in our material bodies from their beginnings. These are in charge of us. Thus we hope—we long—for ultimate union with the essence within us. Our incarnation rests in his Incarnation: the potentiality of all creation made manifest through the Spirit dwelling in us and in whom we dwell. As our essence is in God, God is in our bodies. God never leaves our souls. Since our souls reside in our bodies, as long as we live, God never leaves us. What is in Jesus the Christ is in every one of us. We contain him as much as he contains us. The growth of full one-ing, the process of total union, is a ripening. When we are fully completed, the soul returns home to its essence; Godself goes back to God. We exist in relation to God as he exists in relation to us: in the Trinity of God the creator, Jesus the brother who is our true self, and the Spirit's work of mercy and grace leading our soul to its origin.

Julian distinguishes between the higher and lower parts of humanity—the soul versus the body. She does not denigrate the body as much as she celebrates the primacy of the soul. Material creation, the body, is exalted because God does not simply realize his potentiality through individual acts of making. God rests in each specimen of humanity. Our souls are not random manifestations of God; our bodies are not arbitrary objects of creation. Rather, they are one-ed in the experience of incarnation that unifies and enlivens where creator and creature meet. The divine reason nourishes our understanding, inviting us to ask the questions that shine light in our understanding for which Jesus the Christ is the answer. As the Word was with, in, and of God in the beginning, so our souls look back to that origin. It is striking how active—breathing and pulsing—the movement of soul into body is. As if going under water and coming up for air, we return to our beginning. The soaring of Christ's body is our soaring from the depths into the true breath of God, a kiss of the soul. Victorian poet and theologian Christina Rossetti indicts the "sensual Christian" whom she compares to a sea anemone. In the depths it grows and blows—but what shall it do in a world where there is no sea? Lest we ask a similar question when we contemplate our frail human form, Julian assures us that God is in our very fleshliness. So much for gnashing of teeth and rending of garments—so much for detesting these dry bones. We may be "dust" and we may return to "dust," but that dust is infused with the glory of God. For all time, God is rooted there. Our experience of humanity is the ripening. Our pilgrimage here is not for nothing; we could not be ready for the promise of salvation without that "basis of human nature"—visited, once again, by the action of mercy. May we pray and discern how we need to take action—even if it is to keep still.

৬ **56** ৩

Thus I saw most surely
> that it is easier for us to come to the knowledge of God than to
> > know our own soul,
> > for our soul is so profoundly based in God,
> > and so endlessly treasured,
> > that we may not come to the knowledge of it
> > until we first have knowledge of God,
> > who is the Creator to whom it is one-ed.

But, nevertheless, I saw that we have by our human nature a fullness
> > of desire wisely and truly to know our own soul,
> > and by this desire we are taught to seek our soul where it is,
> > and that is in God.

Thus by the gracious leading of the Holy Spirit,
> > we must know them both in one,
> > > whether we are stirred to know God or our soul.
Both stirrings are good and true.
God is nearer to us than our own soul,
> > because He is the foundation on which our soul stands
> > and He is the means that keeps the essence and the fleshliness
> > > together so that they shall never separate.

For our soul sits in God in true repose,
and our souls stands in God in true strength,
and our soul is naturally rooted in God in endless love.
> > And therefore if we wish to have knowledge of our soul and
> > communion and conversation with it, it behooves us that we search
> > into our Lord God in whom it is enclosed.

> > (And of this enclosing I saw and understood more
> > in the sixteenth showing, as I shall say.)

And regarding our essence, it can rightly be called our soul, and
regarding our fleshliness, it, too, can rightly be called our soul
   (and that is because of the one-ing that it has in God).

The honorable City that our Lord Jesus sits in,
      it is our fleshliness in which He is enclosed;
and our natural essence is enclosed in Jesus with the blessed soul of
      Christ sitting in repose in the Godhead.

I saw most surely that it is inevitable that we must be in yearning and
in penance until the time that we are led so deeply into God that we
honestly and truly know our own soul.

And truly I saw that into this great divine depth our good Lord Himself
   leads us
      in the same love in which He created us,
      and in the same love that He bought us by mercy and grace
         by virtue of his blessed Passion.

Notwithstanding all this,
      we can never come to full knowledge of God
      until we first know clearly our own soul,

      for until the time that the soul is in its full powers,
      we cannot be all fully holy—
         and that is as soon as our fleshliness
         (by the virtue of Christ's Passion)
         is brought up into the essence
            with all the benefits of our tribulation
            that our Lord shall cause us to gain
            by mercy and grace.

I had a partial touching, and it is grounded in nature (that is to say,
         our reason is based in God who is essential nature).
      From this essential nature of God mercy and grace spring and expand
         into us,
            accomplishing all things in completing our joy.

These three are our foundations on which we have our being, our
growth, and our fulfillment—
      for in our human nature we have our life and our being,
      and in mercy and grace we have our growth and our fulfillment.

These are three aspects of one goodness,
and where one works, all work,
in the things which are now proper to us.

God wills that we understand,
desiring with all our heart and all our strength
to have knowledge of these three more and more
until the time that we are fulfilled.
   For fully to know them
   and clearly to see them
   is nothing else but the endless joy and bliss
   that we shall have in heaven
      (which God wills we begin here in knowledge of His love).

For by our reason alone we cannot benefit,
   unless we have memory and love with it equally;
nor can we be saved only with reference to our natural origin that we have
   in God,
   unless we have, coming from the same origin, mercy and grace.

From these three acting all together we receive all our goods;
   the first of which is the good of human nature
      (for in our first creation God gave to us as many good and even
      greater goods than we could receive in our spiritual essence alone,
      but His foreseeing purpose in His endless wisdom willed that we
      be two-fold in our human natures).

            ಬಂ   ಬಂ   ಬಂ

We cannot know our own soul without first knowing God. The God-in-us is so much more "God" than "us" that to know our deepest essence, our truest reality, is to know God. We desire to know our soul; we want to know our deeper self. Julian asserts that in and of that incarnational essence we crave to know our God, but in our humanness we long to discover who we are. What drives us to explore our inner self leads us to know God. This is a statement of profound psychological health. Were we to look for God outside ourselves, we would miss the reality of God-in-us. We would fail to see our particular experience of incarnation, the wisdom and experience that is unique in each of us. That practice leads to bad theology and a distorted spiritual life. We forget who we are; we forget that we have bodies, and we forget that in our souls God already rests. Looking for God outside of us fails to respect the mystery of the Incarnation: we ignore the depth of our union with God, we denigrate our created selves. We must know both God and our souls, that the desires to know ourselves and our God are both worthy. God is nearer to us than our own soul because our soul is built on God. He is our foundation, what holds soul and body together in the mystery of the Incarnation. Since we are enclosed in God, we find our souls when we look to God. Were we able to look directly into our souls, we would see our God there. Through the working of mercy and grace, like Julian, we receive insight in our bodies, minds, and understandings. This enables us to glimpse who we are: to see our souls and to better know God.

The soul is that place where our essence, the Godself-in-us, and the fleshliness are one-ed. Our bodies are enclosed in the incarnating flesh of Jesus as the soul of Christ is in God. Our yearning is for the plain sight of our soul, where God leads us. Julian articulates the trinity of our being as human nature worked upon by mercy and grace. This we know as the Incarnation: the action of the Spirit in the material world. The understanding of our soul, our understanding of God, comes through these three. Reason alone fails; we need the memory of who we truly are—that God is our essence residing in our soul—and love. That love is the action of mercy and grace; mercy and grace are what saves us. These are the goods we receive.

How well do we know our souls? Some of us get there with a conscious awareness of God's guidance; many of us benefit from psychotherapy and spiritual direction. Few of us get to spirituality's treasures without first knowing our baggage, some of it marked by religion's dark side. Psychotherapy and spiritual guidance shy away from too much identification with one another—perhaps for good reason, because it would be unhelpful to put forth one when a person really needs the other. But when we are more fully aware that any of these processes that lead to greater soul-depth inevitably lead us to God—and that, in Julian's words, God is leading us into and through the entire process—a stronger integration can be imagined.

ᛆ **57** ᛒ

Regarding our essence, He made us so noble and so rich that we
*   constantly work His will and His honor.*
*   (When I say "we," it means "men who will be saved"; for truly*
*   I saw that we are what He loves, and we do what He desires*
*   constantly without any ceasing.)*

And from these great riches and from this high nobility, virtues
*   beyond measure come to our soul when it is knit to our body*
*   (in which knitting we are made fleshly).*

Thus in our essence we are complete,
and in our fleshliness we are insufficient.
*   This insufficiency God will restore*
*   and make complete*
*   by the action of mercy and grace*
*   plenteously flowing into us from His own natural goodness.*

So His natural goodness causes mercy and grace to work in us, and the natural
goodness that we have from Him enables us to receive that working of mercy
and grace.

I saw that our human nature is completely within God. In this human nature
*   He makes diversities flowing out of Him to work His will;*
*   nature protects it,*
*   and mercy and grace restore and complete it,*
*   and of these none shall perish.*

For our human nature (which is the higher part) is knit to God in creation; and
God is knit to our human nature (which is the lower part) in the taking of our
flesh.

Thus in Christ our two natures are united,
> *for the Trinity is encompassed in Christ in whom our higher part is*
> > *based and rooted,*
> *and our lower part the Second Person has taken, which human*
> > *nature was first assigned to Him.*

I saw most certainly that all the works God has done, or ever shall do,
were completely known to Him and foreseen from without beginning,
> *and for love He made mankind*
> *and for the same love He Himself was willing to be man.*

The next good that we receive is our Faith in which our benefiting begins;
> *and it comes from the high riches of our natural essence into our*
> > *fleshly soul;*
> *and it is based in us and we in it*
> > *through the natural goodness of God*
> > *by the working of mercy and grace.*

From Faith come all other goods by which we are guided and saved.

The commandments of God come in our Faith
> *(about which we ought to have two kinds of understanding which are:*
> > *His bidding to love them and to keep them; the other is that we*
> > *ought to know His forbiddings in order to hate and to refuse them;*
> *for in these two are all our actions contained).*

Also in our Faith come the Seven Sacraments
> *(each following the other in order as God has ordained them to us)*
and all manner of virtues
> *(for the same virtues that we received from our essence, given to*
> *us in human nature, by the goodness of God, these same virtues,*
> *by the action of mercy, are also given to us in grace, renewed*
> *through the Holy Spirit).*

These virtues and gifts are treasured for us within Jesus Christ,
> > *for at that same time that God knitted Him to our body*
> > *in the Maiden's womb, He assumed our fleshly soul.*
> *In taking this fleshly soul, He, having enclosed us all in Himself,*
> *one-ed our fleshly soul to our essence.*
> *In this one-ing He was complete humanity, for Christ, having knit*
> *unto Himself all men who shall be saved, is Perfect Man.*

Thus Our Lady is our Mother in whom we are all enclosed and out of
  her we are born in Christ
  (for she who is Mother of our Savior is Mother of all who shall be
  saved within our Savior).

And our Savior is our true Mother in whom we are endlessly born
  and never shall come to birth out of Him.

Plenteously and completely and sweetly was this shown
  (and it is spoken of in the first showing where He says that we are
  all enclosed in Him and He is enclosed in us; and it is spoken of in
  the sixteenth showing where it says that He sits in our soul).

It is His delight to reign in our understanding blissfully,
  and to sit in our soul restfully,
  and to dwell in our soul endlessly,
    drawing us all into Him.

In this drawing He wishes that we be His helpers,
  giving Him all our attention,
  learning His lesson,
  keeping His laws,
  desiring that all be done which He does,
  honestly trusting in Him—
    for truly I saw that our essence is in God.

ಬ ಬ ಬ

The completion of our incomplete selves—our outer reality, the
"fleshliness"—is restored by God's "goodness"—the working of mercy
and grace. This does not just happen. We must be ready to receive God's
goodness. Julian asserts that we are able to do so because of the "natural
goodness" we have from him. But surely there are those times when
this goodness is blocked. The Spirit has to work harder to break through,
to make us remember who we are, to call us to return. To God, it is worth
it. God saw everything he would create. Because of love, he made humanity; because of love, he became human. These are profound statements about our being and purpose. We are not here by accident, nor is
the Incarnation some kind of divine rescue. God moved creation, fully
aware of how it would unfold. God made us because of his great love,
and the act of the *Logos*, the work of the Spirit in the world, was fully

intended. Faith is another means of Incarnation: it is part of that continued one-ing. Faith draws creator and creature closer; the essence within us remembers home. Faith is not an act of will but a biological determinism accomplished by God, hardwired into our souls and bodies in the Incarnation. Jesus the Christ is "complete humanity": in him the one-ing of soul and flesh is total.

Mary is our mother because the union of soul and body accomplished through her in Jesus the Christ encloses us all in God. His Incarnation knits together our discrete entities. Thus he mothers us. Hers was the flesh from which he was made, so we are as enclosed in her in our flesh as we are enclosed in God in our soul. We are born in the Christ because of this act of the Incarnation that one-ed us together. Our wounds were healed as the split between body and soul was sealed, as mercy and grace continue this work of realization on an external level. We are endlessly born in the Christ because the Incarnation is ongoing. It is never finished as long as creation exists. We never come to birth out of him because we are always contained in him, in soul and body. We created beings, the entire world, rest in the womb of our mother Jesus. His fleshly body rests in the womb of Mary as his soul rests in God. We are always to be born in the flesh; we are already born in the Spirit, which labors to knit together our sins, our separations. This story of life and birth, enclosure and mothering, is unique to Julian's showings. In it creation is unending parturition. We are never not in Christ's womb. His Incarnation cannot be a single, simple act of giving birth, but is a continuous, permanent act of holding us there in him. We may be birthed into life, but our life in Christ is an ongoing journey back into him. By this incarnate one-ing with him that was done once and for all eternity, that is unchanging for all without end, we received faith literally *in* him. Faith is not something we need to find, or proclaim, or even define abstractly. It just *is*, in Christ's Incarnation, forever calling us to return.

☙ **58** ❧

God, the blessed Trinity (who is everlasting Existence)
  just as He is endless from without beginning,
  just so it was in His endless purpose to create mankind.

This fair human nature was first assigned to His own Son, the Second Person.
  And when He wished, by full accord of all the Trinity,
  He created us all at once,
  and in our creation He knit us and one-ed us to Himself.

By this one-ing we are kept as pure and as noble as we were created.
By the virtue of the same precious one-ing,
    we love our Maker
    and delight Him,
        praising Him,
        and thanking Him,
        and endlessly rejoicing in Him.

And this one-ing is the action which is done constantly in every soul
        that shall be saved
        (which is the divine will in the soul mentioned before).

Thus in our creation,
    God All Power is our natural Father,
    and God All Wisdom is our natural Mother,
    with the Love and the Goodness of the Holy Spirit—
        who is all one God, one Lord.
And in the knitting and in the one-ing,
    He is our most true Spouse,
    and we are His beloved Wife and His fair Maiden.
        With this Wife He is never displeased, for He says:
        "I love thee and thou lovest me,
        and our love shall never be separated in two."

227

I beheld the action of all the blessed Trinity. In that sight I saw and
understood these three aspects:
    the aspect of the Fatherhood,
    the aspect of the Motherhood,
    and the aspect of the Lordhood,
      in one God.

[handwritten margin note: maintain traditional language w/o dominion]

In our Father Almighty we have our protection and our bliss as regards our
    natural essence (which is ours by our creation from without
      beginning);
and in the Second Person, in understanding and wisdom, we have our protection
    as regards our fleshliness, our redeeming and our saving,
  for He is our Mother,
    Brother,
    and Savior.

And in our good Lord the Holy Spirit, we have our rewarding and our
    recompense for our living and our trouble—
    endlessly surpassing all that we desire,
    in His amazing courtesy, from His high plenteous grace.

For all our life is in three.
    In the first, we have our being;
    and in the second, we have our growing;
    and in the third, we have our completing.

The first is nature;
the second is mercy;
the third is grace.

As for the first: I saw and understood that
    the high Power of the Trinity is our Father,
    and the deep Wisdom of the Trinity is our Mother,
    and the great Love of the Trinity is our Lord;
and all this we have in our human nature and in our essential creation.

And furthermore, I saw that the Second Person, who is our Mother
  in essence,
    that same dearworthy Person has become our Mother in flesh.

    For we are two-fold in God's creation: That is to say, essential and fleshly.
    Our essence is the higher part, which we have in our Father,
      God Almighty;

and the Second Person of the Trinity
    is our Mother in human nature in our essential creation. In
       Him we are grounded and rooted,
    and he is our Mother in mercy by taking on our fleshliness.

And thus our Mother is to us various kinds of actions
       (in Whom our parts are kept unseparated)
    for in our Mother Christ, we benefit and grow,
    and in mercy He redeems and restores us,
    and, by the virtue of His Passion and His death and
       resurrection, He ones us to our essence.
In this way, our Mother works in mercy to all His children
    who are submissive and obedient to Him.

And grace works with mercy, and namely in two properties as it
       was shown (which working belongs to the Third Person,
       the Holy Spirit). He works, rewarding and giving;
    "rewarding" is a great gift of trust which the Lord gives to
       him who has labored,
    and "giving" is a gracious action which he does freely of grace,
       fulfilling and surpassing all that is deserved
       by creatures.

Thus in our Father, God Almighty, we have our being;
and in our Mother of mercy we have our redeeming and restoring,
    in whom our parts are one-ed and all made complete man;
and by the repaying and giving in grace of the Holy Spirit, we are fulfilled.

And our essence is in our Father, God Almighty,
and our essence is in our Mother, God all Wisdom,
and our essence is in our Lord the Holy Spirit, God all Goodness,
    for our essence is total in each Person of the Trinity, which is One God.

But our fleshliness is only in the Second Person, Christ Jesus
       (in whom is the Father and the Holy Spirit)
    and in Him and by Him we are mightily taken out of hell
    and out of the misery on earth,
    and honorably brought up into heaven
    and full blessedly one-ed to our essence, increased in riches and nobility,
by all the virtue of Christ and by the grace and action of the Holy Spirit.

ಬಿ   ಬಿ   ಬಿ

Julian calls the Trinity "everlasting existence," articulating forever being. God is "endless from without beginning." In a reversal of what we typically imagine, the second member of the Trinity was created before us. Christ the Son was not developed to fix what creation had damaged. Rather, Existence so valued creation that it chose to create "fair human nature." We came next. Christ is not simply the ideal for our imitation; he is the prototype of the human. It was Existence's "endless purpose" to create humanity. We are so important to our God; we are not errors or general/particular falls from grace. The metaphors of pregnancy developed in Chapter 57 apply to the will to creation as we are knit and one-ed to him, both collectively and individually in every soul. We are married to him through this union as much as we are created by him in our birth. Julian elaborates her Trinitarian theology in terms of familial roles and the three aspects of existence. She observes that "all our life is in three": being, growing, and completing. She elucidates motherhood in Christ, the "Mother in essence" and "Mother in flesh." Our essence, the God-in-us, is not limited to one aspect of the Trinity. It comes of God the Father, Creator and Power; God the Son, Mother and Wisdom; and God the Spirit, Goodness working through mercy and grace. Our essence is of every part, but our fleshliness is Christ alone.

What would it mean to live out our essence? Is the way to our essence blocked? Can we see the union between essence and fleshliness—or do we dismiss our fleshliness as somehow getting in the way of a greater call? Julian asserts that we cannot have one without the other. Even if the essence is higher, in Christ we are one-ed to both. How well do we know our own soul—our "essence" in Christ? What would it mean to be Christ in the world today, to be Christ in *our* world this very day? This is not an "imitation" of Christ, following his actions and teachings, but *being* Christ—whatever that means for our particular living-out of the Incarnation, this specific instance of the essential Godself. Oscar Wilde stated that the madman is the person who thinks he really is Jesus Christ and tries to live out the literal life of Christ. In divine madness, can we discern how we need to release Christ into the world, to be Christ for the world? In the Incarnation Christ has one-ed our personal fleshliness. How can we liberate the Christ-essence enclosed in us?

◦ **59** ◦

All this bliss we have by mercy and grace,
> *which kind of bliss we might never have known if the quality of goodness*
> *which is in God had not been opposed—*
>> *by which goodness we have this bliss.*

For wickedness has been permitted to rise in opposition to that goodness,
and the goodness of mercy and grace opposed against the wickedness,
and transformed all into goodness and into honor for all those that shall be
  saved,
for that is the quality in God which does good against evil.

Thus Jesus Christ who does good against evil is our true Mother—
we have our being from Him where the basis of motherhood begins,
with all the sweet protection of love that accompanies it endlessly.

As truly as God is our Father,
so truly God is our Mother.
> *(And that He showed in all the showings, and*
> *particularly in those sweet words where he says*
> *"It is I"—that is to say:*
> *"It is I: the Power and the Goodness of the Fatherhood.*
> *"It is I: the Wisdom of the Motherhood.*
> *"It is I: the Light and the Grace that is all blessed Love.*
> *"It is I: the Trinity.*
> *"It is I: the Unity.*
>> *"I am the supreme goodness of all manner of things.*
>> *"I am what causes thee to love.*
>> *"I am what causes thee to yearn.*
> *"It is I: the endless fulfilling of all true desires.")*

For the soul is highest, noblest, and worthiest
> *when it is lowest, humblest, and gentlest.*

From this essential foundation we have
  all our virtues
  and our fleshliness
    by the gift of nature and
    by the help and assistance of mercy and grace, without which
      we cannot benefit.

Our high Father, God Almighty, who is Being itself, knew us and loved us
from before any time,
  and from this knowledge in His wondrous profound love, by the
  foreseeing endless agreement of all the Blessed Trinity,
  He wills that the Second Person should become our Mother, our
  Brother, and our Savior.

  Whereof it follows that as truly as God is our Father,
  so truly God is our Mother.
    Our Father wills,
    our Mother acts,
    our good Lord the Holy Spirit strengthens.

And therefore it is right for us
  to love our God in whom we have our being, reverently thanking
    and praising Him for our creation,
  powerfully praying to our Mother for mercy and pity,
  and to our Lord the Holy Spirit for help and grace, for in these
    three is all our life—nature, mercy, and grace—from which
    we get humility,
        gentleness,
        patience,
        and pity,
        and hatred of sin and wickedness
        (for it is right and proper for the virtuous to hate sin and
        wickedness).

Thus is Jesus our true Mother in nature,
  from our first creation,
and He is our true Mother in grace
  by His taking our created human nature.

All the fair action and all the sweet natural function of dearworthy motherhood
is attached to the Second Person; for in Him we have this divine will whole and
safe without end, both in nature and grace, from His own excellent goodness.

I understood three ways of looking at motherhood in God:
    the first is the creating of our human nature;
    the second is His taking of our human nature (and there
        commences the motherhood of grace);
    the third is motherhood of action (and in that is a great reaching
    outward, by the same grace, of length and breadth and of
    height and of depth without end)
and all is one love.

ჵ   ჵ   ჵ

We have bliss because "the quality of goodness . . . in God" was "opposed." Mercy and grace countered wickedness (which had been permitted to develop) and transformed all into goodness. Julian identifies that force as maternal action. These are powerful words, because they speak to the origin of all created matter and the ultimate setting-things-right of the "all shall be well." This mothering power is always at work in the world from the very beginning, the "basis," to lead all to good. Julian reminds us of God's power working in and through the world as in the hands of a loving parent. The Protector-Mother is this force moving, pulsating in all things, leading to goodness. It does not matter that we cannot understand or see it all—it has been set in motion at the very beginning and will continue to be. In a litany of all that is contained in the Godhead, all leads to God's transforming goodness. God causes us to love and yearn and is the fulfillment of our desires. If Unity seems to fracture in Julian's hierarchical description of the various aspects of the Godhead, ultimately it is preserved through the mode of mothering. This mother acts. From the Mother we receive the mercy and pity that create bliss and transform all to goodness. This Mother is the agent and means of change. In the creation, when the Word was with God and was God, God was Mother. In the Incarnation, God was Mother actively living out grace in order to transform all to goodness. In God-made-flesh the divine will is enfolded in love.

Motherhood of God began with creation, continued with the Incarnation, and is finally fully released and liberated in "motherhood of action": salvation. In the transformative power-to-goodness in all these acts, "all is one love." As we contemplate the grace released in the Passion, the mercy expressed in the redemption, may we know the Mother's love and creation working through it all. We rarely see the transformations moving in the big and small "wickednesses" we encounter in our lives. May God's love enfold us in assurance that supreme acts of mercy and grace charge within each and every aspect.

❧ **60** ❦

*But now it is appropriate to say a little more about this reaching
outward, as I understood it in the meaning of our Lord—
how that we are brought back by the Motherhood of mercy
and grace into the womb of our human nature where we were
created by the Motherhood of natural love, which natural
love never leaves us.*

*Our Mother in human nature, our Mother in grace—because He wished
to completely become our Mother in everything, He accepted the foundation
of His work most lowly and most mildly in the Maiden's womb.*

*(And that He showed in the first showing, where he brought that
meek Maid before the eye of my understanding in the simple state
she was in when she conceived.)*

*That is to say, our high God, the supreme Wisdom of all, in this lowly
womb clothed Himself and enclosed Himself most willingly in our
poor flesh, in order that He Himself could do the service and the duty
of motherhood in everything.*

*The mother's serving is most near,
most willing,
and most certain*

*("near" because it is most human nature; "willing," because
it is most loving; and "certain," because it is most true).*

*This duty no one can, nor could, nor ever did to the fullest,
except He alone.*

*We are aware that all our mothers give us birth only to pain and
dying; and what is it but that our true Mother Jesus, He—all love—
gives us birth to joy and to endless life. Blessed may He be!*

Thus He carries us within Himself in love, and labors until full term
  so that He could suffer the sharpest throes
    and the hardest pains that ever were
    or ever shall be,
    and die at the last.

And when He had finished, and so given us birth to bliss, not even all
this could satisfy His wondrous love.
  (And that He showed in these high, surpassing words of love: "If I
  could suffer more, I would suffer more.")

He could die no more, but He would not cease working; therefore
    it behooved Him that He feed us
  (for the dearworthy love of motherhood has made Him owe us that).

The mother can give her child suck from her milk, but our precious
Mother Jesus can feed us with Himself;
  and He does it most graciously and most tenderly with the Blessed
  Sacrament which is the Precious Food of true life.

    And with all the sweet Sacraments He supports us
    most mercifully and graciously.
        (And thus meant He in this blessed word where He said: "It
        is I that Holy Church preaches to thee and teaches to thee";
        that is to say, "All the wholeness and life of Sacraments, all
        the virtue and grace of my Word, all the goodness that is
        ordained in Holy Church for thee, it is I.")

The mother can lay the child tenderly on her breast,
but our tender Mother Jesus can more intimately lead us into His
blessed Breast by His sweet open Side,
  and show therein part of the Godhead
  and part of the joys of heaven,
    with spiritual certainty of eternal bliss.
        (And that was shown in the tenth showing, giving the same
        understanding in this sweet word where He says, "Lo, how I
        love thee," gazing into His side and rejoicing.)

This fair lovely word "mother" is so sweet and so kind in itself, that
it cannot truly be said of anyone nor to anyone except of Him and to
Him who is true Mother of life and of all.

To the quality of motherhood belongs natural love, wisdom, and knowledge—
and this is God;
>> *for though it is true that our bodily birth is but little, lowly, and*
>>> *simple as compared to our spiritual birth,*
>> *yet it is He who does it within the created mothers by whom it is done.*

The kind, loving mother who is aware and knows the need of her child
protects the child most tenderly as the nature and state of motherhood wills.
>> *And as the child increases in age, she changes her method but not her love.*
>> *And when the child is increased further in age, she permits it to be*
>> *chastised*
>>> *to break down vices and to cause the child to accept virtues and graces.*
This nurturing of the child, with all that is fair and good, our Lord does
in the mothers by whom it is done.
Thus He is our Mother in our human nature by the action of grace in the lower
>> *part,*
out of love for the higher part.

>> *And He wishes us to know it; for He wishes to have all our love*
>>> *made fast to Him.*

In this I saw that all our debt that we owe by God's bidding to
fatherhood and motherhood (because of God's Fatherhood and Motherhood)
is fulfilled in true loving of God which blessed love Christ works in us.

>> *(And this was shown in all the showings and specifically in the*
>> *high bountiful words where He says: "It is I whom thou lovest.")*

ജ   ജ   ജ

Incarnation is God "reaching outward." The womb is a place of safety; it is also the pierced side of Christ. Through his suffering we are reborn; through our suffering we enter into rebirth in him. The "reaching outward" refers to the length, breadth, and extent of love found in Chapter 59. This "reaching outward" is a reaching inward as the motherhood of mercy and grace brings us into the womb of our human nature, where we were created by a motherhood of natural love that never leaves us. Julian talks about being born again. We are always already born again. We do not need a call to salvation; we need awareness. We have received birth in Christ. Through our human sufferings we reenter the womb of his wounds. Through our sufferings as well as His we are reborn. A conscious act of will declaring Jesus our personal savior is unnecessary since he has already done the work, whether we realize it or not. We are one-ed; mercy and grace operate within us; God is our essence. The thoroughly abstract *Logos* becomes the "most near, most willing, and most certain" of human nature.

Julian describes the crucifixion as a labor scene. In Julian's time the physical agony and mortal combat present in the act of giving birth—the sheer corporeality that we have sanitized by antiseptic hospital rooms—emphasized the way this saving action exists at the very center of everything. The crucifixion was at the center of life in Julian's medieval world as it is in our lives. The crucifixion and the birth it makes possible are life: our life. God's love surrounds and enfolds us throughout our mortal existence. Our lives, our sufferings, are experiences of utter protection in love. We are nourished and surrounded by God throughout the whole of our earthly, earthy journey until we are born into "bliss." To say that he has taken on our pains, our sufferings, our sorrows in this way no longer limits him to a role of servant. He literally bears the world's grief because it is contained in him, all-carrying mother. It is his and not distinct from him and his struggle. The agony of giving birth is the release of all our woes. The process is active: "He had finished." It is not that he had died, or that he had served His purpose. He has completed the birth for us. Yet the end is only the beginning: "He could die no more, but he would not cease working." God-in-the-world is ongoing and dynamic. The Mother must now feed her young. While she is not the only medieval writer to make such a comparison, in Julian the extension of this image into a systematic theology is extraordinary. The Eucharist is claimed as the vehicle for the constant work of love within creation. It is there, always being made, as the way in which God supports us. Mercy and grace are the hallmarks of the motherhood of God. The sacraments of the church are not simply the means *to* the motherhood of God: Christ as mother *is* the sacrament. All is for love: if he could suffer more, he would suffer more.

We are placed at the foot of the cross, gazing into the wounds of Christ's body that are the womb of motherhood. God invites us in. Will you accept his hospitality? Will you move into his welcome to let the pain of his mothering life be your own? To say yes does not mean that we are forced into a reluctant space of making every day Good Friday. Rather, it means that we can let our Mother make every day Easter Sunday. The wounded side is our pain, our sufferings and grief. It is there inside the body of God that enfolds us and is ready to nourish us with its own flesh. We can seek refuge because we are already enclosed in this body of love. It is a question of awareness. We rejoice as we return to the womb we never left, the womb that forever sustains us. Julian offers a literal version of the popular devotional story about the foot-prints in the sand, God carrying us through the tough times in our lives. Our Mother God bears us in her womb for our ultimate salvation. Our "sins" and woes are not separate from her; they are in her flesh and her pain. We have only to rest in the loving motherhood that cares for us and births us into bliss, the nurture of God that continues within and without throughout all of our lives.

61

In our spiritual birthing, our Mother uses more tenderness for our protection without any comparison

(by as much as our soul is of more value in His sight than the flesh).

He kindles our understanding,

He directs our ways,

He eases our conscience,

He comforts our soul,

He lightens our heart,

and He gives us partially knowledge and love of His blessed Godhead—along with gracious remembrance of His sweet manhood and His blessed Passion,

with gracious wonder at His high, surpassing goodness,

and He makes us to love all that He loves because of His love,

and to be satisfied with Him and all His works.

If we fall, quickly He raises us by His loving calling and merciful touching.

And when we are thus strengthened by His sweet action, then we willingly choose Him, by His sweet grace, to be His servants and His lovers everlastingly without end.

After this He permits some of us to fall more severely and more grievously than ever we did before, as it seems to us.

And then we believe (we who are not all-wise) that all was naught that we had begun.

But it is not so,

because it is necessary for us to fall,

and it is necessary for us to see it.

For if we fell not, we would not know how weak and how miserable we are by ourselves—nor also would we so thoroughly know the amazing love of our Creator.

For we shall see truly in heaven without end that we have grievously sinned
in this life, and, notwithstanding this, we shall see that we were never lessened
in His love, nor were we ever of less value in His sight.
   By means of the test of this falling,
      we shall gain a high, wondrous knowledge of love in God without end.
         For strong and wondrous is that love which cannot nor will not
            be broken because of trespass.
And this is one understanding of our benefits from falling.

Another is the lowliness and humility that we shall gain by the sight of
   our falling,
      for thereby we shall be highly raised in heaven
      and we might never have come to this raising without that humility.
         And therefore it is necessary for us to see our fall,
            for if we see it not, though we fall, it would not benefit us.

And usually, first we fall, and afterwards we see it—and both by the mercy
   of God.
The mother can allow the child to fall sometimes and to be distressed
               in various ways for its own benefit, but she can never permit any kind
               of peril to come to the child, because of her love.
But even if our earthly mother could allow her child to perish,
our heavenly Mother Jesus cannot allow us that are His children to perish.
He is all Power,
   all Wisdom,
      and all Love, and so is none but He. Blessed may He be!

But often when our falling and our misery is shown us, we are so
sorely frightened and so greatly ashamed of ourselves that scarcely
do we know where we can hide ourselves away.
   Then our courteous Mother wills not that we flee away—for Him
      nothing would be more distasteful—
   but He wills then that we follow the behavior of a child, for when
      a child is distressed or afraid, it runs hastily to the mother for help
      with all its might.
   So wishes He that we act as a humble child, saying thus: "My kind
         Mother, my gracious Mother, my dearworthy Mother, have
         mercy on me. I have made myself foul and unlike to Thee,
         and I am neither able nor know how to amend it except with
         Thy secret help and grace."

And if we do not feel ourselves eased very quickly, we may be
sure that He is practicing the behavior of a wise mother, for if He
sees that it would be more benefit to us to mourn and weep, out of
love He permits it with compassion and pity until the best time.

And He wills that we betake ourselves strongly to the Faith of Holy
Church and find there our dearworthy Mother in the solace of true
understanding with all the Blessed Communion of Saints.

For one particular person can often be broken, as it seems, by
himself, but the whole Body of Holy Church is never broken, nor
ever shall be, without end.

And therefore a certain thing it is, a good and a gracious thing, to
will humbly and strongly to be made fast and one-ed to our Mother,
Holy Church, that is, Christ Jesus.
For the flood of mercy that is His dearworthy Blood and precious
Water is adequate to make us fair and pure.
The blessed Wound of our Savior is open and rejoices to heal us.
The sweet gracious hands of our Mother are already and diligently
    about us.
For He in all this action practices the duty of a kind nurse who has
nothing else to do except to attend to the safety of her child.

It is His function to save us,
It is His honor to do it,
and it is His will that we acknowledge it.

For He wills that we love Him sweetly
and trust in Him humbly and strongly.

    (And this He showed in these grace-filled words: "I keep thee
    full safely.")

       ಬಿ   ಬಿ   ಬಿ

Christ shows a mother's love even at the cross. As we children fall,
Mother Christ holds us in his arms and saves us. Our falling helps us
to better know our dependence on God; it leads to knowledge experienced in our understanding. We gain humility by falling. Jesus falls
carrying his cross. He falls for our fallenness. By our fall, and his, we
are healed. Whenever we fall, we have to land somewhere. For Julian it
is in the arms of the Mother God. Though a mother forsake her child,

God will not abandon us. We walk the way of the cross, despising ourselves for our weakness, our sin, our doubt. It seems that our falls hammer in the nails of Jesus' cross. In Julian, this voice is only our limited human perception. We feel not only guilt but also revulsion and embarrassment at what we have done to Jesus' body. We must not run from the foot of the cross because of our shame. We need to stand right there—and receive His love by mercy.

Redemption is here all the time. It has been done once and for all. It was done even before the world had begun. But in our human psychology and spiritual journey we need to be able to accept it when the time is right for us, when we are ready to receive it. Jesus could die on the cross every moment of every day, and if we are not prepared to receive his forgiveness—a mother's love—we will not be healed. The intensity of Holy Week is the awareness that Jesus is dying every moment of every day. The transformative potential is the understanding—in our hearts, minds, and souls—that so too does he rise every moment of every day. God's time is not always our time, but redemption is offered all the time. May we be ready to receive it. Let nothing separate us from the love of Christ. The love of God is Mother Christ, the love of God is the communion of saints, the love of God is the collective body of the faithful. When we are alone our individual guilt or grief rarely allows us to know that love; in community we might be made whole. This is the value of *communitas*. Even if the only society we know is the presence of our Savior, it can be enough for us. Human institutions are always fragile; the Body of Christ is stronger than anything. Many of us come to know that Body not through the formal institution of the Church but through any community of love—even in solitude, if that is where we need to be at the time.

Salvation comes at all times and in all places. God's love was revealed as truly at the Passover as it is revealed on the cross. It is revealed as much at the Seder table as it is in the Eucharist. May we break through the bonds of our limitations to love in an exodus of forgiveness—of self, whatever blocks of sin make us "take flight" from God. May we flee with him and to him. "The blessed wound of our Savior" is our Promised Land. Let us accept reconciliation. From the desert of our wandering, the Lents of our lives, may we know the kindly light that leads us on, that says "I keep thee full safely." May we recognize in those words our God, the "sweet gracious hands of our Mother" always and "already diligently about us." At the foot of the cross, in the empty tomb, bless us with this knowledge, O Mother God. As we abandon the Egypts of our lives, may we remember we are enfolded in love. Let the liberation begin!

❧ 62 ❧

At that time He showed
  our frailty and our failings,
  our betrayals and our denials,
  our despisings and our burdens,
  and all our woes
      to whatever extent they could befall us in this life, as it seemed
        to me.

And along with that He showed
  His blessed Power,
  His blessed Wisdom,
  His blessed Love in which
      He keeps us in these difficult times just as tenderly and as
        sweetly for His honor and as surely for our salvation
      as He does when we are in the most solace and comfort.

To do that He raises us spiritually and nobly into heaven, and
transforms all our woe into His honor and our joy without end.

His love never permits us to lose opportunity.
And all of this is from the natural goodness of God, by the working of grace.

God is natural in His very being—
that is to say, that goodness which is of nature,
it is God.

  He is the ground;
  He is the essence;
  He is the same thing as nature;
  and He is true Father and true Mother of human nature.

All natures that He has caused to flow out of Him to accomplish His will
      shall be returned and brought again into Him
        by the salvation of man through the working of grace.

For of all natures that He has placed partially in various created
> *things, only in man is all the whole*
in fullness,
in strength,
in beauty and in goodness,
in majesty and nobility,
in all manner of solemnity,
>> *of preciousness,*
>> *and of honor.*

Here we can see
> *that we are fully bound to God because of our human nature,*
> *and we are also fully bound to God because of grace.*
Here we can see that we need not intensely search
> *far away to discover the different vital powers,*
>> *but only as far as Holy Church—into our Mother's breast*
>>> *(that is to say, into our own soul, where our Lord dwells),*
> *and there we shall find everything—now in faith and belief, and*
> *afterwards, truly in Himself clearly, in bliss.*

But let no man or woman take this particularly to himself, for it is
not so—it is general!

For it was our precious Mother Christ for whom this fair human
> *nature was prepared,*
> *for the honor and nobility of man's creation,*
> *and for the joy and the bliss of man's salvation—just as He*
>> *understood,*
>> *knew,*
>> *and recognized from without beginning.*

⁋ ⁋ ⁋

Julian investigates where we look for true knowledge and wisdom. The working of grace in the world is responsible for all. God shows Julian our weakness, our mistakes; how we fail to keep our vows; how we harbor ill will and how it is harbored against us—all the heavy weights we carry. These are joyfully balanced, like a set of scales embodied as our God. On the one side are those burdens; on the other is that Holy Trinity of Power, Wisdom, and Love. Our sins and sadness are contained in him; they too are a part of his blessed body. God's nature is goodness;

nature is God; nature is goodness. Julian echoes yet challenges the Aristotelian view of the natural world embraced by Aquinas. The "natural" is God, and it is goodness. The "natural" is not simply in harmony with some remote, abstract idea of God: God is Nature and natural goodness. God is the source of all creation, but God also is creation. This operates as a unified system. There is no "outside" in God's world. We are all "inside." We are literally inside the Body of Christ. Julian's nature theology establishes that all that exists is of God—coming from and returning to God. When she speaks of the transformation of woe into joy, that occurs from the natural goodness of God by the working of grace. It is rooted in the body, in the natural world—the cycle of creation that redeems just as the vegetative world returns from death back to life.

This process in God is a kind of agricultural cycle. It happens of its own accord—it is natural—but it also involves intervention, that of the nurturing Godhead. God is the image of us, and we are the image of God. Julian's glorification of humankind might sound too human-centric to the contemporary mind. We are uncomfortable with viewing humanity as the center of all creation. We must be good stewards of creation, but we cannot abuse our planet or think it is here only for our use and exploitation. For Julian, human-centeredness is less about exploitation than connection with the embodied, incarnate Godhead. Humanity is glorified because therein lies the Incarnation. We need only look within in order to find all the answers. The journey inward is not solipsistic; rather, it is the heart of Julian's theology. Enclosed in the Body of Christ, we go inside our souls to find him. We do not reject human knowledge. How could we, since knowledge of anything and everything is knowledge of God! But we must know ourselves first, know our minds and souls first and best. We must be at peace with our self-knowledge, our God-knowledge, before we move outward to other forms of learning. Inside our soul is everything to be found. In the fullness of transfiguration, when we butterflies emerge from our cocoons, we will know not only God fully but ourselves more fully as well. We are limited in how much we may know our souls as we journey. But our true soul, God's self, awaits us in full revelation. Father-Mother God, who is all Nature, All Created Thing, and the process of creation itself, may we seek to know ourselves first, so that through knowing You and us we might see the union of ground and essence that is your goodness. May we remember that all we come in contact with—human and nonhuman—is part of your Body.

༂ **63** ༃

Here we can see
>*that we truly have it from our human nature to hate sin,*
>*and we truly have it from grace to hate sin—*
>>*for human nature is all good and fair in itself,*
>>*and grace was sent out*
>>>*to preserve human nature*
>>>*and to destroy sin*
>>>*and to bring back fair human nature*
>>>>*and to the blessed point from whence it came—*
>>>>*that is, God—*
>>>*with more nobility and honor*
>>>*by the virtuous working of grace.*

For it shall be seen before God in regard to all His holy saints in joy
>*without end*
>>*that human nature has been tested in the fire of tribulation and no lack,*
>>*no flaw found in it.*

Thus are human nature and grace of one accord—
>*for grace is God*
>*as human nature is God.*
>>*He is double in His way of working*
>>*but single in love,*
>>*and neither of these two works without the other,*
>>*nor is either separated from the other.*

When we by the mercy of God and with His help come to harmony
with both our human nature and grace,
>*we shall see honestly that sin is truly more vile and more painful*
>>*than hell, without comparison,*
>*for sin is opposite to our fair human nature!*

247

For as truly as sin is impure,
just as truly is it unnatural,
 and thus it is a horrible thing to see for the beloved soul that
 wishes to be all fair and shining in the sight of God as both human
 nature and grace direct.
But let us not be afraid of this (except in so much as fear could help us);
  but humbly let us make our moan to our dearworthy Mother,
 and He shall all besprinkle us with His Precious Blood
 and make our souls very pliant and very gentle,
 and restore us to health most gently in the course of time,
  in whatever way as it is most honor to Him and most joy to us
  without end.

He shall never cease this sweet, fair working, nor pause, until all His
 dearworthy children are birthed and brought forth.
 (And He showed that where He showed the interpretation of
 spiritual thirst: that is, the love-longing that shall last until
 Doomsday.)

Thus in our true Mother, Jesus, our life is grounded,
 in His own foreseeing Wisdom from without beginning,
 with the high supreme Goodness of the Holy Spirit.

In the taking of our human nature He restored life to us, and in His
 blessed dying upon the cross, He birthed us into endless life.

And from that time, and now, and until Doomsday,
 He feeds us and helps us
 just as the high matchless nature of motherhood wills
 and as the natural need of childhood requires.

Fair and sweet is our heavenly Mother in the eyes of our soul;
precious and loving are His grace-filled children in the eyes of our
heavenly Mother,
 with gentleness and humility and all the fair virtues that are proper
 to children in nature.

Furthermore,
 by nature the child does not despair of the mother's love;
 by nature the child does not take responsibility upon itself;
 by nature the child loves the mother
  and each one of them the other.

These are the fair virtues (with all others that are like them)
with which our heavenly Mother is honored and pleased.

I recognized no state in this life
greater in weakness,
and in the lack of power and intelligence than our childhood,
until the time that our grace-filled Mother has brought us up to our
Father's bliss.

And then truly shall be made known to us His meaning in these sweet
words where Christ says:
"All shall be well;
and thou shalt see for thyself that all manner of things shall be well."

And then shall the bliss of our Motherhood in Christ be begun anew
in the joys of our Father God
and shall continue being renewed without end.

Thus I understood that all His blessed children which have been
birthed from Him by nature shall be brought back into Him by grace.

⁞ ⁞ ⁞

Amazing Grace is Jesus Christ. The focus is not on Adam's fall and the long continuum of original sin. Rather, our true reality is the goodness of human nature—something we have been unable to establish even in secular thinkers like Freud, let alone theologians who have been too apt to focus on humanity's fallenness. Grace as superhero, Christ performing a salvific role, is really just about getting rid of the villain. It is perfectly natural that human nature is all goodness. We have been taught to see our wickedness, our fallenness, as our truest selves. But our truest self is God; our truest human nature is goodness. Grace is God as human nature is God. There is no separation here. Just as we are he, he is we. Christ is fully human and fully God; so are we through his Incarnation. The process by which, through mercy and grace, we come into harmony with our real human nature—that outward in sync with the inward—is not an "if" but a "when." We need to do this; we need this integration. How much bad theology has thwarted this—teaching us to hate our sinful bodies—when for Julian sin is nothing of the body, nothing essential to the soul. It is most foreign, as she sees it. The existent disruption that is sin is much worse than its threatened consequence of hell because it is opposite to our nature. We are not punished for our sins; we are punished by our sins. Suffering comes not from outside as punishment; it comes from the presence of sin interfering with our glorious selves. Sin is defined as "unnatural": it is *contra naturam*, totally in opposition to nature—especially the goodness that is our human nature.

The Incarnation of Christ is constantly working grace, continuously in the process of making all things well. We will all be born again in Christ, return to our truer nature as we enter the wound/womb. The antifeminism of medieval theology essentialized the notion that being born of woman condemned human nature to be fallen humanity locked in original sin. Through Holy Mother Jesus, Julian reclaims birth and, by extension, women's bodies, their pregnancies, their menstruation. Through literal birth into Jesus' body, sin is shed. Since we are he, and we are all goodness, how can human birth ever truly bear with it the blight of "original sin"? Salvation is "love-longing"—the desire, the processing "workingness" of ongoing literal "labor" in Christ's body. The drama of the Triduum, the Easter mystery, is a never-ending series of contractions. The goodness of human nature ensures that it is only natural for us to totally trust in God's salvific working of grace. Any deviation from that is missing the mark—is sin, is unnatural. This does not make us terrible sinners if we doubt; we only need to be reminded that our rightful place is in love, in the arms of God. Our despair—our discouragement, even our grief over our sins—is not where God wants us to be. Faith and trust need not be earned; they are literally our birth-right. We do not have to do it ourselves; we rest in God's arms and let it be done for us by the work of grace. Love is natural. Anything that blocks love is sin—and even that is not our fault. God's maternal love is there for us at all times and in all ways; we must accept it as the worthy, deserving children we are.

Christ our Mother continues to make all things well by grace. While the ongoing work may be a process, not complete all at once, how could anything be left out of this picture of salvation? Perhaps all the apocalyptic things that are supposed to happen are included in that promise of the long-term, not the immediate, completion of grace's mission. But here in this moment, at this space in her text, Julian wants us to know that as she understood it we are all already saved, and we need do nothing to affect, effect, or change that. What a different view of Lent and Easter we receive when the lesson of love takes our sin and guilt away!

∞ **64** ∞

Before this time, by the gift of God, I had a great yearning and desire
to be delivered from this world and from this life,
> for frequently I beheld the woe that is here,
> and the well and the bliss that exists there.

>> And even if there had been no pain in this life except the
>> absence of our Lord, it seemed to me that that was sometimes
>> more than I could bear.

And this absence made me mourn and earnestly yearn—and also my
own misery, sloth, and weakness—so that I had no delight in living
or laboring as it fell to me to do.

To all this our gracious Lord answered for the sake of comfort and
patience, and He said these words:
"Without warning thou shalt be taken
> from all thy pain,
> from all thy sickness,
> from all thy distress,
> and from all thy woe,
and thou shalt come up above,
and thou shalt have me for thy reward,
and thou shalt be filled full of love and bliss,
and thou shalt never have any manner of pain,
> nor any manner of sickness,
> nor any manner of displeasure,
> nor any lack of will,
but always joy and bliss without end.
Why then should it bother thee to suffer awhile, seeing that it is my
Will and to my honor?"

In this word: "Without warning thou shalt be taken . . ." I saw that

God rewards man for the patience that he has in awaiting God's will,
  and for his lifetime (if that man extends his patience over the time of
    his life)
  because of not knowing the time of his passing away.

This is a great benefit, for if a man knew the time of his passing, he
  would not have patience concerning that time.

Also God wills that while the soul is in the body, it seems to itself
that it is always at the moment of being taken.

For all this life and this languishing that we have here is only a
moment, and when we are taken without warning out of pain into
bliss, then the pain shall have been nothing.

At this time I saw a body lying on the earth
  which appeared thick and ugly and fearsome,
  without shape and form,
  as it were a bloated heap of stinking mire.

And suddenly out of this body sprang a most fair creature,
  a tiny child,
  well-shaped and formed,
  quick and lively,
  whiter than a lily,
    which neatly glided up into heaven.
  The bloatedness of the body symbolizes the great misery of our mortal
    flesh,
  and the tinyness of the child symbolizes the clearness and purity of our
    soul.

And I considered:
  "With this body remained none of the fairness of the child,
  not on this child did there remain any foulness of the body."

It is most blessed for man to be taken from pain,
more than for pain to be taken from man;
for if pain is taken from us, it can come again.
Therefore is it an unequalled comfort and a blessed awareness for a
loving soul that we shall be taken from pain,
    for in this promise I saw
        a merciful compassion that our Lord has to us in our woe and a
        gracious promise of pure deliverance,

for He wills that we be comforted in surpassing joy.

> *(And that He showed in these words:*
> *"And thou shalt come up above;*
> *and thou shalt have me for thy reward;*
> *and thou shalt be filled full of joy and bliss.")*

It is God's will that we fix the point of our concentration on this blessed sight as often as we can and for as long a time as we can keep ourselves therein with His grace.

For this is a blessed contemplation for the soul that is guided by God and very much to its honor for the time that it lasts.

And when we fall again into ourself
> *by sluggishness and spiritual blindness*
> *and the experiencing of spiritual and bodily pains*
> > *because of our frailty,*
it is God's will that we recognize that He has not forgotten us.
> *(And this He means in these words He says for the sake of comfort: "And thou shalt never more have pain, nor any manner of sickness, nor any manner of displeasure, nor lack of will, but ever joy and bliss without end. Why should it bother thee to suffer awhile seeing that it is my will and to my honor?")*

It is God's will
> *that we accept His promises and His comfortings*
> *as broadly and as powerfully as we can receive them.*
And He also wills
> *that we accept our waiting and our distress*
> *as lightly as we can take them, and pay no attention to them—*
> > *for the more lightly we take them,*
> > *and the less value we place on them for the sake of love,*
> > > *the less pain shall we have in experiencing them,*
> > > *and the more favor and regard will we have because of them.*

ಡಿ   ಡಿ   ಡಿ

Chapter 64 is a meditation on how we deal with the fear of death. Much ink has been spilled trying to understand how Julian could have prayed for illness. We get a better sense of how she could have prayed for death—and for life. Julian longed to escape the woe of this life, to have the well that exists in the next world. She knew a dark night of the soul, a spiritual depression. Julian the mystic observes her pain in separation from full union with God. The "absence" made her "mourn" so that she had no delight in living. Milton described hell as "darkness visible." For Julian, life on earth is absence tangible. God's answer to Julian is all about the nick of time. God relies on the element of surprise. "Without warning" we are taken from this absence into full presence. Julian seems most impressed with how we do not know when we are going to die. That makes the waiting more livable. She had a near-death experience; she had prayed for death. But impatience keeps us from living our lives in the present moment. To know that one day we will be with God has to be enough. The mystic cannot make it happen instantaneously. If we knew when we would die, we would waste our lives in preparation for that very moment. We would lose the blessings inherent in life on earth. Patience in awaiting the final complete union means we must be willing to live through pain and strife, sickness, distress, and woe. Pie-in-the-sky might be tempting, but it would be sin: premature separation from our souls-in-progress, where the one-ing of our inner and outer natures is still being made well. We have work to do here: on our fragmented selves and in our broken world, with the help of mercy and grace. Union with God is the "reward," not the avoidance of mortal life.

For the mystic—for anyone deeply living the spiritual life—we have one foot here, one foot there. We are aware of the transience of life— whether we work with the sick and "actively dying" or contemplate Christ on the cross. Some of us feel this urgency viscerally; some of us are acutely aware of loss, and fear it terribly—the loss of ourselves, our loved ones, our way of life. Christians live a faith whose central metaphor is that we must die in order to live, yet we fight so hard against this letting go. At our most sacramental moments we can see the bridge between the two worlds—life and death, this world and the next. Those vantage points can be moments of terror or celebration. Julian does not speak doctrinally, saying that it is somehow good for us to cultivate the horror of sin and fear of judgment that lay at the heart of much of the spiritual practice of her day, intended to bring the soul to a state of compunction and thus open a doorway to God. Rather, she observes the soul's longing and says rather humbly that in our experiences we are already there—living at the cusp of the mundane and the celestial; that holiness is breaking through every moment of our days. We are "always at the moment of being taken."

Being "taken" suggests divine rapture, when we receive God as the "reward," "joy and bliss without end." The suddenness Julian describes makes this a climactic moment when full sacramental union becomes possible. The love of God is love-making here. The French expression for sexual climax, "the little death," is apt in the mystic's attainment of presence rather than absence. Yet in the midst of highly sensual language depicting our crossing-over, Julian remains painfully aware of the human suffering we experience in life. That must have been so real to her that she built it into her imagery. Given this reality of suffering, death is a gift. Death offers a good, not a loss. Her focus is not on the loss of life, but rather the removal of pain. Life's potential for, if not reality of, suffering is always present. Death is a blessing, another lesson of love to bring the soul to full union with God. It is God not forgetting us as we labor here in our sorrows. God cannot take our sufferings away from us, but He can offer unending bliss. This action is not an abstract expression of just desserts. Rather, it is direct and personal motion of love, remembrance, and being drawn nearer. These words are not easy for those of us who grieve, who love others, who are attached to our lives in this world. Our culture has many ways of preserving and extending life. We see death as a failure on our parts or on the parts of our "saviors" in science or medicine. Julian was surrounded by deaths her culture had no control over: infant and maternal mortality alone, not to mention the lack of medical treatment for the plague, made death much more "natural" than we experience it now. Perhaps her words—coming out of a very different time and place, and the mystic's longing for the love of God—can make us a bit less afraid of being drawn nearer, letting go of our loved ones or ourselves.

୧ **65** ଓ

Thus I understood that whatever man or woman willingly chooses
God in this life for the sake of love, he can be certain that he is loved
without end with endless love which creates in him that grace.

He wills that we hold on to this trustfully—
> that we are all in as certain hope of the bliss of heaven
> > while we are here,
> as we shall be in certainty when we are there.

And the more delight and joy that we take in this certainty with
reverence and humility, the better it pleases Him, as it was shown.
> This reverence that I mean is a holy, gracious fear of our Lord,
> to which humility is knit:
> > and that is, that a creature sees
> > > the Lord as wondrous great,
> > > and the self as wondrous small.

For these virtues are possessed eternally by the beloved God, and
this can be understood and experienced now in some measure by the
presence of our Lord when that presence occurs.
> This presence in everything is most desired,
> > because it produces wondrous reassurance,
> > in true faith and certain hope by the greatness of love,
> > in fear that is sweet and delightful.

It is God's will that I see myself just as much bound to Him in love
as if He had done all that He has done just for me.
> > And thus should every soul think in regard to His Love: that is
> > > to say,
> > > > the love of God creates in us such a unity that when it is truly
> > > > understood, no man can separate himself from any other.
And thus ought our soul to understand that God has done just for
itself all that He has done.

This He shows in order to make us love Him and fear nothing but
  Him; for it is His will that we be aware that all the power of
  the Enemy is held in our Friend's hand.

Therefore the soul that surely recognizes this shall fear nothing
except Him whom it loves.
  All other fears the soul reckons along with passions and bodily
  sickness and fantasies, and therefore, although we may be in so
  much pain, woe, and distress that it seems to us that we can think
  of absolutely nothing except what we are in or what we are experiencing,
  as soon as we can, we pass lightly over it and we set it at nought.

And why? Because we know God's wish that
  if we know Him
  and love Him
  and reverently fear Him,
    we shall have peace and be in great repose,
    and all that He does shall be a great pleasure to us.

        (And this showed our Lord in these words: "Why should
          it bother
          thee to suffer awhile, since it is my will and to my honor?")

Now I have told you of fifteen revelations as God granted to deliver
them to my mind,
  renewed by enlightenings and inspirations
    (I hope, from the same Spirit who showed them all).

Of these fifteen showings the first began early in the morning, about
the hour of four, and they lasted, appearing in a most beautiful order
and solemnly, each following the other, until it was three in the
afternoon or later.

꙰   ꙰   ꙰

The suffering we experience is overcome, like the "fiend," by the love of God. We need only answer the call to choose God, choose love, choose life. He first loved us, that we might love him. That "endless love" is our God who kindles in our hearts and souls a desire for him to love and be loved. Liberal Christians are apt to distinguish ourselves from fundamentalists who talk too much of a "personal savior." We would also be suspicious of any modern-day Margery Kempe who thought she could experience the love of God directly—the mystic is dismissed as deranged. Julian says that the love of God creates unity in us. When we truly understand it, we no longer see ourselves as separate—sinful, in sin. The Incarnation and redemption are for each of us and for all of us. There is no "them" versus "us"; there is only "us." In Christ we are all one. None of us is "special," uniquely privileged—yet each of us is special, particular. This experience of body and soul is known through Julian's "understanding," the rational mind. That is what makes her story worth telling. We are taught that humility is the only decent virtue to cultivate. We had better make ourselves as "less-than" as possible, because, don't forget, Jesus made himself a suffering servant. Women get drummed into their heads a distorted Marian "let it be done to me according to Thy will." Yet some subvert this teaching. The nineteenth-century "girl-saint" Thérèse of Lisieux is remembered as the "Little Flower." We rarely recall that in her prayers to become the smallest of the small, the weakest of the weak, she claimed greater authority than priests or even the pope, observing that her littleness brought her closer to Jesus than they. Julian wants the soul to understand that God has done just for itself all that he has done. This does not leave much room for damaging humility. We cannot allow our false selves—our self-deprecating, dysfunctional habits—to prevent that light from shining through. Each of us is chosen, each of us is blessed with the redemption and singled out in the Incarnation. Every one of us is the most loved child of God. May we love ourselves as much as we love our neighbors—not in arrogance, but with a self-love that nurtures and nourishes so that our light—God's light in us—will be strong enough to shine out into the world. As the parable tells us, hiding it does no good; that denies our God. The rejection of the divinity within our own souls effects the separation of sin.

Julian expresses the love of God as the love of a friend. The power in the hand of the "fiend" is exchanged for the hand of a friend; God holds our hand. Julian's earthly relationships must have been deeply loving ones. How could someone have been able to write so purely amatory a theology without the sacramental bliss that is human love? It is worth clarifying the discussion of the "fear" of God, a subject Julian talks a lot about. When Julian speaks of fearing nothing but God, she emphasizes the first part of that equation: fear nothing. The "fear" of God is the awe we have of God's power, God's amazing grace. As she says elsewhere, by that is the fiend overcome. To "know him and love him and reverently fear him" is more about trust than fear. This is hard for our modern minds to grasp, as we are conscious of dysfunctional fear in intimate relationships. Given the "fears" Julian names—of pain, bodily sickness, and so forth—if our awesome God is all-powerful, then what power can these have over us? Just as Julian says these will all be over in the blink of an eye (that is how much God loves us—can we see them through for a short time?), she puts forth the idea that our personal salvation is built on trust. Chapter 64 made death God's gift of love. Here our sufferings—our "fears"—are as nothing compared to a God whose blessed assurance promises triumph over sin and death. He offers "peace" and "great repose"—hardly the work of a God who wants us to literally be afraid of him. Julian's language shows the loving bliss of our God who makes all things well for each of us, every one a friend. She offers us something to hold on to—the hand, and love, of our God. Clinging to the everlasting arms is "in true faith and certain hope by the greatness of love." The "sweet and delightful" "fear" can only be the tremor of awe we feel when we touch the fringes of the garment of our Savior.

❧ **66** ❧

*After this, the good Lord showed the sixteenth showing on the
    following night, as I shall say later,*
and the sixteenth was the conclusion and confirmation of all fifteen.

*Except first it behooves me to tell you about my weakness, misery,
    and blindness.*
> *I have said in the beginning, "And in this all my pain was suddenly
>   taken from me." From this pain I had no grief and no distress as
>   long as the fifteen showings lasted one after another, and at the
>   end all was concealed and I saw no more.*

*And soon I sensed that I would live and linger on, and immediately
    my sickness came again—first in my head, with a sound and a
    noise, and without warning all my body was filled full of sickness
    just as it had been before, and I was so barren and so dry that I
    had but little comfort.*

*And as a wretch I moaned gloomily because of the experience of my
bodily pains and for the lack of comfort, spiritually and bodily.*

Then a member of a religious order came to me and asked how I fared.

> *And I said that I had been raving today, and he laughed aloud and
>   inwardly.*
> *I said, "The cross that stood before my face, it seemed to me that
>   it bled profusely."*
> *And with this word, the person that I spoke to grew all serious and
>   marveled.*
> *And immediately I was sore ashamed and amazed at my recklessness,
>   and I thought,*
> *"This man takes seriously the least word that I could say" and
>   then I saw no more of him.*

But when I saw that he took it seriously and with such great respect,
I grew most greatly ashamed,
> *and I would have been shriven,*
> *except at that time I could tell it to no priest,*
> *for I thought, "How would a priest believe me when, by saying I raved,*
> *I showed myself not to believe our Lord God?"*
>> *(even though I believed Him truly during the time that I saw*
>> *Him, and so was then my will and my intention to do so*
>> *forever without end—but, like a fool, I let it pass from my*
>> *mind).*

Ah, behold me, a wretch!
> *This was a great sin, a great unkindness, that I, out of folly, out of*
> *feeling a little bodily pain, so stupidly lost for the time the comfort*
> *of all this blessed showing of our Lord God.*
>> *Here you can see what I am by myself.*

But even in this our gracious Lord would not leave me.
And I lay still until night, trusting in His mercy,
> *and then I began to sleep.*

In my sleep, at the beginning, it seemed that the Fiend fixed on my
> *throat, thrusting forth a face like a young man's very near to my*
> *face; and the face was long and wondrous thin. I never saw any such.*
> *The color was red like the tilestone when it is new fired, with*
>> *black spots in it like black holes, fouler than tilestone.*
> *His hair was red as rust, clipped off in front, with side locks*
>> *hanging on the temples.*
> *He snarled at me with an evil expression, showing white teeth,*
>> *and so much that I thought it even more repulsive.*
> *He had no fit body nor hands, but with his paws he held me by the*
>> *throat and would have strangled me, but he could not.*

> *(This horrible showing was given in sleep, as was no other.)*

And during all this time,
> *I trusted to be saved and protected by the mercy of God.*
And our gracious Lord gave me grace to awaken,
> *and scarcely had I any life.*

The persons that were with me watched me and wet my temples,
> *and my heart began to relax.*

Immediately a little smoke came in the door with a great heat and a foul stink.
   I said, "Benedicite domine! Everything here is on fire!"
      And I imagined that it was a physical fire that would have burnt
         us all to death.

I asked those who were with me if they sensed any odor.
   They said no, they smelled none.
      I said, "Blessed be God!"
         because then I was well aware that it was the Fiend that had
         come only to tempt me.

And immediately I betook myself to what our Lord had shown me on that
   same day,
      with all the Faith of Holy Church
         (for I look upon them as both the same),
and I fled to that as to my comfort.

And soon all vanished away,
   and I was brought to great repose and peace
      without sickness of body or fear of conscience.

ર૭   ર૭   ર૭

We are back in the sickroom with Julian; she narrates her experiences of the showings and her encounters with others. This is the human Julian, not the eloquent voice of the theologian or the passionate voice of the mystic. We find a suffering, confused, and *doubting* person who attempts to rationalize the events that have happened to her, perhaps out of embarrassment. In a dramatic gesture—one that can be attributed to anxiety, guilt, or God bursting through—we then have a return to the fierce narrative commitment to take these visions seriously. I am glad that Julian wavers in her certainty about how to understand what happened to her. If she were so sure, it would be difficult to relate to her. She struggles as we do. Julian points out that her period of visions was a pain-free time. She laments not the loss of the direct experience of God and the sweet sharing she had with him, but rather the physical reality that she is back in the bodily world where suffering is tangible instead of being glimpsed spiritually or intellectually. Her story is not "would I were in heaven with him," but "this really hurts." Still, she notes that the "lack of comfort" is spiritual as well as corporeal. Perhaps the most important external event of the *Showings* is chronicled here. When Julian tells a religious brother that she had been "raving" in her illness and describes briefly what has happened, he is stunned. She feels guilty that she may have trivialized the experience. She is ashamed and wants to confess her light treatment of it as a sin. From this moment we move to an intensely personal and psychological reflection. Julian's old life is over. She can never go back to it. When she tries to return to that old way of life she is struck by the magnitude of what has happened to her. As we know from her subsequent autobiography, the showings were her defining event.

Julian sleeps. In her dreams she has a vision of a devil—a literal "anti-Christ": an active foil to the suffering body of Jesus she had experienced in her visions. She sees this as a temptation. The real temptation, the real "devil," is the desire to forget. It would be easy to go about one's quotidian existence and put behind oneself the memories of illness. Julian is called to do more—to say more. Her heart has turned: she has "converted." Julian inserts herself into the narrative of salvation; like Christ, she has fought the good fight. An unawakened consciousness of God is no longer possible. She has become aware of the mercy of God working within her. She smells, feels, and sees smoke. Julian interprets this as the fire of hell that threatens, the danger of damnation. She recalls her visions and faith and is healed. Her new life must not only be with God; it must also be in the Church. Did heresy beckon? Must orthodoxy be confirmed, if the "fiend" tempts? In any case, the Church becomes a sanctuary for Julian, a place for her to tell the story of her life, the narrative of her showings. Julian's story is ours in every way. How many of us have felt the stirrings of the Spirit? How has God called us for some purpose to tell a message the world needs to hear? How easy would it be to simply forget, to return to our predictable lives with their duties, plans, and desires! Chapter 66 narrates "the call of Julian," comparable to the call of men and women of the Bible. Her visions contain all sorts of images, but it is up to her to share them. She must process them through her "understanding" to make them meaningful and relevant to those who need to hear their message. We may not all have visions while lying in a sickbed. That does not mean we are not all called to listen for the voice of God speaking in our hearts, to allow God to break through to us so that his message may be transferred, translated, carried through to the world. May we be good listeners, and may we have the courage to say "yes" to the call.

☙ 67–68 ☜

[Chapter 67]
And then our Lord opened my spiritual eye and showed me my soul
in the midst of my inner self.

I saw my soul as large
  as if it were an endless castle
    and as if it were a blessed kingdom;
and by the circumstances I saw in it
 I understood that it is an honorable City.

In the midst of that City sits our Lord Jesus Christ,
  true God and true man,
  a handsome person,
  and of tall stature,
   a most exalted Bishop,
   a most solemn King,
   a most honorable Lord.

How would Jennings answer [handwritten annotation]

And I saw Him arrayed with great pomp and honor.
 He sits in the soul calmly upright in peace and repose, and He
 rules and guards heaven and earth and all that exists.

The Manhood sits with the Godhead in repose,
and the Godhead rules and guards without any agent or activity.
And the soul is all occupied with the blessed Godhead, who is
 supreme Power,
 supreme Wisdom,
 and supreme Goodness.

The place that Jesus takes in our soul,
 He will never move it away forever, as I see it, for in us is His
 most familiar home and His eternal dwelling.

And in this He showed the delight that He has in the creating of man's soul
   —for as well as the Father had the power to make a creature,
   and as well as the Son had the knowledge to make a creature,
   equally well did the Holy Spirit have the wish that many souls be made;
   and so it was done.

And therefore the blessed Trinity rejoices without end in the creating of
   man's soul,
      for He saw from without beginning
      what would please Him without end.
Everything that He has made shows His Lordship.

   An understanding was given at the same time by the illustration
   of a creature that was led to see great nobility and kingdoms
   belonging to a lord, and when he had seen all the nobility below,
   then, marveling, he was moved to go above to the high place
   where the lord dwells, knowing by reason that his dwelling is in
   the most honorable place.

And thus I understood truly that our soul can never have rest in
   things that are beneath itself.
And when it comes above all created things into the self, still it
   cannot remain in the contemplation of the self, but all its
   contemplation is blissfully fixed on God who is the Creator
   dwelling in the self (for in man's soul is His true dwelling).

The highest light and the brightest shining of the City is the glorious love
   of our Lord,
as I see it.

And what can make us rejoice in God more than to see in Him that
He rejoices in us, the highest of all His works?
For I saw in the same showing
      that if the blessed Trinity could have made man's soul any better,
         any more beautiful, any nobler than it was made,
      He would not have been wholly pleased with the creation of man's soul.

But because He made man's soul as fair, as good, as precious a
creature as He could make it,
      therefore the Blessed Trinity is wholly pleased without end in the
         creation of man's soul,

and He wills that our hearts be powerfully raised above the depths
    of the earth and all vain sorrows,
and rejoice in Him.

[Chapter 68]

This was a delightful sight and a restful showing that is without end,
    and the contemplation of this while we are here,
    that is most pleasant to God
    and very great help to us.

And the soul that thus contemplates it makes itself to be like Him
who is contemplated, and ones itself in rest and peace by His grace.
It was a particular joy and bliss to me that I saw Him seated, because
the steadiness of sitting suggests endless dwelling.

And He gave me knowledge truthfully that it was He who showed
me everything before,
    for when I had watched this,
    with time for consideration,
    then our good Lord revealed words most humbly
    without voice and without opening of lips,
    just as He had done before,
    and said most sweetly:
    "Be well aware that it was no raving that thou sawest today,
    but accept it,
    and believe it,
    and keep thyself in it
    and comfort thyself with it
    and trust thyself to it,
    and thou shalt not be overcome."

These last words were said to teach true certainty that it was our Lord Jesus
    who showed me everything.

And just as in the first word that our good Lord revealed, referring
    to His blessed Passion: "With this is the Devil overcome"—
just so He said in this last word with completely true faithfulness,
    referring to us all: "Thou shalt not be overcome."

And all this teaching and this true comfort is universal for all my
fellow Christians as was said before—and this is God's will.

These words: "Thou shalt not be overcome," were said very sharply
and very powerfully, for certainty and comfort against all tribulations
that can come.

> *He said not*
> > *"Thou shalt not be tempted;*
> > *thou shalt not be troubled;*
> > *thou shalt not be distressed,"*
> *but He said,*
> > *"Thou shalt not be overcome."*

God wills that we take heed to these words,
and that we be very strong in certain trust,
in well and in woe,
> *for as He loves and delights in us,*
> > *so He wills that we love Him and delight in Him*
> > > *and strongly trust in Him;*
> > > *and all shall be well.*
And soon after all was concealed, and I saw no more.

ಬ   ಬ   ಬ

How often we quote the famous line, "Thou shalt not be overcome."
We sometimes cite that phrase out of context. In considering these words
as they follow Julian's moving narrative of illness, doubt, fear, and commitment in Chapter 66, they take on a wholly different meaning. The
journey inward is not easy. We do not always like what we find. There
are hurts and other parts of ourselves we would prefer not to see. But
Julian's soul, her inner reality, is not a place of wrestling, fear, doubt,
and pain. Rather, it is the glorious space that joins her to Christ through
his Incarnation into her very being. Julian elaborates extensive imagery
of God's habitation in the city of her soul. Julian is reassured that God
is seated there: He is at home. In turn, the soul rests in God in understanding. God shows Julian how she might go on after what has happened to her—something that she cannot rationally explain, easily part
with, or make peace with. How do we rebuild our lives once we have
been through great trauma, and perhaps felt the hand of God touching
us? Julian will not be overcome if she accepts and believes. She must
keep herself in the experience, trust herself to it, and comfort herself
with it. This advice is for all of us as we feel the Spirit working in our
lives. How easily we might be overcome and give up! We want to avoid

the pain of remembering. The call and the fearful desire to answer the call have the power to overturn our lives. Julian's eyes have opened to what this life will entail for her. God's words concern how Christ's Passion overcame the power of evil. This is the reminder that if we accept, believe, and rest in our own passion, neither will we be overcome. Christ did it first by suffering on the cross. We must do it now, as his incarnate spiritual progeny living out our passions, whatever they might be. God does not will us to suffer. We cannot accomplish any God-willed acts of redemption and transformation in the world and in ourselves without the pain and growth of change. We live not for our crucifixions but for the resurrections that God invites us to allow in our lives and the world around us. God's strength will work within us and through us, but we must trust that God "sits" in our soul and that we likewise rest and trust in him. The "devils" we encounter include the challenges to accept, believe, rest, and trust in God. We need his comfort to sustain us if we are going to answer his call.

Julian is strengthened; we are strengthened. Come what may, she will not, we will not, be overcome on the journey. This is the evolution of an assurance that comes over time. One cannot expect to maintain such certainty except for brief, intense glimpses. Julian reminds us that "He said not 'Thou shalt not be tempted; thou shalt not be troubled, thou shalt not be distressed,' but He said, 'Thou shalt not be overcome.'" Thus she sets out to have a life far different from what she had imagined, one she hardly had been prepared for. Can we have the courage to say yes and trust that we shall not be overcome? Do we have a choice? We may be tempted to give up, we may be troubled, we may be distressed—but can we accept that we shall not be overcome? At times depression, anxiety, disease, and affliction of every kind seem to overcome us. Even then, can we believe that the kindly light still leads us on?

☙ **69** ❧

After this the Fiend came again with his heat and with his stink, and
made me most anxious.

> The stink was so vile and so painful,
> and the physical heat was fearful and troublesome also.

Also I heard a physical chattering as if it had been from two bodies,
and both, it seemed to me, chattered at one time as if they were
holding a parliament with a great business; and all was soft muttering,
since I understood nothing that they said.

All this was to move me to despair, as I thought, seeming to me that
> they ridiculed the saying of prayers
>> (as when prayers are said coarsely with the mouth, without the
>> devout intention and wise effort which we owe to God in our prayers).

Our Lord God gave me grace to trust in Him,
> and to comfort my soul with physical speech
> as I would have done to another person who had been troubled.
>> (It seemed to me that their carryings-on could not be agreeable
>> to any physical activity of mine.)

My physical eye I fixed upon the same cross where I had been in
> comfort before that time,
my tongue I occupied with speaking of Christ's Passion and reciting
> the Faith of Holy Church,
and my heart I made fast to God with all my trust and with all my might.

And I thought to myself, saying:
> "Thou has not a great duty to keep thyself in the Faith in order
> that thou shouldst not be seized by the Enemy;
> if thou wouldst now from this time onward be as busy to keep thyself
> from sin, this would be a good and a most excellent occupation,"

{ *for it seemed that if I were truly safe from sin, I would be*
} *completely safe from all the fiends of hell*
{   *and the enemies of my soul.*

And so he occupied me all that night, and in the day until it was
    about six in the morning.

And immediately they were all gone,
all passed away,
and they left nothing but the odor;
and that still lasted awhile.

{ *I scorned that Fiend, and so was I delivered from him by the virtue*
}   *of Christ's Passion, for with that is the Fiend overcome,*
{   *as our Lord Jesus Christ said before.*

ಖಾ   ಖಾ   ಖಾ

Of course, after the blessed assurance of Chapters 67–68, it stands to reason that the next step in the process would be a visit from the devil, worse than ever. We may interpret this in a few different ways. On the one hand the mind is apt to create the test of the assertion of security that was put forth. The question here is, "Will I really not be overcome?" It is another manifestation of fear and perhaps good for building confidence. On the other hand, if we locate the powers of evil, the "fiend" in this chapter, as outside of Julian, then her story reflects a typical heroic narrative. She must do battle, like Christ, with the forces of darkness and be tempted in some manner. In answering the call, what stands in our way? Is it a crowded schedule, an unaccepting family—or just a needy one—or some unwillingness in our lives to make or accept the changes that heeding a spiritual yearning might require? Is it our attachment to the things of this world, our pride, keeping up with the Joneses? We each have our dragons to slay, fiends to do battle with. It is worth noting that the worst fiend could be our sense of unworthiness. "God wants me to do what?!! Surely not I!" This distorted humility is a real sin because it prevents us from living out God's call to us, God's need for us, God's plan for our lives. God cannot repair the world without our special gifts and talents. God really will not do it without us. As long as we hold onto the notion that we are not good enough or smart enough or resourceful enough, we are rejecting the power of the Incarnation working in us and through us. That one-ing with God is a blessing that Julian demonstrates throughout the *Showings* and is meant to give us courage.

Julian's fiend is a supremely carnal manifestation. Our troubles are experienced through living lives in this world; they are the anti-types of the blessing of the Incarnation that "ones" us. This is not a discourse of dualism; all our problems cannot be blamed on our having bodies. Much bad Christian theology has already made that faulty assertion. Rather, the physicality of the mystical experience as well as Julian's struggle with evil remind us that we *are* our bodies. We live in the world; with and through the very circumstances we encounter we can help to heal it. For some of us this means understanding and accepting our bodies and the human experiences of people like us and different from us. For others it may mean healing relationships or reaching out to improve the material circumstances of people near or far. This is a broad lesson from Julian's self-enclosed, mystical experience but it can help us on our spiritual journeys just as Julian articulates her personal struggle. Incomprehensible voices cause her to despair, fearing that her prayers were ridiculed. Julian literally struggles with the noises in her head. What is God trying to tell her, and who is speaking? Is this all her imagination at work, or should she take it seriously? Doubt rears its head again. Is she devoutly praying, or is her experience just a lot of mumbo jumbo? One might call the noise "static"—racing thoughts that take one away from important messages. We can almost taste Julian's frustration when she tells us she understood nothing. Her book is the narrative of the life and spiritual experience of an extraordinary person trying to make sense of the irrational, attempting to discern God's will for her life. Julian craves understanding; she craves meaning. Years after her illness, she was finally able to conclude that "Love was His meaning." That is what it all boils down to, not extensive theological explanations about the world or our lives. But this realization did not come overnight, and we too must be patient on our journeys.

Julian talks to herself. She attempts to reason out her experience and give herself courage. Surely no one else is going to understand. If they do listen to her, they may suspect her of being mad or dangerously misguided. This journey inward to the "understanding," to the conversation with the self, opens the door to the composition of her text. Julian did not know where to go or what to do, but she solves it in a trinity. She looks to the cross (with her physical eye), she speaks of the Passion (giving language to, making meaning of, its message), and she wills her heart and soul to trust in God (through her soul's determination). Her narrative is anxious lest she be labeled a heretic but it also expresses concerns about blocks that might get in her way. If Julian is really going to follow this path she had better find the inner tools to clear away the barriers, the "sins" that could distract her. She details a dark night of the soul as she fights the good fight. Here is the spiritual struggle to set oneself on the path one is determined to follow, to seek out God. We may look to the human struggle of Jesus, his passion and death, to inspire us as we take up our crosses. That story is mythologized in Christian theology as the battle between good and evil that our God fights for us. In his heroic death he wins life for us. In our human way we can carry that story with us to give us the courage to follow the voices calling us on. May Julian's message give us strength to listen to God's desires for us.

∞ **70** ∾

In all this blessed showing, our good Lord gave me understanding
that the vision would pass (which blessed showing the Faith holds to)
with His own good will and His grace,
> for He left with me neither sign nor token by which I could know this,
> but He left me His own blessed word in true understanding,
> bidding me most powerfully that I should believe it.
> And so I do!

Blessed may He be!

I believe that He is our Savior who showed it,
and that it is the Faith that He showed.

And therefore I believe it, rejoicing; and to it I am bound by all His
own intention, with these next words that follow: "Keep thyself
therein and comfort thyself with it and trust thyself to it."

Thus I am bound to maintain it in my Faith.

For on the same day that it was shown, as soon as the vision was
passed, like a wretch I forsook it and openly said that I had raved.

Then our Lord Jesus of His mercy would not let the vision perish,
> be He showed it all again within my soul,
> with more fullness,
> with the blessed light of His precious Love,
> saying these words most strongly and most humbly:

"Know it with certainty now that it was no raving that thou sawest
> this day."
> > As if He had said:
> > > "Because the vision was passed from thee, thou didst let it go
> > > and knew not how to preserve it; but know it now, that is to say,
> > > now that thou dost understand it."

273

This was said not only for that particular time,
but also to fix it there upon the foundation of my Faith
where He says immediately following:
   "But accept it, believe it, and keep thyself in it and comfort thyself
   with it and trust thyself to it; and thou shalt not be overcome."

In those six words which follow where He says "accept it,"
His intention is truly to make this fast in our heart,
   for He wills that it dwell with us in Faith until our life's end,
      and afterwards in fullness of joy,
         willing that we always have certain trust in His blessed promises,
         knowing His goodness.

For our Faith is opposed in various ways by our own blindness and by
      our spiritual Enemy, within and without,
   and therefore our Precious Lover helps us with spiritual insight
      and true teaching in equally different ways, within and without,
      by which we can know Him.

And therefore in whatever manner He teaches us,
      He wills that we perceive Him wisely,
         receive Him sweetly,
         and keep ourselves in Him full of faith—
for beyond the Faith is no goodness preserved in this life,
      as I see it,
and below the Faith is no health for souls,
but in the Faith there the Lord wills that we maintain ourselves.

   For we must by His goodness and His own working maintain
      ourselves in the Faith,
   and by His permitting it, we are tested in the Faith by spiritual
      opposition and made strong.

If our Faith had no opposition, it would deserve no reward, as far as
the understanding I have of all our Lord's meaning.

ॐ   ॐ   ॐ

Just as we celebrate Christ's ascension, as we rely on the truth of
Pentecost, Julian tells us that God gave her "understanding" that her
vision would pass, and "his own blessed word in true understanding"

that she should believe it. Here we stand at the empty tomb; here we meet him on the road to Emmaus. We touch his wounded side; we live in his word, and we celebrate the Eucharist of his Word. "And so I do." And so we believe; and so we receive the Spirit into our midst. The fire of Pentecost burns a remembrance that he is with us always. Such Spiritual evangelism is all well and good, but what do we do—what does Julian do—with the absence? We may know those times of the Spirit in our midst—when we are living fully in the present moment. For Julian, that is her visionary experience. But what can we do with, how do we handle, those times of recollection when we are living in the absence and might only recall the experiences of bliss and reassurance? Can we make it real enough for ourselves that we can assert "And so I do"? Wordsworth calls poetry "emotion recollected in tranquility." An experience so bright and intense when it is perceived cannot be put into words at that time. It takes the vivid imagination at a later date—when the climax has passed—to remember the experience more fully and give voice to it. Doing so makes it real. Feeling it in one's heart, the "I am with you always, even to the end of time," is living the "And so I do." For Julian, this meant entering into her body's/soul's/understanding's grasp of God—where God literally "sits"—again and again to write the poetic revelation that is her book. This is a firmly incarnational experience. The vision is over, the Presence seems absent. But it rests in her just as God rests in our souls; it comes to rest in Julian's text. Can we trust with courage to shout the "And so I do!" in those diastoles, those pauses between beats? Fundamentally, God is with us always in our soul's memory that is the "seat" of the Incarnation.

Julian again laments her doubt and trivialization of the experience she had dismissed as "raving." She regrets, but God cannot let the vision perish and shows it all again within her soul. He literally lifts a lamp to illuminate Julian's darkness and affirm for her that what she saw was true. In our times of bleakness, the Light shines. What more can we ask for than a God who again and again moves our hand into the glory of his wounded side to strengthen our belief? Such is the sacrifice of the Mass. For us it is easier said than done. It would be lovely to say that whenever and wherever we doubt, God is there with a Zeppelin to say "Fear not, it is I!" Usually it is a bit subtler. Otherwise there would be no "dark nights of the soul." Those dry terrains, Milton's "darkness visible," are part of the growing cycle for our souls. There is nothing wrong with looking more closely for God's light in the darkness; there is nothing wrong with lighting a candle ourselves and sharing it with others. That is what we are called to do. Julian was in the process of becoming a lamp to enlighten her world through the composition of her text. It has lived for six hundred years and deepened the spiritual lives of many. Julian's visionary experience was not for herself alone. Her call was to share God's message with the rest of humanity. Over a period of decades she discerned this call as she wrote her book. She may not have known immediately that it was God's will for her to speak out. Indeed, we will never really learn how Julian viewed her own text. Given the years she spent making it, we have to believe that she saw it as a major part of what she was here to do. The message had been fixed in her understanding; Julian's job was to unravel it. She then wove a narrative to explain its meaning to others.

We suffer within; we may be victims of circumstances outside ourselves. While our reflection, contemplation, and prayer can lead to "spiritual insight," it can also come from outside. God's love is revealed to us in community, not just in solitude. We learn "love's meaning" in our discourses with others and our blessings of *communitas* as much as we learn them through our quiet understanding. Julian affirms that she is within the orthodox Church and trusts its guidance and teaching. She is careful to ensure that no one could label her a heretic. Exchange with the outside world is important to her. If she is going to share the Word, she needs to hear and understand the words of others. Trials come from within (doubt, the absence of an immediate Presence), but they also come from without. We do not speak exclusively to ourselves or for ourselves, but in and for community. There are times our challenges are for the good. May we rest in the knowledge of an indwelling—and outdwelling—Presence that accompanies us all our days, to the end of time. May we see the light in the darkness or light a candle to share with others. May we raise a pen or a voice to help the light of assurance to shine within and without.

৪ **71** ৶

Glad and merry and sweet is the blessed loving face our Lord turns to our souls;
 for He sees us always living in love-longing,
  and He wills that our soul be of glad expression to Him
   in order to give Him his reward.

And thus I hope with His grace that He has—and shall even more—
draw in our outer expression to the inner demeanor and make us all at one
with Him and each of us with the other, in the true lasting joy that is Jesus.

I understand three kinds of expressions from our Lord.
  The first is the face of passion as He showed it while He was here
   in this life, dying. (Though this sight is mournful and sorrowful, yet
   it is also glad and merry, for He is God.)

  The second kind of face is pity and sympathy and compassion; and
   this He shows to all His lovers who have need of His mercy,
   with certainty of saving.

  The third is the full blessed face as it shall be without end; and
   this was continued most often and longest.

And thus
  in the time of our pain and our woe,
   He shows us the face of His Passion and of His cross,
   helping us to bear it by His own blessed strength.

And in the time of our sinning,
  He shows us the face of compassion and pity,
   mightily protecting us and defending against all our enemies.

    (And these two are the usual faces which He shows to us in
    this life; with them mixing the third.)

  And this third is His blessed face, partially like what it will be in heaven.

And that face is a gracious inspiration and sweet enlightening of
the spiritual life by which we are saved in certain faith, hope
and love, with contrition and devotion and also with contemplation
and all manner of true solace and sweet comforts.
The blessed face of our Lord God accomplishes that inspiring
and enlightening in us by grace.

ᛞ   ᛞ   ᛞ

Julian moves from trial and uncertainty back to the relationship with
God, the contemplative mode. The fear and doubt give way to theological commentary that is less personal and autobiographical, if no less
penetrating. Her narrative concerns the face of God, a powerful thing
to consider. The Hebrew scriptures are obsessed with a God who cannot
show his face. In contrast, we have the God whose face never leaves us
in the human incarnation that is Jesus. Earlier chapters have been preoc-
cupied with the suffering body of Christ—the figure on the crucifix—but
this one is all about the loving face of Jesus. What can know us better
than that which literally sees us "face-to-face"? Julian does not "see
through a glass darkly." She moves into the experience of Christ's subjectivity as he gazes into her own. It is grace to behold the face of Christ.
It is this turning that is the act of the redemption; it is the taking flesh
in the Incarnation. The death on the cross is a turning of his face toward
us. Our desire is "love-longing," encompassing our want of transcendence, our need for salvation, and the confirmation that all is one in
love. God is love; we desire God. Every act of God is of love; we desire
God's love. It is God's will that our souls literally "smile" back at him,
love back at him for the love that he is giving. It is his reward that we do
so; the love relationship, that God needs us in his act of redemption, is
his reward as we gaze at him face-to-face. The working out of our lives
in the world, the Spirit incarnate present—thus is the smile returned.

With grace our outer expression draws closer to its inner demeanor:
the smile of the face looking up at God will "one" us to him in love. That
inner one-ing also has the graceful power to one us with one another.
Anyone who thinks Christianity is not joy is missing Julian's point.
Teresa of Avila might have said that the resurrection is the divine joke
on the devil (and Julian laughs as the devil is overcome), but Julian
makes our one-ing with God an exterior and interior smile. We are back
in endless joy, having returned from the dark night. This icon of con-

templation that is Christ's face is a trinity: the passion and suffering, the face of compassion, and the unchanging changelessness that is the face of God. Julian can see these in her "understanding." The dying face is also a glad, merry face because of what it enacts in the divine plan. This is the will of God carried out in the salvific act, putting all things right, returning the smile to the broken face of creation. The second face is Jesus' humanity: his compassionate glance offers sympathy to all his lovers who need his mercy. This is the face we know best. It offers us comfort in our pains and promises that "all shall be well" in the grand scheme. The third is the face of divine revelation that unites the first and second. Mercy and grace are joined together in the *Logos* that is and was and ever shall be. This face is that of the Spirit unceasingly working with, and within, the created world toward its repair. Julian glosses these faces as comfort in joining our sufferings to his by gazing at his Passion, forgiveness of our sins protecting us from evil, and the heavenly face that is not of this world. The third face overcomes. Jesus' sufferings on this earth—our sufferings, our sins—his forgiveness and protection are no-thing. In all the world's sufferings it is this face we are led to— through and past the falls of Jesus and ourselves. We move beyond the world's "all shall be well" to a place where truly all is well. This is the end of the love-longing: this is the space where it is taking us, from the faces of passion and compassion to the face of the "I AM." In our prayer, literally and figuratively gazing at our icon Christ, we may occasionally catch a glimpse of this everlasting.

May we find our rest in looking upon the loving face of God who understands and supports—who needs us to "smile" back at him, who pulls us through and away from all our cares to rest in his unmitigated gaze. In going inward, seeking gracefully our God for growth and comfort, we must smile outward at the world by action and work. How does the world perceive our faces? How do we perceive others'? How do we judge others, or privilege certain kinds of faces—by age, color, cleanliness, culturally specific standards of beauty or gender? We know the love-longing of God; we hear that call. In seeing his face we are refreshed and nourished to return and share it with others, one-ing them to us and to him. All our faces are one in Christ; this is Incarnation. We are inspired to act. We see his face in the faces of all we encounter. May we smile the love-longing of one-ing inclusion back into the world.

⟨ **72** ⟩

*But now it behooves me to tell how I saw mortal sin in those creatures
who shall not die because of sin, but live in the joy of God without end.*

*I saw that two opposites should never be together in one place.
The greatest opposites that exist are the highest bliss and the deepest pain.
    The highest bliss that is, is to have God in the radiance of endless life,
        seeing Him truly,
        experiencing Him sweetly,
        all peacefully enjoying Him in fullness of joy.
            (And thus was the blessed face of our Lord shown, but only
            partially.)*

*In this showing I saw that sin is most opposite to this, to such an
        extent that as long as we are mixed up with any part of sin,
        we shall never see clearly the blessed face of our Lord. And
        the more horrible and the more grievous our sins are, the
        deeper distance are we from this blessed sight for that time.*

*Therefore it seems to us frequently that we are in peril of death,
    in some part of hell,
    because of the sorrow and pain that the sin is for us.*

*And thus we are deadened for the time
    from the very sight of our blessed life.*

*But in all this I saw truthfully that we are not dead in the sight of God,
    nor does ever He pass away from us,
    but He shall never enjoy His full bliss in us
    until we enjoy our full bliss in Him,
    truly seeing His fair, blessed face,
        for we are ordained to that in nature,
        and get to it by grace.*

*Thus I saw how sin is mortal for only a short time in the blessed
creature of endless life.*

*And ever the more clearly that the soul sees this blessed face by
     grace of loving, the more it yearns to see it in fullness;
for notwithstanding that
     our Lord God dwells in us
     and is here with us,
     and calls us
     and enfolds us to tender love so that He can never leave us,
     and is nearer to us than tongue can tell or heart can think, yet we
          can never cease moaning nor weeping nor yearning until the
          time when we look at Him clearly in His blessed face; for in
          that precious, blessed sight there can remain no woe nor any
          lack of well-being.*

*In this I saw cause for mirth and cause for mourning:
     cause for mirth because our Lord our Creator is so near to us and
          within us, and we in Him, by the faithfulness of His great
          goodness in protecting us;
     cause for mourning, because our spiritual eye is so blind and we
          are so borne down by the burden of our mortal flesh and the
          darkness of sin that we cannot look our Lord God clearly in
          His fair blessed face.*

*No, and because of this murkiness, scarcely can we even believe and
trust His great love and His faithful protection of us.*

That is why I say that we can never cease mourning nor weeping.

*This "weeping" does not wholly signify pouring out of tears by our
physical eyes, but also intends more spiritual interpretation,
     for the natural desire of our soul to see His face is so great and so
          immeasurable that if all the splendor that ever God made in
          heaven and on earth were given to us for our solace, but we
          saw not the fair, blessed face of Himself, still we would not
          cease from mourning nor from spiritual weeping (that is to
          say, out of painful yearning) until the time we truly see the
          fair, blessed face of our Creator.
     And if we were in all the pain that heart can think and tongue can tell,
          if we could at that time see His fair, blessed face, all this
          pain would not bother us.*

*Thus is this blessed sight the end of all manner of pain to the loving
soul, and the fulfillment of all manner of joy and bliss.*

> *(And that He showed in the high, wondrous words where He
> said, "I am He who is highest; I am He who is lowest; I am
> He who is all.")*

It is proper for us to have three kinds of knowledge:
> *the first is that we know our Lord God;*
> *the second is that we know ourselves, what we are by Him in
> nature and grace;*
> *the third that we know humbly what we ourselves are as regards
> our sin and our weakness.*

And the whole showing was given for these three, as I understand it.

ଽ   ଽ   ଽ

We struggle all our lives to make metaphor of the icon of Chapter 71.
As the people who long to see his face, we are faced with those things
that impede our vision. Sight matters so much to Julian; she is a "visionary," after all. Yet her experience did not concern the physical, literal
picture but the essence of its meaning in her understanding. The icon
works as a means of explanation. Sin stands in juxtaposition to sight; it
is the un-sight of God, anything that separates us from a clearer perception of him. The mental static that gets in the way of good contemplation
and prayer is sin. It rarely is the fault of our will *per se*. It just is, as a
consequence of being human. Julian the contemplative longs to see the
face of God. But Julian the theologian desires to see that face as metaphor,
to understand God's meaning in her understanding. Whatever gets in
the way of this, whatever clouds over that holy face, is not of God. She
illustrates many uses of sight. When we cannot see God because of sin
we feel "deadened . . . from the very sight of our blessed life." For God,
this is not so. Even when we feel dead—separated from God, unable to
see his face—God sees us, God is with us. It is God's will that we see one
another face-to-face: for all the garbage, the murkiness, to be cleared
away. It is his bliss and is ordained in nature and enabled by grace. The
physical order wills that we see ourselves in the mirror of God's face and
the spiritual order makes that possible. As we are made in God's image
and Christ's body is our body, the full union enacted by his salvation
creates this mirror moment for the soul. One glimpse and we want more
of our indwelling, enfolding God who can never leave us.

The icon ceases being a remote image of an unspeakable divine and becomes the face of God that is within our very souls, in every one of us. God sees through our bodies; seeing him, getting to know him, is again a process of seeing ourselves. This can be difficult and painful. We crave greater union with God; we long to see his face. To move in that direction, we must go inward. There is too much murkiness, too many things that obscure our sight. The consolation found in the eye of the storm is to be treasured. Have you ever caught such a glimpse? The voice of love that reassures can sustain us through our worst moments. Julian's "whole showing" was given for a trinity of knowledge: of God, of our inner selves (by nature and grace), and of our outer selves (by sin and weakness). Remembering that we are his in nature—in our physical incarnation as part of his body and in grace that saves—we are better able to cope with the "sin" and "weakness" we inevitably experience. We cannot despair because of those things; they are a part of our journey. May we recall, no matter what the temporary feeling, that we are his in nature and grace—especially in those moments when we feel we have no hope of seeing his face.

(margin annotation: bodily vision / words / spiritual insight)

*All this blessed teaching of our Lord God was shown in three parts:
that is to say,*
> *by bodily sight,*
> *and by word formed in my understanding,*
> *and by spiritual insight.*
>> *As for the bodily sight, I have told it as I saw as truly as I can;*
>> *and as for the words, I have spoken them just as our Lord*
>>> *showed them to me;*
>> *and as for the spiritual insight, I have said somewhat, but I can*
>>> *never fully relate it, and therefore I am moved to say more*
>>> *about this insight (as God wills to give me grace).*

God showed two kinds of sickness of soul that we have:
> *the one is impatience or sloth (for we bear our labor and our pains*
>> *gloomily);*
> *the other is despair or doubtful fear (as I shall say later).*

In general, He showed sin with which everyone is involved, but in
> *particular He showed none but these two sins.*
And these two are those which most trouble and tempt us (according to what
our Lord showed me),
from which He wills that we be put right.
>> *(I speak of such men and women who because of God's love*
>> *hate sin and dispose themselves to do God's will; then by our*
>> *spiritual blindness and our bodily gloom, we are most inclined*
>> *to these sins, and therefore, it is God's will that they be known*
>> *and then we shall refuse them as we do other sins.)*

For help against this, full humbly our Lord showed
> *the patience that He had in His cruel Passion,*
> *and also the rejoicing and the delight that He has from that*
>> *Passion because of love.*
And this showed by example that we should gladly and wisely bear our pains,

*for that is greatly pleasing to Him
and endless benefit for us.*

*And the cause why we are troubled with these sins is because of our
ignorance of Love,*
> *for though the three Persons in the Trinity are all equal in
> themselves, the soul received most understanding in Love;*
*yes, and He wills that in everything we have our contemplation and
our enjoyment in Love,*

To this knowledge we are most blind;
> *for some of us believe*
>> *that God is all Power and is able to do all,
>> and that He is all Wisdom and knows how to do all,
>> but that He is all Love and wills to do all, there we stop.*

This ignorance is that which most hinders God's lovers, as I see it,
> *for when we begin to hate sin and amend ourselves by the
> command of Holy Church,*
still there persists a fear that hinders us,
> *because of paying attention to ourselves and the sins
>> we have done in the past*
>> *(and some of us because of our present every-day sins),*
>>> *for we keep not our covenants
>>> nor maintain the purity in which our Lord places us,
>>> but we fall frequently in so much misery that it is shame to
>>> see it.*
>>> *And the recognition of this makes us so sorry and so sorrowful
>>> that scarcely do we know how to find any comfort.*
>>> *And this fear we mistake sometimes for a humility, but this is
>>> a shameful blindness and a weakness.*
>>> *And we do not know to despise it as we do another sin which
>>> we recognize (which comes through lack of true judgment)
>>> and it is against truth, for of all the properties of
>>> the blessed Trinity, it is God's will that we have most
>>> certainty and delight in Love.*

For Love makes Power and Wisdom wholly submissive to us;
> *for just as by the graciousness of God He forgives our sin after the
> time that we repent us,*
*just so He wills that we forgive our own sin in regard to our
> unreasonable sorrow and our doubtful fears.*

ဢ   ဢ   ဢ

One can give voice to mysticism, but the whole picture (or icon?) is first and foremost an experiential concern. In Julian's Christian theology of embodiment, a phenomenon so dependent on our perception can only be felt; it cannot be described. Julian seeks to capture this idea: that our God is beyond language, beyond the human mind/spirit/body's capacity to ever really name. Yet she speaks to us in a most personal voice what happened to her. The soul's progress is explained and generalized in Chapter 73. Impatience and despair are two pitfalls. What else is there in the spiritual struggle? The hopeful desire to want to push things forward, to force winter bulbs before they are ready, possible apathy or lack of discipline; finally, giving way to depression or anxiety. As for the longing for God, it is all there is. Julian speaks to those who want to do God's will. They are the ones who by "spiritual blindness or bodily gloom" suffer in this way. Christ teaches patience, a strong statement of God's love for the spiritual seekers—those plodding the way, trying to make sense of things as Julian sought to do. She reminds herself that suffering comes from forgetting God's love for us. We fall off the wagon and get discouraged because we fail to remember the supreme love of God. It is very difficult when pursuing a solitary spiritual life not to fall prey to these kinds of sins. We need reassurance from somewhere, and it is often sadly lacking. We are fortunate when we find an understanding listener—someone who will encourage us onward toward our practice and remind us that our falls are not our faults. We can apply Julian's understanding to other situations in life, in the "secular" spiritual journey. Those who struggle with depression and anxiety do not lack worthiness (or even serotonin) but perhaps fail to remember that our very coming into existence means that we are deeply loved. Not all emotional struggles should be treated with good theology alone, but a healthy dose of right thinking can contribute to spiritual well-being in many ways besides religious growth.

Julian speaks from her experience to address those in need of her words to elucidate this "understanding in Love." God wills that "in everything we have our contemplation and our enjoyment in Love." We are "most blind" if we focus solely on the "power" or even "wisdom" of God and forget "that He is all Love and wills to do all." It refreshes the soul to recall that the workings of the universe are moved by love. Forgetting hinders us; we become self-absorbed, solipsistic, and scrupulous. We do not have to be "good enough." We need not despair on the path because we imagine that we are not. God's love is enough for all of us to conquer our struggles with what we wish we could do better and to avert the tendency to give up. Julian warns against preoccupation with our unworthiness. She experienced this when she felt guilt over trivializing her visions. We suffer and regret, and in fear we mistake such misery of falling for humility. We glorify it and stay in that muck. To miss the forest of love for the sake of the humble trees is blindness. We must learn to "despise" the tendency that is "against truth." We must forgive our own sin in this regard—we should not blame ourselves for wallowing—because it will get us nowhere.

Can we forgive ourselves? Julian suggests that we must do so if we are going to deliberately travel the spiritual journey. We are called to forgive ourselves once and for all as God forgave us through love. Perhaps we need to give up bad habits of excessive self-criticism. Many medieval people were repeatedly "shriven" for the same sin. Julian's message here of "don't get stuck" challenges the notion that we get to God through focus on our human weaknesses, errors, and failings. She insists that we not get bogged down in the dangerous place of fear (perhaps the famous state of "compunction" meant to bring the soul out of torpor, ready to flee to God for mercy). If we do get lost there we have forgotten God's love. Julian posits an entirely different theology: that the longing soul should instead always remember God's love. An unhealthy attachment to our particular human weaknesses is a block rather than an avenue to greater awareness and spiritual growth. Julian recognizes that the spiritually focused are most liable to this temptation, and it is therefore important to dismiss it. One wonders what direction the history of Christianity might have taken had there been more Julians. Indeed, what transformations will contemporary spirituality undergo if Julian's message continues its diaspora to an ever-widening audience?

∝ **74** ∾

I understand four kinds of fear.

*One is the fear of fright which comes to a man suddenly through
weakness. This fear does good, because it helps to purge man
(as does bodily sickness or such other pain which is not sin), for
all such pains help man if they are patiently taken.*

*The second is fear of pain by which a man is stirred and awakened
from the sleep of sin; for man that is hard asleep in sin is not
able, for the time, to perceive the gentle comfort of the Holy
Spirit until he has understanding of this fear of pain, of bodily
death, and of spiritual enemies. And this fear stirs us to seek the
comfort and mercy of God; and thus this fear helps us as an
entry place, and enables us to have contrition by the blessed
inspiration of the Holy Spirit.*

*The third is doubtful fear. Doubtful fear, insofar as it draws us to despair,
God wills to have transformed in us into love by true
acknowledgment of Love; that is to say, that the bitterness of
doubt be turned into the sweetness of natural love by grace; for
it can never please our Lord that His servants doubt His
Goodness.*

*The fourth is reverent fear, for there is no fear in us that fully
pleases God except reverent fear; and this is most gentle, for
the more of it one has, the less it is felt because of the sweetness
of love.*

*Love and fear are brothers;
and they are rooted in us by the Goodness of our Creator
and they shall never be taken from us without end.*

We have it from our human nature to love
and we have it from grace to love;
> *and we have it from human nature to fear*
> *and we have it from grace to fear.*

It is part of the Lordship and of the Fatherhood to be feared,
as it is part of the Goodness to be loved;
> *and it is as proper for us who are His servants and His children to*
> > *fear Him for His Lordship and His Fatherhood,*
> *as it is proper for us to love Him for His Goodness.*

And although this reverent fear and love are not separated, yet they
are not both the same, but they are two in character and in operation
(but neither of them can be had without the other).

Therefore I am certain that he who loves, fears—
even though he feels it only a little.

All fears other than reverent fear that are offered to us, although
they come under the pretense of holiness, yet are not as true;
and by this can they be known apart:
> *that fear which makes us quickly to flee from all that is not good*
> > *and fall onto our Lord's breast*
> > > *as the child into the mother's arms,*
> > > > *with all our intention and with all our mind acknowledging our*
> > > > > *weakness and our great need,*
> > > > *recognizing His everlasting Goodness and His blessed Love,*
> > > > *seeking only Him for salvation,*
> > > > *cleaving to Him with certain trust—*
the fear which brings us into this process is natural, merciful, good, and true.
> *And all that opposes this, either it is wrong, or it is mixed up with wrong.*

Then this is the remedy—to know them both and refuse the wrong.

For the natural benefit that we have in this life from fear
> *(by the merciful action of the Holy Spirit)*
that same benefit will be in heaven before God, noble, gracious,
> *and totally delightful.*
And thus we shall in love be intimate and near to God, and we shall
> *in fear be noble and gracious to God; and both equally.*

We desire of our Lord God
> *to fear Him reverently*

and to love Him humbly
and to trust Him mightily;
  for when we fear Him reverently and love Him humbly,
  our trust is never in vain;
  for the more that we trust—
  and the more strongly that we trust—
  the more we please and honor our Lord in whom we trust.

If we lack this reverent fear and humble love (as God forbid we
should) our trust shall soon be misdirected for that period of time.

Therefore we much need to beseech our Lord for grace that we may
  have this reverent fear and humble love as His gift,
  in heart and in deed—
for without this no man can please God.

ഇഗ   ഇഗ   ഇഗ

Julian defines four kinds of fear. The first we might call anxiety, what she names as "the fear of fright." As she describes it as cathartic or purgative, it is in line with our understanding of the "fight or flight" instinct that helps to rid the body of excess adrenaline produced under stress. Julian's second fear is a familiar one to her culture: that by which one is "stirred and awakened from the sleep of sin," understanding the "fear of pain, of bodily death, and of spiritual enemies." It "stirs us to seek the comfort and mercy of God." This fear is an "entry place": the open door through which one must pass on the soul's journey to the love of God. Medieval discourses on the spiritual life presume this awakening from the sleep of torpor to a state of compunction for one's sins. This primal scene of horror is meant to rouse the soul to decisive action in pursuit of God. The third and fourth fears are complementary, inasmuch as they are doubt and that which leads to faith, trust. Doubtful fear draws us to despair; God wills that it be "transformed in us into love by true acknowledgment of Love." God as love can break through bleak moods. Julian states that "there is no fear in us that fully pleases God except reverent fear; and this is most gentle." It can be hard to read this if we were taught a God of traumatic fear, if we have had to unlearn a dysfunctional relationship of "sinners in the hands of an angry God." A distorted parental figure of authority who wounds bodies or spirits is not Julian's God. This rhetoric of fear corresponds with her ongoing depiction of the "lordliness" of God, employing notions of power based on hierarchies in the social contract. In a society in which a feudal system of exchange remained the cultural paradigm for how people at all levels experienced good in their lives, it is not surprising that Julian's God is a lord who provides his vassals with all their needs. In turn, such a God deserves awe and respect. That is "reverent fear" in this text.

Julian articulates the union of love and fear that we have from nature and grace. As the mundane lord is to be loved and feared, so too is God in the impersonal aspect of his office. Julian never suggests that we should fear the Incarnate One who is one of us, the literal means of our subjectivity. Her love and fear are complementary rather than dichotomous. "I am certain that he who loves, fears" is "he who loves, respects," with the inflection that is particular to her culture. Besides the glorification of awe/respect, Julian has more to say about other kinds of "fear." Good fear drives us to the loving arms of God our mother when we awaken to our need. Thus it is not fear itself but the outcome of fear that is meaningful. Julian celebrates not our vulnerability but rather our ultimate trust and faith in God. Fear helps us to realize our dependence on God not because it makes us weak, incapable, powerless people. Rather, we can better claim our own strength through trust in God that empowers us. Even vulnerability can operate as a good through the action of grace. Anything that blocks this process, that prevents us from becoming all we are called to be, is the opposite of good. Within her awe and respect for authority, Julian's amatory theology creates a radical intimacy with the divine for which there is little precedent except perhaps in the literatures of courtly love or affective piety. Julian articulates a trinity of fearing, loving, and trusting God—leading to faith. Faith provides the appropriate reverence for the grandeur of God. Julian uses her culture's metaphors of authority to aggrandize the power of love and trust in this faith, whereby personal vulnerability is of value only insofar as it brings us to God. Failure to honor the trust and faith God gives us, which transform our lives and enable us to "be all we can be," breaks the social contract between lord and vassal and is false pride.

~ 75 ~

I saw that God can do all that we need; and these three which I shall
say we need:
love,
yearning,
and pity.
Pity in love protects us in the time of our need, and yearning in
the same draws us into heaven.

For the thirst of God is to have the whole of mankind within Himself;
in this thirst,
He has drawn and drunken His Holy Souls who are now in bliss;
and, gathering in His living members,
He continually draws and drinks,
and still He thirsts and yearns.

I saw three kinds of yearning in God (and all for one purpose), of
which we have the same in us
(and of the same strength and for the same purpose).
The first is that He yearns to teach us to know Him and to love
Him for ever, since that is suitable and advantageous to us.
The second is that He yearns to have us up into His bliss as souls
are when they are taken out of pain into heaven.
The third is to fill us with bliss; and that shall be completed on the
Last Day to last for ever.

For I saw (as it is known in our Faith) that the pain and sorrow shall be ended
for all that shall be saved.
And not only shall we receive the same bliss that souls have had in
heaven before,
but also we shall receive a new bliss, which shall be abundantly
flowing out of God into us and filling us up.

292

*These are the good things which He has prepared to give us from
    without beginning.*
*These good things are treasured and hidden in Himself, for until
    that time, a created being is not strong or worthy enough to
    receive them.*

In this we shall see truly the reason for everything He has done,
    and, even more,
    we shall see the reason for all things that He has permitted.

And the bliss and the fulfillment shall be so deep and so high
    that out of wonder and amazement
    all created being shall have for God so great a reverent fear
        (surpassing what has been seen and felt before)
    that the pillars of heaven shall tremble and quake.

But this kind of trembling and fear shall have no pain—rather it is
part of the noble majesty of God to be seen this way by His creatures,
    fearfully trembling and quaking,
        for abundance of joy endlessly marveling at the greatness of God
            the Creator, and at the smallness of all that is made,
        for the sight of this makes the creature wondrous humble and subdued.

Wherefore God wills (and it is also proper to us both in nature and
    grace) that we be aware and know of this experience, desiring
    this sight and this deed,
for it leads us in the right way
and preserves us in true life and ones us to God.

God is as great as He is good;
    and as much as it is part of His Goodness to be loved,
    equally much it is part of His Greatness to be feared;
        for this reverent fear is the fair courtliness that is in heaven
            before God's face.

And just as much as He shall then be known and loved far more than
    what He is now,
to the same extent He shall be feared far more than what He is now.

Therefore it is inevitable that all heaven and earth shall tremble and quake when
the pillars shall tremble and quake.

ဢ   ဢ   ဢ

God is all we need: not only for our human desires but also from a cosmological, eschatological perspective. This is not pie-in-the-sky, wait till you get to heaven. God, the ground of our being, is all there is. Julian presents a trinity of needs: love, yearning, and pity. She does not attribute these to us, but rather to God. God loves us, yearns for us, pities us. Rather than projecting onto God our human desires, this chapter cites these all-too-human-sounding emotions in the service of salvation and union with God. In the short focus, such a trinity is what the suffering, longing soul needs to hear. If we are striving for the love of God and struggling with our weaknesses, it is a glorious gift to imagine that God desires us too. God-essence taking material form is this divine who then subsumes us in longing. At the foot of the cross, where lovers of Christ long to enter the wounded side, Julian goes further: to tell how he hungers to be inside us. This powerful statement keeps us traveling on the road. We do not just serve our needs in the process. We are led by a need greater than our own, in whose service we joyfully follow.

It makes sense that God wishes to "teach us to know him and to love him" if God wants us to rejoin with him in eternity. But that teaching also offers something else: the promise of justification of the intellectual hunger, the desire for understanding that Julian exudes. God wants us to come to him, "to have us up into his bliss." He wants us in heaven. He wants to "fill us with bliss," which will happen on the "last day." Julian's showing promises that the eternity of the end of time is not just about being with God. It is fully receiving him in the "we are his bliss, his reward." He desires us, longs for us, and at the end of time completely gives us himself, which is all joy—offered even more fully than he could on the cross. How can we have even more—"a new bliss, which shall be abundantly flowing out of God into us and filling us up"? Apart from the obvious erotic metaphors of divine penetration, this new bliss suggests complete union, becoming part of God in a greater way than is possible through the Incarnation, atonement, redemption, or resurrection alone. The trajectory of this discourse is logical for the intellectual Julian: final entry into the heart and mind of God so as to understand. It is not just being close to the heart of God in love. It is about making sense of her visions, what Julian spent decades working at. She also struggled to understand the workings of her world, the meaning not only of the revelations that happened to her but of all the events of life. It is perfectly well and good to be taken to the Lover's bed, to fully enjoy him in body. To know one is loved and to love in return is a beautiful thing. But Julian always needs to know why. The promise of the afterlife is almost enough in the union she will experience there. Yet the crown comes on the Last Day when everything will make sense. We will know God's mind and heart.

As in the "reverent fear" of Chapter 74, Julian underscores the hierarchy that "all created beings" should have such awe for God, lacking "pain." That keeps us on the straight and narrow, one-ing us to God. This "new bliss," this one-ing with God makes us even more/ever more part of him. In the glory of the last day, when the lovers of God will be fully joined to him, "reverent fear" can no longer maintain the distinctions known in the world. As Paul writes, the categories that separate us will not apply in Christ. Awe will melt away for those loved, yearned for, and pitied as they become part of what God is, as they are one-ed. Before that time we are not able to receive it. Here is fulfillment, an "abundance of joy endlessly marveling at the greatness of God the creator." In this *jouissance* of bliss, a literal second "coming," there will be no more separation between us and him since "sin" will be gone. God wants us to know about this experience, to contemplate it, as it ones us to him. Why does he need us so badly? What does it take to imagine him as need? It is fine to awaken to the fact that it is our job to work on fixing a broken world. Do we also need to fulfill a broken God?

ೞ **76** ಬಿ

I speak but little of reverent fear, for I hope it can be understood in this previous matter, but I am well aware that our Lord showed me no souls except those that fear Him.

I am also well aware that the soul that truly accepts the teaching of the Holy Spirit, hates sin more for its vileness and horribleness than it does all the pain that is in hell.

For the soul that beholds the good nature of our Lord Jesus,
hates not hell, but sin, as I see it.

And therefore it is God's will that we recognize sin, and pray
diligently and labor willingly, and seek teaching humbly, so that we
do not fall blindly into sin;
 and if we fall, that we rise quickly (for it is the worst pain that the
 soul can have to turn from God any time there is sin).

When other men's sins come to mind, the soul that wishes to be in repose
 shall flee from that as from the pain of hell, searching in God
 for remedy for help against it,
for the beholding of other men's sins
makes, as it were, a thick mist before the eye of the soul,
and we cannot for the time see the fairness of God
  (unless we can behold another's sins
  with contrition with him,
  with compassion on him,
  and with holy desire to God for him,
 for without this it troubles and tempts and hinders the soul that
 beholds those sins).
   (This I understood in the showing about compassion.)

In this blessed showing of our Lord, I have an understanding of two opposites:

the one is the most wisdom that any creature can do in this life;
the other is the most folly.

> *The wisdom is for a creature to act following the will and advice*
> *of his highest supreme Friend. This blessed Friend is Jesus;*
> *and it is His will and His advice that we bind ourselves with*
> *Him and fix ourselves intimately to Him ever more in*
> *whatever state we are. For whether we are filthy or pure,*
> *we are always the same in His love. For well or for woe,*
> *He wills that we never flee from Him.*

> *However, because of our changeability within ourselves we fall*
> *frequently into sin. Then we have this by the guidance of*
> *our Enemy, through our own folly and blindness; for they*
> *say thus: "Thou art well aware that thou art a wretch, a*
> *sinner, and also untrue; for thou keepest not thy covenant;*
> *thou dost promise our Lord frequently that thou wilt do*
> *better, and immediately afterwards, thou fallest into the*
> *same—especially sloth into the wasting of time" (for*
> *that is the beginning of sin, as I see it, and especially to*
> *the creatures who have given themselves to serve our Lord*
> *with inner contemplation of His blessed goodness).*
> *And this makes us fearful to appear before our gracious Lord.*

Then it is our Enemy who will set us back with his false fear
concerning our sinfulness because of the pain with which he threatens
us. It is his intention to make us so gloomy and so weary in this that
we would forget the fair, blessed beholding of our everlasting Friend.

ॐ   ॐ   ॐ

Fear of coming before God because of our sense of unworthiness is
sin. Again, Julian's notion of fear is not the trembling and terror that
paralyze us. That condition blocks us on our path to God; it is the real
sin. In reverent fear Julian seeks to convey what the Romantic poets
described as the sublime, grasping at the skirts of the infinite. No one
can be drawn nearer to God without such holy breathlessness at the
Everest he or she longs to ascend. Julian describes what it means to look
at another: "The beholding of other men's sins makes . . . a thick mist
before the eye of the soul, and we cannot for the time see the beauty of
God." Whether we become obsessed with our sins or those of another,

we stare in the face of that which separates us from God. By this we cannot see his face. As with the beam in our eye in the gospel parable, we must be cautious we do not turn ourselves into judges lest we be judged likewise. This point would have been very important for Julian to remember as she moved into the role of spiritual counselor. Whether we are serving as spiritual directors exclusively to our own souls or to others' as well, we must beware in contemplating sin. The goal for another is, as Julian describes, "contrition with him, compassion on him, and holy desire to God for him." We must put ourselves in the other's place and know compassion for the person. This is a form of "love thy neighbor as thyself." In viewing another's falling we should neither bring ourselves up to an exalted state of pride and judgment nor pull ourselves down in finding ourselves so unworthy. This experience presents a lesson on how to live in full communion. We learn strength for our own souls, because otherwise the trinity of "troubles . . . tempts . . . and hinders" to the soul beholding another's sin will bring us down. That depth can be despair, as any good adviser knows. This passage on compassion serves as a model for the Christian life. As we seek to understand another's experience that may be different from ours, we must not be swift to judge. We need to grow mindful of what aspects of their "sin" bring up "issues" for us. We also should remember first and foremost that any and all abstract definitions of "sin"—which we may be fast to condemn—have an individual human story. That requires listening and understanding before we make sweeping generalizations.

Jesus the "blessed Friend" wills and advises "that we bind ourselves with him and fix ourselves intimately to him ever more, in whatever state we are." God does not want us to wait until we are perfect before we feel acceptable to come before him. God wants (and needs) us to present ourselves just as we are. Here is the choice to participate in actively one-ing ourselves to him, saying yes to his call. To think we are not good enough is to separate ourselves from him; it is sin. "For whether we are filthy or pure, we are always the same in his love. For well or for woe, he wills that we never flee from him." God will take care of it all if we will turn over to him our awareness of the imperfect external self. It is easy for us to fall into self-blame. This is especially true for those "creatures who have given themselves to serve our Lord with inner contemplation." Scrupulosity sets in; discouragement, despair, "is the beginning of sin." When we labor in this meaningless waste of time we reject God. We miss the mark by dwelling on our inadequacies. We are prevented from living out our vocations and serving God in the way that he has called us. Here is the real "fear," the "bad fear," this preoccupation with a sense of our unworthiness that keeps us from showing up before God. Such breast beating is not of God, it is from those forces that separate us from him. It makes us "gloomy and so weary" that we move into that space of forgetting the face of our Friend. We must not glorify it because it is an occasion of sin. It is more of Julian's "static," the voices she understands as sources of temptation, the devil pulling her away from God.

It is easy for a solitary contemplative like Julian to fall victim. In our contemporary world we are equally vulnerable. Sin comes in many different forms. The devout can become bogged down with rules and regulations that create the idea that we are miserable sinners. Our "fear" of God cannot then be that "awe" on the cusp, glimpsing from afar the glory of God. We are too caught up in our small fear, our solipsistic preoccupation with the unworthy self. Many people feel separated from traditional religions because they think they will never be good enough, they could never approach the throne of the Almighty. They suffer from having internalized a belief in a God who will forever judge them like the dangerous spiritual counselor Julian warns against. They are thwarted from coming nearer. Even in the most secular space of modern psychotherapy one encounters scrupulous, striving individuals who sabotage opportunities for growth, self-realization, or happiness. When they claim this "less-than" status they commit sin—whether or not contemporary psychology would use that vocabulary. No child of God should feel so unworthy. May we approach our awesome God with the heart-pounding sense of his immanence, knowing that he calls us to him just as we are.

❧ **77** ❧

Our good lord showed the enmity of the Fiend,
    by which I understood that everything that is in opposition to love
    and to peace, it is the Fiend and of his party.

We both must fall because of our weakness and our folly;
and we must rise to more joy
    because of the mercy and grace of the Holy Spirit.

And if our enemy wins anything from us by our falling
    (for it is his delight),
he loses many-fold more in our rising by love and humility.

This glorious rising is such great sorrow and pain to him, for because
    of the hate that he has for our soul, he burns continually in envy.
And all this sorrow that he wishes to make us have,
    it shall turn upon himself.

And it was because of this that our Lord scorned him;
and this made me laugh mightily.

This, then, is the remedy:
    that we be aware of our sinfulness
    and flee to our Lord,
        for ever the more quickly we do so,
        the more advantageous it is for us to be near Him.

And this is what we say in our intention:
    "I know well I have deserved an evil pain,
    but our Lord is all Power and can punish me mightily,
    and He is all Wisdom and knows how to punish me with reason,
    and He is all Goodness and loves me tenderly."

And in this awareness it is necessary that we remain, for it is a loving
humility of a sinful soul (wrought by the mercy and grace of the Holy

Spirit) *when we will willingly and gladly accept the scourging and
chastening that our Lord Himself wishes to give us.*

> *(And the chastening shall be wholly tender and very gentle if we will
> only consider ourselves pleased with Him and with all His works.)*

*For the penance that man takes upon himself was not shown to me—
that is to say, it was not shown in particular—*

> *but it was shown particularly and highly and with full lovely
> demeanor that we shall humbly and patiently bear and suffer the
> penance that God Himself gives us, with remembrance of His
> blessed Passion.*

*For when we have remembrance of His blessed Passion, with pity
and love, then we suffer with Him as His friends did who saw it*

> > *(and this was shown in the thirteenth showing,
> > near the beginning, where it speaks of pity).*

For He says,

> *"accuse not thyself overly much,*
> > *questioning if thy tribulation and thy woe is all because of thy
> > > sinfulness;*
> > *for it is not my will that thou be gloomy or sorrowful
> > > undiscerningly;*
> > *for I tell thee, whatsoever thou doest, thou shalt have woe.
> > And therefore I will that thou wisely recognize thy penance
> > > which thou art in constantly,*
> > *and that thou dost humbly accept it for thy penance,
> > and thou shalt then truly understand that all thy living is
> > > beneficial penance."*

*This earth is imprisonment,
and this life is penance,
and in this remedy He wills that we rejoice:*

> *that our Lord is with us,
> guarding us
> and leading us into the fullness of joy—for it is an endless joy to
> > us in our Lord's purpose:*
> > *that He shall be our bliss when we are there,
> > that He is our protector while we are here,
> > our way,*

and our heaven
  in true love
  and certain trust.

  (He gave understanding of this in all the showings, and
    particularly in the showing of His Passion where he caused
    me mightily to choose Him for my heaven.)

If we flee to our Lord, we shall be comforted;
if we touch Him we shall be made pure;
if we cleave to Him we shall be secure and safe
    from all manner of peril.

For our gracious Lord wills that we be as friendly with Him as heart
can think or soul can desire.
    But beware that we take not so recklessly this friendliness that we
    refrain from courtesy; for while our Lord Himself is supreme
    friendliness, He is also as courtly as He is friendly,
    for He is true courtesy.

And the blessed creatures that shall be in heaven with Him without end,
He wishes to have them like Himself in all things, for to be like
our Lord perfectly, that is our true salvation and our complete bliss.

And if we do not know how we shall do all this, let us desire it from
          our Lord and He shall teach us, for that is His own delight and
          His honor.

Blessed may He be!

ॐ   ॐ   ॐ

Evil is everything that is not love and peace. Julian encourages us to
rise up when we fall. She personifies evil as the "Fiend." He takes pleasure in our falling. Our rising up, like Christ's resurrection, accomplishes
so much more than our falling can ever do. Julian's use of personification
serves her well in her strength of psychological insight. She writes that
"all this sorrow that [the fiend] wishes to make us have, it shall turn upon
himself." When we experience and then express malice, anger, and re-
sentment, these have the potential to hurt us more than they hurt those
against whom we harbor "un-love" and "un-peace." Julian develops her
idea of fallenness with respect to love and peace. God is Power, Wisdom,

and Goodness. Because of the first two we could be punished. He has the strength, and he also has the understanding of our fallenness. But his goodness makes him all love. The "penance that man takes upon himself" was not shown to Julian. Rather, God's will is that we suffer the penance God gives us of himself. This is not self-punishment, physical or mental. It is not God's will that we take that upon ourselves. Rather, we do penance when we look to his Passion with pity and love. We suffer with him "as his friends did who saw it." What could be more perfect than to be invited to be his friend, to contemplate what he suffered? When we do so, we understand our own pain. This lesson is for our souls. We consider his loss and our gain, and know ultimately that the salvation he wrought means so much more than our small fall. The Passion puts everything into perspective. It brings to mind God's love for us.

Julian offers a particular interpretation of the prevailing belief that we are punished in this life for our sins. God tells us not to be so hard on ourselves. As long as we live, "whatsoever" we do, we shall have "woe." That is what it means to be human: to face challenges. God suggests that this experience is a penance that we are in constantly. We do not need to do anything more. We only need to accept it, to take up our crosses. All living is "beneficial penance." Of course, this is easier said than done. How we fight our trials and tribulations, not just to right their wrongs! Rather, we fight against them, fail to accept, and whimper "why me?" Facing and accepting, taking up that cross, requires courage. This is how transformation happens. This is how we are saved and changed. These are moments of sacrament, transcendence—opportunities to heal ourselves, others, and our world. There is already enough suffering here. We do not need to make any more for ourselves or for others. We need to help repair the world. God "wills that we rejoice"— he leads us to the fullness of joy. This is not pie-in-the-sky theology. Julian states that God "caused [her] mightily to choose him for [her] heaven." That is here and now. We can have our hell on earth—a hell of our own making, with the "fiend" tempting us to wallow in suffering and create more pain and self-punishment. We can also have our heaven on earth in answering God's loving call to choose him for our heaven. It is literally evil to imagine that doing so requires self-inflicted misery. God is all generosity, hospitality, and welcome. Our God invites us to the table. If we hold back or indulge in a meal of self-punishment, we are being selfish and dishonoring our host. He offers us a journey of personal perfection; he wants us to be like him in our outer selves as we already are in our inner nature. He leads us there. This is salvation. This is our journey, if we accept his hospitality and say yes to the call. This way of perfection requires us to take up our crosses. The Incarnation made him like us as the redemption makes us like him. Fortunately, we do not need to have all the "understanding" Julian craves, all the answers, to begin. "And if we do not know how we shall do all this, let us desire it from our Lord and he shall teach us, for that is his own delight and his honor." A desire is a prayer.

‹ **78** ›

Our Lord of His mercy shows us our sin and our weakness by the
sweet gracious light of Himself,
> *for our sin is so vile and so horrible that He of His courtesy will*
> *not show it to us except by the light of His grace and mercy.*

It is His will that we have knowledge concerning four things:

> *the first is that He is our ground from whom we have all our life*
> > *and our being;*
> *the second, that he protects us mightily and mercifully at the time we are*
> > *in our sin and among all our enemies who are most fierce against us*
> > *(and so much the more are we in greater peril because we*
> > *give the enemy occasion for that and know not our own need);*
> *the third is how courteously He protects us and lets us know when*
> > *we go amiss;*
> *the fourth is how steadfastly He waits for us and does not change*
> > *His demeanor, for He wills that we be transformed and*
> > *one-ed to Him in love as He is to us.*

Thus by this grace-filled knowledge
> *we can see our sin beneficially without despair*
> > *(for truly we need to see it)*
> *and by that sight we shall be made ashamed of ourselves,*
> *and our pride and presumption shall be broken down.*

It truly behooves us to see that by ourselves we are just nothing but
sin and wretchedness.
> *And thus by the sight of the less which our Lord shows us,*
> *the more which we do not see is diminished, for He of His courtesy*
> > *adjusts the sight to us (for it is so vile and so horrible that we would*
> > *not endure to see it as it is).*

And by this humble knowledge thus, through contrition and grace,
we shall be broken away from all things that are not our Lord,
and then shall our blessed Savior perfectly heal us and one us to Himself.

This breaking and this healing our Lord means with reference to all mankind,
    for he that is highest and nearest to God, he can see himself sinful
        and needy with me,
        and I who am the least and the lowest of those that shall be saved,
        I can be comforted along with him that is highest.
So has our Lord one-ed us together in love.

When He showed me that I would sin, because of the joy that I had
in beholding Him, I did not readily pay attention to that showing, and
our courteous Lord stopped then, and would not teach me further
until He gave me grace and the will to pay attention.

From this I was taught that although we are nobly lifted up into contemplation
        by the particular gift of our Lord,
        yet it is necessary for us along with that to have knowledge and
        awareness of our sin and our weakness.

Without this knowledge we cannot have true humility,
and without this humility we cannot be saved.

And also I saw that we cannot get this knowledge from ourselves,
nor from any of our spiritual enemies, for they do not will us very
much good (for if it were by their will, we should not see our sin
until our ending day).

Then we are much beholden to God that He will Himself out of love
show our sin and weakness to us in time out of mercy and grace.

ℝ   ℝ   ℝ

We glimpse our great need for God and know his compassion. On the surface we are grimly reminded of how far we have to go. But through that awareness comes the invitation to change, to grow, to be one-ed with him more than we already are. We sin; we are weak and flawed. But God wills that we know that "he is our ground from whom we have all our life and our being." Before we contemplate our distance from where we could be, we have to call to mind that he is our foundation. We are already there, one-ed with him. There is nothing that we can do that could change that. Nothing can "separate us from the love

of God in Christ Jesus our Lord" (Rom 8:39). He protects us in our brokenness. God is with us *when* we sin and in our sin. He holds us and
cares for us there lest we come to harm. We are never alone or uncon-
nected. He grants us awareness of our transgressions. Without that, we
can never be more fully one-ed with him. In love He waits for us to come
to him and glimpse his unchanging face. God is patient. When we are
ready to make a change he is there to help us. We choose him as he has
chosen us so that we might join him more fully through our will.

Sin, our missing the mark, is not an occasion for shame; it is an opportunity for growth. We need to see it; to do so offers hope, not despair.
We know we cannot dwell on it or view ourselves as unworthy. Sin
simply is not of the nature that ones us to God. To recognize it breaks us
away from our hindrances. This is an act of healing: integration, making
whole the union of the one-ing, not condemnation. We ourselves are not
condemned; that which is not of God is. We are most fully of God. His
humanity shares this difficult conversion with us. His compassion sustains us as we turn away from what is not of God and move more fully
into the oneness that is him. Jesus the Christ "can see himself sinful and
needy with me." Such is the miracle of the Incarnation: we are comforted
as he is. This is all human feeling; this is what it means to share in a God
who feels as we feel, who suffers as we suffer. There is nothing we experience that is beyond his compassionate understanding.

Julian did not want to be shown that she would sin. Who would
choose to look at the reality that we willingly refuse and deny what God
has offered us? But God would go no further in the showings until
through grace and will Julian would pay attention. Spiritual growth is
simply not possible without our willingness to know ourselves utterly,
to look at ourselves more deeply. The courage to do so increases with
our trust in the Spirit leading us on. We must know who we are and
recognize our Achilles' heels. These may not be the obvious occasions of
sin. They could be resentments we hold against others or psychological
hurts from pain and trauma of the past. Anything that keeps us from
loving ourselves as children of God will hinder our spiritual growth. The
knowledge of ourselves comes from God. We cannot trust this awakening
to come from anywhere else. The God-driven grace of waking up can
come in unlikely places. An insight we get in a relationship, in a work
situation, or through secular psychotherapy is as truly of God as when
we are on our knees in prayer. When we realize that whatever leads us
to greater self-knowledge, whatever helps us on our spiritual journey, is
the work of the Spirit in the world we see more clearly the hand of God
ever laboring in this transcendental Incarnation we call creation.

☙ **79** ❧

Also I had in this showing more understanding—when He showed me that I would sin, I applied it simply to my own individual self, for I was not otherwise stirred at that time,

> but by the high gracious comfort of our Lord which followed afterward, I saw that His meaning was for all mankind—that is to say, all mankind which is sinful and shall be until the Last Day (of which group I am a member, as I hope, by the mercy of God)— for the blessed comfort that I saw is large enough for us all.

And here I was taught that I ought to see my own sin, and not other men's sins (unless it could be for the comfort and help of my fellow Christians).

Also in this same showing where I saw that I would sin, was I taught to be cautious of my own uncertainty,

> for I am not aware of how I shall fall,
> nor do I know the measure nor the greatness of my sin.
> > (For I fearfully wished to have known that,
> > but to that I received no answer.)

Also our gracious Lord, at the same time, showed me most certainly and powerfully the endlessness and the unchangeability of His love.

> And also, by His great goodness and His grace inwardly guarding, that His love and that of our souls shall never be separated in two, without end.

Thus in this fear I have cause for humility that saves me from presumption; and in the blessed showing of love I have cause for true comfort and joy that saves me from despair.

All this friendly showing of our gracious Lord is a loving lesson and a sweet, gracious teaching from Himself in the comforting of our soul.

For He wills that we know, by His sweetness and familiar loving,
    that all that we see or sense, within or without, which is in
    opposition to this is from the Enemy and not from God—
such as this: if we are moved to be more heedless of our living or
    the keeping of our hearts because we have knowledge of this
    plenteous love, then we need greatly to beware, for this
    inclination, if it comes, is untrue, and we ought greatly to
    hate it, for none of it has any similarity to God's will.

When we are fallen because of frailty or blindness,
    then our gracious Lord inspires us,
        stirs us,
        and calls us;
    and then He wills that we see our wretchedness
    and humbly let it be acknowledged.

But He does not wish us to remain thus,
nor does He will that we busy ourselves greatly about accusing ourselves,
nor does He will that we be full of misery about ourselves;
    for He wills that we quickly attend to Him;
    for He stands all alone and waits for us constantly, sorrowing
        and mourning until we come,
    and hastens to take us to Himself;
    for we are His joy and His delight,
    and He is our cure and our life.

(Though I say that He stands all alone, I leave out speaking of the
Blessed Company of heaven, and speak of His function and His working
here on earth, in respect to the circumstances of the showing.)

ᏞᎤ   ᏞᎤ   ᏞᎤ

Julian observes that "the blessed comfort that I saw is large enough for us all." How difficult it is to remember that at times! We live in an economy of scarcity and lack. Our human minds want us to believe that there is not enough, that there never will be enough. We live in a "dog-eat-dog" world where we are supposed to fight the ruthless rat race to get our piece of the pie. This is not just in the realm of material things. We seek to distinguish ourselves so that we might feel "special." We want to do the reading, or give the lesson, or receive particular thanks or praise for the gift of our unique contribution. Indeed, in religious milieux humility and individuality often do battle. We even long for the pride of being seen as exceptionally humble. Julian's message that there is enough reminds us that we really are all one. Whatever happens to one of us happens to all of us because we are all one in Christ. We can rejoice at others' successes as we can join together in celebration of our common salvation. We can stop fighting: we need not struggle so hard. Believing that there is enough for everyone commands us to the radical welcome God offers. The gate cannot be narrow. There are no blocks to our salvation. The distinctions and separations we wish to construct are decidedly not God's will. It is hard for us to remember this when we get into an "us versus them" mentality. We all do that at some level. We set ourselves up as righteous judges to exclude and close the doors of the kingdom. Even when we are fighting for justice we may be encouraging a worldview that sees separation rather than common humanity. We become so convinced that what we have to say is not only right but also crucial for protecting the rights and loving place at the table for everyone that we see oppressors everywhere. Yet Julian writes, "I ought to see my own sin, and not other men's sins." The more we commit to a spiritual path, the more aware we become of how often we violate that precept. Religion and social justice create spaces for us where we can easily label right versus wrong. We take to it ferociously. Then we find we have sadly fostered division rather than built the healing we want to create.

God offers us more than this. God can bridge what we cannot. "His love and that of our souls shall never be separated in two." The "large enough" comfort happens in the context of community. God heals rifts. In God we can never be truly separate from one another any more than we can be distinct from him. In our world, factionalism and hatred exist within and between peoples of different faiths. In God's promise to humanity we are healed, boundaries do not exist, and hateful divisions melt. When we pray for peace, may it be a loving-kindness that allows all of our hearts in, however we worship our God. God calls us home from division, separation, condemnation. We realize our mistakes, but God does not command or commend the paralysis of self-blame. He calls us to healing, to come to him right here and now as we are. We need not be changed, prepared, or converted in order to look to God. We are always already there just as we are. God calls the one through the many, the range and diversity of who we are. He is One, but he is also many. We often forget that. The categories and distinctions we have created are nothing in God's love. We do not have to break down the barriers ourselves; we cannot. God has already done it for us. When we want healing, we look to him. When we crave healing for our broken world, we are called to awaken to our oneness through him, the one-ing he has accomplished. That is "his function and his working here on earth." May we see the One in the face of our brothers and sisters who are different from us. May we remember that there is nothing we need do to break down our separations. We are one, as we are one-ed in the One.

❧ **80** ❧

By three things man is grounded in this life, and by these three God is honored and we are aided, protected, and saved.

> The first is the use of man's natural reason;
> the second is the common teaching of Holy Church;
> the third is the inner grace-filled working of the Holy Spirit;
>   and these three are all from one God.

> > God is the ground of our natural reason;
> > and God is the teaching of Holy Church;
> > and God is the Holy Spirit.

All are different gifts which He wills that we have great regard for and pay attention to, for these work in us constantly all together, and these are important things.

He wishes us to have knowledge of these things here as it were in an ABC—that is to say, that we have a little knowledge, of which we shall have fullness in heaven, and that is to further us.

We acknowledge in our Faith
>   that God alone took our human nature
>   and none but He;
and, furthermore,
>   that Christ alone did all the works that are part of our salvation,
>   and none but He;
and just so He alone acts now in the last end—that is to say,
>   He dwells here with us and rules us
>   and governs us in this life,
>   and brings us to His bliss.

And this shall He do as long as any soul is on earth who shall come to heaven—to such an extent that if there were no such soul but one,

He would be with that one all alone until He had brought it up
to his bliss.

I believe and understand the ministration of angels as the priests
relate it, but it was not shown to me,
> for He Himself is nearest and humblest,
>> highest and lowest,
>> and does all;
>>> and not only all that we need,
>>>> but also He does all that is honorable for our joy in heaven.

Where I say that He awaits us, sorrowing and mourning, it means
>> that all the true feeling that we have in ourselves in contrition
>> and compassion,
> and all the sorrowing and mourning because we are not one-ed
> with our Lord,
and all such which is beneficial, it is Christ in us.

And though some of us sense it seldom, it passes never from Christ
> until the time that He has brought us out of all our woe.

For love never allows Him to be without pity.

And whenever we fall into sin
and give up the remembrance of Him
and the protection of our own soul,
> then Christ alone takes care of the responsibility of us.
> And thus He stands sorrowing and mourning.

Then it is proper for us, for the sake of reverence and kindness,
to turn ourselves quickly to our Lord and not leave Him alone.

> He is here alone with us all—that is to say, only for us is He here.

And whenever I am alienated from Him by sin, despair, or sloth, then
> I allow my Lord to stand alone, inasmuch as He is in me—
> and so it goes with all of us who are sinners.

But though it is true that we act this way frequently,
> His goodness never allows us to be alone,
> but He is constantly with us,
> and He tenderly excuses us,
> and always shields us from blame in His sight.

ဆာ   ဆာ   ဆာ

We are never alone. Our God waits for us, yet it is theologically impossible for us to ever really desert him. God is honored, and we are
aided, protected, and saved by our reason, the Church's teaching, and
the "grace-filled working of the Holy Spirit." This is a profound set of
guides. Julian shares with the great philosophers a belief in the importance of human reason. In an age in which spirituality was set against
reason, Julian maintained a commitment to both. Her text is an attempt
to reconcile the two—an anomaly among "mystical literature." Julian
observes that the use of reason honors God. At the same time, she expresses her trust in grace, trust in the Holy Spirit. She believes in the
Spirit's work in the world. The human mind must be guided to discern.
We must be open and receptive to where the Spirit is leading us, intellectually and otherwise. The church's teaching is part of Julian's trinity,
but reason and Spirit share this "grounding." Theologically, Julian
"ones" them by observing that they are "all from one God." The three
"work in us constantly all together." Even if bliss is our end point, God
still "wishes us to have knowledge" here on earth. Julian affirms that
"God is the ground of our natural reason." Our God saves all of us and
each of us; this is no contradiction. It is not sentimentality for her to
suggest that "if there were no such soul but one, he would be with that
one all alone until he had brought it up to his bliss." Rather, this is at
the very center of her theology. There is only one manifestation of the
Incarnate. We are all examples of that One; we all share in that One; we
all are that One. The theological depth of the affective claim of individual
salvation is no saccharine platitude. It is rooted in Julian's understanding of the Incarnation.

    We need no mediation because in every encounter God is there. By
the Incarnate Word, God is manifest in relationship, speech, love with
each one. He awaits us in our pain because his grief is our own: it is our
sorrowing and mourning because we are not one-ed with our Lord on
the external level as we are in our interior reality. There is no distinction
between our suffering and his. He feels lack and separation from us
because he completely and utterly experiences everything we know. We
suffer because we long for him; "all such which is beneficial, it is Christ
in us." Our desires, our hopes and aspirations, our connections with
others and the words we speak—they are all one in his Incarnate Word.
Christ remembers us when we cannot remember him. This statement is
not meant to evoke guilt. It demonstrates how deeply we are one-ed

with him, and "love never allows him to be without pity." Forgetting is "whenever we fall into sin and give up remembrance of him." Whenever our craving for him diminishes, if even for a little while and no matter how slightly, he takes over the job. Julian inverts our typical depiction of sin. God neither stands pointing a finger of judgment nor wringing his hands in guilt-giving grief when we deviate from the path to him. Rather, our desire for him is his desire for us, and when we pause or slow this dynamic flow toward the divine—expressed as lack and longing—he takes over. There is no distinction between him and us. God needs us in contemplation and in action. This is not about blame. We must not leave our God waiting alone, because he is alone with each of us and for each of us alone he is here. Human nature stands exalted in God's purpose: us. The point is not that every one of us *shares* in this salvation. It is *for* every one of us particularly because his one-ing is unique to us. God needs us, saves us, and is us. When we desert him through sin, we stand up the best date we ever could have. This comparison is inadequate, for it is impossible to "allow my Lord to stand alone, inasmuch as he is in me." We can never walk away from him because he never leaves us.

❦ **81** ❧

Our good Lord showed Himself to His creature in various ways,
    both in heaven and in earth,
but I saw Him adopt no resting place except in man's soul.

    He showed Himself on earth in the sweet Incarnation
        and in His blessed Passion.
    And in other ways He showed Himself on earth where I say:
        "I saw God in a point."
    And in other ways He showed Himself on earth thus, as it were on
        pilgrimage: that is to say, He is here with us, leading us, and
        shall be until the time He has brought us all to His bliss in heaven.

He showed Himself reigning at different times, as I said before,
but primarily in man's soul.
    He has adopted His resting place there and His honorable City,
    out of which honorable throne He shall never rise
        nor move away without end.

    Wondrous and splendid is the place where our Lord dwells.

Therefore He wills that we pay attention to His grace-filled
    inspiration, more rejoicing in his undivided love
    than sorrowing in our frequent fallings.

For it is the most honor to Him of anything that we can do that we
live in our penance gladly and merrily because of His love,
    for He looks upon us so tenderly that He sees all our living here to
    be penance.

The natural yearning in us for Him is a lasting penance in us,
    which penance He produces in us
    and mercifully He helps us to bear it.

> His love makes Him to yearn,
> His wisdom and His truth with His rightfulness makes Him to put up
>   with us here,
> and this is the way He wants to look at it in us.

For this life is our natural penance and the highest, as I see it,
    for this penance never goes from us,
    until the time that we are fulfilled
    when we shall have Him for our reward.

And therefore He wills that we fix our hearts on the transition—
that is to say, from the pain that we feel into the bliss that we trust.

ဢ   ဢ   ဢ

Julian and Christ trade places. In the theology of the creation, we are one in God; Julian demonstrates that we are one-ed in him. While all things may be made by God, it is by that divine breath into us that the Word becomes flesh. We exist in the divine mind and our minds share something of him, a connection to God. It is not a simple remembrance of him who made us. The bond is deeper. Julian speaks of our soul as a "resting place," reminiscent of the famous line from Augustine's *Confessions*, "our hearts rest not until they rest in thee, O God." Here it is the reverse. God so loves us that God cannot rest in anything besides our very soul. Julian articulates a desiring God who longs for us more than we long for him. He wants us to yearn for him as he desires us to know him through that Incarnate Word that unites our minds to his. God invites us to remember that even though we cannot fully comprehend how, he abides in us and is hurling himself nowhere else in all of creation. Of course, this is not to say that we humans are to disregard or exploit the created world. Rather, the responsibility and obligation this places on us to be good stewards is all the greater because those actions of our lives are God working through us. Our souls are sites for the expression of God's love and the sharing in his wisdom. God's residence in us and with us through this soul-dwelling is for the repair of the world, *tikkun olam*. It is a pilgrimage. As she inverts Augustinian soul-yearning for God, Julian likewise makes God's mission to us for the good of God. God grows in us and through us. He needs us to make positive change. In Julian's time, pilgrimages were difficult journeys. They were embarked on at considerable cost and physical risk. They took a very long time and were intended to show the soul's devotion to God as a means toward achieving heavenly reward. Christ's Passion, to Julian, is such a pilgrimage. His Incarnation "here" is to bring us to him "there." He is desperate that we may be won over. He loves us that much.

Julian uses this example to deliver another teaching on sin and redemption. Her God wills that we spend our time "rejoicing in his undivided love [rather] than sorrowing in our frequent failings." He has come to do his will. We need do nothing more than accept that our "natural yearning in us for him is a lasting penance . . . which . . . he produces in us." Our lives here and now are how we get to him. God's pilgrimage to us, God's mission, comes in the form of our experiences. Penance changes the understanding of sin and death from an idea of punishment and ending to a means of deeper union, a longing for the divine. Our lives, imperfect as they are, become the ways we know God because they bring us closer. The literature of Julian's time reflected the historical reality of an age of pilgrimage. The quest narrative, the allegory—these belong to a genre that leads to eternal reward. Here Julian participates in that discourse, except the pilgrimage is not "Everyman's." It is God's, who came here in sacrifice and loss so that we might move "from the pain that we feel into the bliss that we trust." Through the suffering and sacrifices of our lives we can make God's world a better place. To live as Julian did, contemplating the Passion of Christ, could have resulted in a much different perspective. She could have become fixated on human failings. She could have been like her contemporaries, attempting to posit a theology of suffering that united our pains with his. Instead, Julian delved into an understanding that led her to imagine God's sufferings and longing as like ours. She teaches how God ones us to himself. Our desire for God is penance enough; we do not need to make ourselves suffer any more than that for our imperfections.

❧ **82** ❧

But here our gracious Lord showed the sorrowing and the mourning
        of the soul, meaning thus:
   "I am well aware that thou livest for my love,
   merrily and gladly suffering all the penance that can come to thee,
   but inasmuch as thou dost not live without sin, therefore thou art
        sad and sorrowful,
   and even if thou couldst live without sin, thou wouldst still suffer
        for the sake of my love
        all the woe,
        all the tribulation and distress that could come to thee.
   And that is true.
   But be not much bothered by sin that comes to thee
        against thy will."

Here I understood that the lord looks upon the servant with pity and not
   with blame,
for this passing life does not require that we live wholly without sin.

He loves us endlessly,
and we sin habitually,
     and He shows the sin to us most gently;
     and then we sorrow and mourn prudently,
         turning ourselves to the contemplation of His mercy,
         cleaving to His love and goodness,
         seeing that He is our medicine,
         aware that we do nothing but sin.

     Thus by the humility that we get from the sight of our sin,
     faithfully knowing His everlasting love,
     thanking and praising Him, we please Him.
        "I love thee and thou lovest me;
        and our love shall never be divided in two,
        and for thy benefit, I suffer."

And all this was shown in spiritual understanding,
  He saying these words:
    "I keep thee full safely."

By the great desire that I saw in our blessed Lord that we should live in this way
      (that is to say, in yearning and rejoicing, as all this lesson
        of love shows)
    by this desire I understood that all that is opposed to this is not
    from Him, but from enmity, and He wills that we know it by the
    sweet gracious light of this natural love.
If there is any such one alive on earth who is constantly kept from falling,
I know it not, for it was not shown me.

  But this was shown:
      that whether in falling or in rising
      we are ever preciously protected in one love.
        In the sight of God we do not fall;
        in the sight of self, we do not stand—
        and both of these are true as I see it, but the way our Lord
          God sees it is the highest truth.

Then are we much bound to God
  because He wills in this life to show us this high truth.

And I understood that while we are in this life, it is most helpful to us
that we see both of these at once;
    for the higher point of view keeps us in spiritual solace
      and true rejoicing in God,
    and the other, that is, the lower point of view, keeps us in fear
      and makes us ashamed of ourselves.

But our good Lord wills always that we see ourselves more from the
point of view of the higher
    (but not give up knowledge of the lower)
until the time that we are brought up above,
where we shall have our Lord Jesus for our reward,
and will be filled full of joy and bliss without end.

଼ଌ   ଼ଌ   ଼ଌ

Julian explains her radical gospel of sin: a God who sees us "with pity and not with blame." The soul regrets that it cannot live without sin. Yet God says not to worry too much about sin, as it comes about without our will. It is the nature of human experience that we know sin whether we like it or not. We inhabit a creation one-ed to God wherein there is sin and death. The God who looks upon "this passing life does not require that we live wholly without sin." We may strive for perfection, but God's gracious love and redemption does not require us to be sinless. If we were, what would be the purpose of the Passion? Sin— humanity, human frailty—humbles us, and in those moments of breakthrough we submit to God's love. If we had our full pride, would we need him so much? If we were perfect, would we still love him? Through "sin" we are one-ed to him. The Incarnation is by means of and because of sin. Our fall is our glory, leading to the full union of love in him. Sin is our way to the experience of God's love. It brings us to a state of "yearning and rejoicing, as all this lesson of love shows." All that is opposed to this is not from God. Thus paradoxically our human fallenness, our sin, comes from him insofar as it is the wound in our own sides that hungers love-longing. Our brokenness is the path to his Incarnation and to singular relationship with him.

Julian's point is not simply that no human being is without sin— comforting in and of itself as we strive for spiritual perfection. Rather, no soul is kept from sin precisely because through sin we come to God's love. To make anyone without sin, to prevent anyone from falling, would be to keep her or him from God's love. Sin is a gift: the doorway to our redemption, the invitation to his love. Sin can never really hurt us because of the all-encompassing love of God. In our sin, we are protected; when we turn to God, we are held near. God does not see us as falling or fallen. In his one-ing love, the fallen state is not real to him. That is why he looks with pity and not with blame. We only see our sins. Our human mind is incapable of God's sight. The mundane blocks to our awareness of his love prevent us from seeing as he sees. In her showings, Julian was given a glimpse of this reality, that God's perception is different from ours. As intermediary, she offers a view through the lens of his love. Despite our limitations, our purpose is to learn this lesson of love, to see as Julian has seen. The one-ing of the Incarnation calls us to this discernment. Through our human struggles we grow toward God. The only important teaching is that God sees us as risen, not fallen. This gives us hope. Julian presents us with what she saw and suggests that we benefit from both forms of sight. Our human perspective maintains us in striving toward the goal of spiritual growth. Seeing through the eyes of God, we find peace and joy in him. We come to know his unconditional love for us and his belief in our perfection. Our souls are already there with him; moving our mortal selves to that place is the work of this world. The reward of full union is put forth as the promise, but not at the expense of human experience.

ᘓ **83** ᘖ

I had a partial inspiration, vision, and sense of three properties of God
of which the strength and outcome of the whole revelation consists
> *(and they were seen in every showing, and most particularly*
> *in the twelfth where it was often said, "I am He"):*

The properties are these:
> *life,*
> *love,*
> *and light.*
>> *In life is wondrous familiarity,*
>> *and in love is gentle courtesy,*
>> *and in light is endless kindness.*

These three properties were seen in one Goodness,
> *to which Goodness my reason wished to be one-ed*
> *and to cleave to it with all my might.*

I beheld with reverent fear (and greatly marveling at the sight and
the feeling of the sweet harmony) that our reason is in God,
> *understanding that it is the highest gift that we have received, and*
> *that it is grounded in human nature.*

Our Faith is a light, naturally coming from our Endless Day—that is
our Father, God;
>> *in this light our Mother, Christ,*
>> *and our good Lord the Holy Spirit*
> *lead us in this passing life.*

This light is meted out prudently,
> *faithfully remaining with us as we need it in the night.*

> *The light is the cause of our life;*
> *the night is the cause of our pain and of all our woe,*

on account of which woe we earn endless reward and
     favor from God,
  for we, with mercy and grace,
     willingly acknowledge and believe our light,
     walking in it wisely and mightily.

And at the end of woe,
suddenly our eye shall be opened
and in clarity of sight
our light shall be full.
This light is God our Creator
and the Holy Spirit
in Christ Jesus our Savior.

Thus I saw and understood that our Faith is our light in our night;
     and the light is God, our Endless Day.

ℚ ℚ ℚ

God is reason. Human beings are made for God; they are made for reason. Faith is not incompatible with reason, for the very highest light is the mind of reason. God is a trinity of "partial inspiration, vision, and sense." Inspiration is the work of the Holy Spirit that breathed life into matter in the creation. It also suggests human acts of creation such as Julian's text, her attempt to write a narrative of her experience. Vision refers to visionary experience as well as literal sight, actual perception as well as metaphorical understanding. Sense leads to both physicality and intuitive thought, reason. These three work together in the trinity "of which the strength and outcome of the whole revelation consists." They "were seen in every showing," especially the "`I am he.'" Herein is the essence of the Godhead. Are we ready to receive it? Another trinity of properties is deceptively simple: "life, love, and light." The most material and literal is placed against the fundamentally abstract and spiritual. We have the living, breathing Incarnation: the life that pulsates, the love we can feel and touch, and the light we can see. In the Godhead we have not only this in Christ but also the cognitive idea: the divine mind that is life, love, and light. This is the source of all creation. "In life is wondrous familiarity": to be one's "familiar" is to be an intimate—a friend, a lover, a spouse. What we call life is not foreign to us: it is our experience, and it is God. God is our familiar, yet wondered at. That is Father God—far away, yet as near as our very soul. To say "in love is gentle courtesy" evokes a whole series of associations for Julian's audience. *Gentilesse,* as Chaucer began teaching this fast-changing world, was not being born into the aristocracy, but rather how one behaved. "Gentle deeds make the gentleman." God's courtesy is not of the old courtly world that separated the few from the many. Christ, love in gentle courtesy, came for all. His love is what we know. Julian's "light is endless kindness," the work of the Holy Spirit in the world. Spirit is light. It is without end. It brings light into the world. To call it kindness is not simply suggesting compassion; it also recalls nature. To be true to one's "kind," or kin, is to follow one's nature. The work of light in the world, the action of the Holy Spirit, is embedded in the natural order.

All three are "goodness"; all three are God. The soul, Julian's "reason," wished to be "one-ed" to such good. The soul desires God; reason longs for the good. The existential reality is such that "our reason is in God." The soul longs for God because the soul-being, reason, is already there. Our reason is "the highest gift that we have received." It is inseparable from godliness. We cannot exist outside of God insofar as our belief and thought are always an extension of the divine mind. In God we have our being because without God we would not be. On a less abstract level, this explanation justifies the work of Julian's book. She demonstrates faith seeking understanding. The answer here is that the understanding is God. Julian brings mystical experience to bear on intellectual thought. Reason is "grounded in human nature." It is given material form as the *Logos,* the Word, was with God, was God, and took flesh. Reason takes flesh in us through the creation. The Incarnation embodies the idea of divine love in the human Christ. The light of reason is connected to the "endless day," the trope of creation associated with Father God the Creator. Julian states that our "faith is a light." Night is not night to God; it is only and always reason because the dynamic process of creation, the unfolding of divine mind, is never ending. The day's work is always being done through the light of reason given to us by God. We cannot labor in the night; the light of God—who said, "Let there be light," creating even reason—is working in us and through us. We are led by "Mother Christ" in this journey: we are led by love. We are led by our reason as we participate in the new creation.

To say as Julian does that "the light is the cause of our life" is to affirm that the First Mover spoke and made us not only for reason and in reason but also by reason. To exclaim that "the night is the cause of our pain and of all our woe" is to indict ignorance. There is no light of God where reason is not present. We suffer because we are un-reason-able. In this dark night of the soul we suffer until we receive God's "mercy and grace"—those two old friends present throughout the *Showings*—that allow us to "willingly acknowledge and believe our light, walking in it wisely and mightily." It is only through mercy and grace that we are able to accept this. God wants us, God needs us, to believe in our reason. Without such understanding we cannot be partners in the unfolding of God's purpose in the world. And yet we see in a glass darkly; our reason is limited. We await the time when we shall see face-to-face. As in Paul's conversion, "suddenly our eye shall be opened and in clarity of sight our light shall be full." This is what we will receive in the afterlife: the complete awareness of divine reason. The whole of the *Showings* has been a desire to explain, to understand. Ultimately Julian must accept that in the end some things cannot be received, cannot be shown, until we cross to the other side. Her awe is tangible as she contemplates the wisdom of God, the light that is divine mind. She can conclude this chapter by saying: "Thus I saw and understood that our faith is our light in our night." She saw, she understood. What more could humanity ask for? Faith is not opposed to reason—it is reason working in us and through us. May we work out the new creation as we live in his "endless day."

❧ **84** ❧

This light is love,
>   and the meting out of this light is done for us beneficially by the
>   >   wisdom of God,
>   >   >   for neither is the light so bright that we can see clearly our blessed
>   >   >   Day,
>   >   >   >   nor is it completely barred from us,
>   but it is such a light in which we live rewardingly with toil,
>   earning the endless honor-filled favor of God.

>   >   >   (And this was seen in the sixth showing where He said,
>   >   >   "I thank thee for thy service and thy labor.")

Thus love keeps us in faith and hope;
and faith and hope lead us to love.

>   >   And at the end all shall be love.

I had three kinds of understandings on this light of love:
>   the first is love uncreated;
>   the second is love created;
>   the third is love given.

>   Love uncreated is God;
>   love created is our soul in God;
>   love given is virtue—
>   >   and that is the grace-filled gift of action,
>   >   in which we love God for Himself,
>   >   and ourselves in God,
>   >   and all that God loves,
>   >   for God's sake.

❧   ❧   ❧

In the fullness of life and creation, in eschatological time, at the end all shall be love. There is nothing left to say or do. If Julian succeeded in arguing for a reconciliation of faith with reason in Chapter 83, where divine mind is holy reason and our human reason is one-ed with that, here she moves from head to heart. The light of reason is no different from love. The kindly light of divine mind is one with divine love. Chapter 83 made plain the sense that on earth we have limited capacity for that light of reason—we have a glimpse of it, but in the fullness of eternal life we will be completely one with it. The same is true for divine love. Light, reason, and love join as divine guidance moving us through the created world. What impels our journey, enlightens our mind, is a wholly loving presence. We are given what understanding we need; we are given the love we need. These are just enough to sustain us but also to keep us hungering and searching for more. We find a specter of the light but not the full light itself. The light is "neither . . . so bright that we can see clearly our blessed day, nor is it completely barred from us." There is greater continuity here in Julian, in both reason and in love, than a simple Platonic distinction between the heavenly ideal and the flawed example. In our participation in the Incarnation we hold within ourselves some of the light that helps us to know that the "blessed day" is a promise that can sustain us. In this light "we live rewardingly with toil, earning the endless honor-filled favor of God." Our souls are perfected; this is the true fruit of the spiritual life. We work, we grow. This in itself is a blessing, our souls' movement toward fuller union with God. Of course, in a far more practical dimension the fallout of our souls' work is more love in the world, more reason. In harmony with divine love, divine reason, glimpsing the light of God helps us to bring that light into the world. We are partners in the new creation by our very longing for the transcendent light. Through God's Incarnation our vision—that is not particular, individual, but wholly God-directed—helps us in the cocreation of a more perfect world through the perfection of our souls.

The contemplative life is connected to our experience in and of and through the world. "Thus love keeps us in faith and hope; and faith and hope lead us to love." Living in and of the divine mind and divine love, we participate in the promise of the endless day. This is our faith; this is the reason leading us on through our individual action. These bring us to and through the partial light—the experience of and participation in love in this world—ultimately to divine love at the end of our individual time and at the end of the world's time. "And at the end all shall be love." We can take that observation out of context and (more than the "all shall be well") it still retains its integrity and meaning. Living and working in and with and through the light, we individually and collectively participate in being led to Love. Regardless of the circumstances of our lives, none of the details really matter. Whether we recognize it or not as we suffer, God is leading us to Love; we need not know that in order for it to be true. "Love uncreated is God." In the beginning was Love, Love was with God, Love was God. Our very existence is an incarnational example of divine love. Through that love we perpetually reside in God. Virtue in Julian is humanity's willingness to make this offering of love, love given. It is a "grace-filled gift of action" that leads us to turn to the light, to be converted by our free will. It is a move from a passive existence of unawareness, inhabiting the love of God without even knowing it or doing anything about it, into a space of greater loving-kindness. We are thus compelled to see that light within ourselves and all creation: "We love God for himself, and ourselves in God, and all that God loves, for God's sake." This is the practice of contemplative life: willfully choosing the love of God, an awareness of our own keeping in that love, and loving ourselves as we reside therein. By extension we love all that God loves because we abide in love and we actively make the move to will such love into service. It is all for God's sake—the primary mover and the source of love in our hearts.

$\text{\small CB}\ \textbf{85}\ \text{\small BO}$

I marveled greatly at this vision,
> *for notwithstanding our stupid living and our blindness here,*
> *yet endlessly our gracious Lord looks upon us in this struggle,*
>> *rejoicing.*
And of all things,
> *we can please Him best*
>> *by wisely and truly believing that,*
>> *and rejoicing with Him and in Him.*

For as truly as we shall be in the bliss of God without end,
> *praising Him and thanking Him,*
just as truly we have been in the foresight of God loved and known
> *in His endless purpose from without beginning.*

In this love without beginning He made us,
and in the same love He protects us
and never allows us to receive harm
> *by which our bliss might be lessened.*

Therefore when the judgment is given
and we are all brought up above,
then shall we clearly see in God
the secrets which are now hidden from us.

> *Then shall none of us be moved to say in any way:*
>> *"Lord, if it had been thus-and-so,*
>> *then it would*
>> *have been all well";*

> *but we shall say all in one voice:*
>> *"Lord, blessed mayest Thou be!*
>> *Because it is as it is; it is well.*
>> *And now we see truly*

that everything is done
as was Thine ordinance
before anything was made."

॰ঌ ৪৩ ৪৩

Julian's endeavor was not simply an intellectual exercise. Her act of writing the book was not a matter of theological pride. It was an act of love for her fellow creatures, to try to share with them God's love that she had known. "And at the end all shall be love" is both narrative and conclusion. The end of her narrative journey, the end of the soul's journey, is love. Chapter 85 is repose. The agony in the garden—what it feels like to try to give voice to the ineffable—has passed. As Julian stands near the end of her text, she can see that God was leading her—in reason and in love—through it all. Hence "notwithstanding our stupid living and our blindness here, yet endlessly our gracious Lord looks upon us in this struggle, rejoicing." God wants us to keep on keeping on. God wants us to follow the call, to embark on the journey. God is there—in us and working through us, watching us—as we try to discern meaning in our lives. God carried Julian through her narrative. It is easy to say that God looks at us with pity and laughs sympathetically at the things we take so seriously. In the light of divine love, the "stupid" things of our lives really do not matter. Yet God rejoices as we make our way through our struggle because God knows we see that there is more to it than just the fight. Our battle scars are our lessons. By his wounds we are healed, but they are our wounds too. That is the Incarnation. God is with us through it all, cheering us on.

A story comes to its conclusion; we return to the one-ing with divine love at the end. But Julian encourages us to focus on our source, our origin in God. Just as much as we will be with him in endless "bliss," so too "we have been in the foresight of God loved and known in his endless purpose from without beginning." Our experience of conversion is not so much a turning, or even a re-turning, as an awareness. If the God who would be the Incarnate has been One from before time, our very existence and God's full "knowledge" of us (the same as full "loving" of us) have been without time. In rejecting the very idea of time, rejecting the linear direction of narrative, we find that there is no beginning, middle, or end. There is just God; there is just "is." "At the end all shall be love" could be rewritten as "love is all that is." This is a perspective our human minds find difficult to grasp. But Julian affirms with certitude that when we finally "get it," we will no longer need a hopeful promise that "all shall be well." We will say "all in one voice" that "it is well." We must treasure Julian's doubt and uncertainty. It is ours. She struggled with her rational mind's fight to deny the love that was presented to her. We do the same. All the nitpicking, all our being thrown here and there by thought, will find its rest in the divine reason that knows "all is well."

☙ **86** ❧

This book is begun by God's gift and His grace,
but it is not yet completed, as I see it.
   For the sake of love let us all pray
   together with God's working—
      thanking,
      trusting,
      rejoicing,
   for thus would our good Lord be prayed to
         (as is the understanding that I received in all His own
         meaning, and in the sweet words where He says most merrily,
         "I am the basis of thy praying").

Truly I saw and understood in our Lord's meaning that He showed it
because He wished to have it known more than it is,
   and in this knowledge He will give us grace to love Him
   and cleave to Him.

For He beholds His heavenly treasure with such great love on earth
         that He wills to give us more light and solace in heavenly joy by
         drawing our hearts from the sorrow and darkness
         which we are in.
From the time that it was shown, I desired frequently to know what
our Lord's meaning was. And fifteen years after (and more) I was
answered in spiritual understanding, saying thus:
   "Wouldst thou know thy Lord's meaning in this thing?
   Be well aware:
      love was His meaning.
   Who showed it thee? Love.
   What showed He thee? Love.
   Why did He show it thee? For love.

Keep thyself in that love and thou shalt know and see more
     of the same,
but thou shalt never see nor know any other thing therein
     without end."

Thus was I taught that love was our Lord's meaning.
     And I saw full certainly in this and in all the showings,
     that before God made us, He loved us
     and this love was never slackened
     nor ever shall be.

In this love He has done all His works,
and in this love He has made all things beneficial to us,
and in this love our life is everlasting.
     In our creation we had a beginning,
     but the love in which He created us was in Him from without
          beginning,
     and in this love we have our beginning.

And all this we shall see in God without end,
which may Jesus grant us. Amen.

⋈ **Colophon** ⋉

(Attributed to the scribe)

Thus ends the revelation of love of the Blessed Trinity
showed by our Savior Christ Jesus
for our endless comfort and solace,
and also to rejoice in Him in this passing journey of life.
Amen, Jesus, Amen.

I pray Almighty God that this book does not come into the hands of anyone except those who are His faithful lovers, and those that will submit themselves to the Faith of Holy Church and obey the wholesome interpretation and teaching of the men who are of virtuous life, settled age, and profound learning, for this revelation is high theology and high wisdom, wherefore it cannot survive with him who is slave to sin and to the Devil. And beware that thou not accept one thing after thine own inclination and preference and omit another, for that is the situation of an heretic. But accept each thing with the other and truly understand that all is in agreement with Holy Scripture and grounded in the same, and that Jesus, our true love, light, and truth, shall show this wisdom and Himself to all pure souls who with humility ask constantly. And thou to whom this book shall come, thank our Savior Christ Jesus highly and heartily that He made these showings and revelations for thee, and to thee, out of His endless love, mercy, and goodness, to be a safe guide and conduct to everlasting bliss for thee and for us—which may Jesus grant us. Amen.

Here end the sublime and wonderful Revelations
of the unutterable love of God in Jesus Christ,
vouchsafed to a dear lover of His and in
her to all His dear friends and
lovers, whose hearts, like
hers, do flame in the
love of our
dearest
Jesu.

∂ℭ ∂ℭ ∂ℭ

To say that "love was his meaning" is a tremendous statement for the contemporary mind. "Meaning" has many different resonances. We speak of humanity's "search for meaning." We long for answers, something to give purpose and direction to our lives. We cope with, and struggle within, clinical anxieties and depressions, spiritual fears and doubts. The postmodern mind is intrigued with the notion of "meaning." Does meaning exist, and can it be found? What is the relationship between the "signifier" and the "signified"—the word or symbol that represents the true "meaning" that lies behind it?

Julian affirms that yes, there is meaning: love is God's meaning. Love is thus all meaning, all there is. There is meaning in our lives of strife, there is meaning behind the words, behind the showings. "Love was his meaning" takes the Word, the *Logos,* and parses it to say that in both the beginning (John's gospel) and the end (Chapter 84), all is only love. We are assured: meaning exists, and it is love. In all those re-presentations that revert, like images that shrink to infinity in mirror tricks' endless progression, the only meaning to be found is love. Our intellectual quest is humbled. In Julian's trinity, love shows, love is the showing, and it is shown for love: God the essence, the Incarnation, and the Spirit at work in the world—all are one Love.

To say "love was his meaning" is an important signification for Julian's age. Texts were always glossed with commentaries, the complementary reactions to the action of the Word. Julian's role as interpreter, the insertion of her self into the narrative as "hermeneut," analyst, affirms her commitment that God wills our knowledge. If reason and love are God, human understanding is his goal. "He showed it because he wished to have it known more than it is." Julian observes that "understanding" does not come overnight. It took over fifteen years for her to comprehend the meaning of her showings.

Interpretation of the "text"—the love of God present in the world—is Love's work. The colophon assures orthodoxy. Julian speaks as a theologian and here she is justified and supported: "This revelation is high theology and high wisdom." She, as a medieval woman, has dared to enter the province of interpreters. To ask questions, to penetrate in search of answers—this is the work of every human and is God's will. The search for meaning is the search for God; it is the search for Love. Through Julian's text, we are led there.